Ink Studies

Everyday Practices of Calligraphy in Contemporary China

Laura Vermeeren

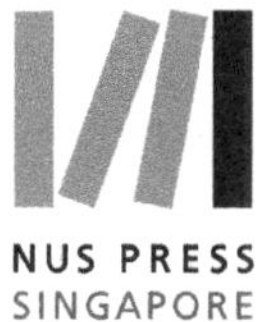

The research for this book was supported by a European Research Council grant [616882].

Published by:

NUS Press
National University of Singapore
AS3-01-02, 3 Arts Link
Singapore 117569

Fax: (65) 6774-0652
E-mail: nusbooks@nus.edu.sg
Website: http://nuspress.nus.edu.sg

print ISBN 978-981-325-297-4 (paper)
ePDF ISBN 978-981-325-298-1

Portions of the arguments and material discussed in this book are based on work I have previously published. Readers may recognize some similarities in the themes and analyses. These include:

- Vermeeren, Laura. "Chinese Calligraphy in the Digital Realm: Aesthetic Perfection and Remediation of the Authentic." *Concentric: Literary and Cultural Studies* 43 (2) (2017): 163–91.
- Vermeeren, Laura. "Evaporating Ennui: Water Calligraphy in Beijing." In *Boredom, Shanzhai, and Digitisation in the Time of Creative China*, ed. Jeroen de Kloet, Yiu Fai Chow, and Lena Scheen. Amsterdam: Amsterdam University Press, 2019, pp. 121–31.
- Vermeeren, Laura, and Jeroen de Kloet. "We Are Not Like the Calligraphers of Ancient Times: A Study of Young Calligraphy Practitioners in Contemporary China." In *China's Youth Cultures and Collective Spaces*, ed. Vanessa Frangville and Gwennaël Gaffric. London: Routledge, 2020, pp. 219–34.
- Vermeeren, Laura. "Locating Vernacular Creativity Outside the 'Urban Cool' in Beijing: Ephemeral Water Calligraphy." *Cultural Studies* 36 (5) (2022): 748–69.
- Vermeeren, Laura. "Unearthing Fonts from a Creative Chinese Past." *European Journal of Cultural Studies* (2025): 1–10.

Cover image: Wang Dongling 王冬齡, *Li Bai, "Drinking Alone in Moonlight: Verse One"* (2016). Ink on paper. 180 × 97 cm. Courtesy of Wang Dongling.

Typeset by: Westchester Publishing Services UK
Printed by: Integrated Books International

Ink Studies

To
Rosie and Noor

Contents

List of All Interviewees (Quoted and Unquoted)

Anonymous	April 6, 2018	Graduate student of Calligraphy at Renmin University
Anonymous	April 6, 2018	Undergraduate student of Philosophy at Peking University and student leader of the Beida Calligraphy Hobbyclub
Anonymous	April 10, 2018	Founder of Dongfang Moyun Calligraphy School
Chen Cong	April 18, 2018	Painter, calligrapher and seller at Liulichang
Chi Ziming	May 29, 2018	MA student of Calligraphy at Renmin University
Da Jingjing	May 27, 2018	Chinese font designer
Deng (Ms)	April 10, 2018	Mother of a child taking calligraphy classes at Dongfang Moyun
Dong Jie, Zhang Yong, Zhen Bo	April 29, 2018	Children from Gansu, participating in calligraphy contest in Beijing
Doris Liu	May 17, 2018	Student of Calligraphy at Central Academy of Fine Arts (CAFA)
Emma	April 10, 2018	Taking calligraphy classes at Dongfang Moyun
Feng Mengbo	April 12, 2018	Artist and teacher at CAFA
Funkie Gao	May 30, 2018	DJ and calligrapher and employee at Yidege

Guo Tong	May 18, 2018	4th-year undergraduate student of Calligraphy, Qinghua
He Hualing	May 18, 2018	PhD student of Calligraphy
He Ruile	April 25, 2018	Calligraphy teacher at Hao Shufa calligraphy school
Hong Liang	February 22, 2016	Calligraphy teacher at Children's Palace School
Jia Ruoceng	April 6, 2018	Undergraduate student of Sociology at Peking University and participant of the Beida Calligraphy Hobbyclub
Jia Zhen	May 24, 2018	Teacher of Art at CAFA
Jian Meng	April 10, 2018	Curator at the Beijing Museum of Art
Jiang Han	April 29, 2018	Propaganda Manager of the Chinese Calligraphy Grade Assessment Center
Jiao Zihui	April 6, 2018	Graduate student of Calligraphy at Renmin University
Li Yuqi	April 9, 2018	Law student at Beijing Jiaotong University, taking calligraphy lessons at Qin Han Hutong Calligraphy School
Li Yushan	April 10, 2018	Taking calligraphy classes at Dongfang Moyun
Lin Du	May 27, 2018	Chinese font designer, designer at Manga APP
Lin Shujie	February 18, 2016	Postdoctoral fellow at the Tsinghua University Academy of Fine Arts
Liu Doris	May 17, 2018	Student of Calligraphy at CAFA
Liu Hanxu	May 16, 2018	Font designer at Founder Company
Meng Dahuai	April 29, 2018	Manager of the Chinese Calligraphy Grade Assessment Center
Meng Lei	May 11, 2018	Art professor at Zhejiang University, Vice President of the Young Calligraphers Association Hangzhou
Pei Lun	April 23, 2018	Traditional calligrapher
Peng Houjian	April 6, 2018	Graduate student of Calligraphy at Renmin University

Qiu Zhenzhong	December 10, 2015	Professor at CAFA, Director of the Center for Comparative Study on Chinese Calligraphy and Painting, author, artist
Shi (Miss)	April 10, 2018	Grandmother of a child taking calligraphy classes at Dongfang Moyun
Tao	April 14, 2018	Calligraphy teacher at Qin Han Hutong Calligraphy School
Tao Di	May 27, 2018	Chinese font designer
Wang Dongling	May 11, 2018	Modern calligraphy artist
Wang Liangliang	May 24, 2018	PhD student of Calligraphy at Capital Normal University
Wang Siqi	April 13, 2018	Calligraphy teacher and manager at Xiao Yunge Academy
Wang Wen	April 21, 2018	Taped lecture at the National Museum in Beijing organized by the Cultural Innovation Center in Beijing
Wen Gongsui	May 27, 2018	Chinese font designer
Xia Pengcheng	June 3, 2016	Modern calligraphy artist
Xu Bing	May 10, 2016	Contemporary artist
Xu Yufeng	April 10, 2018	Master's student of Calligraphy at Beijing Normal University
Xue Fengli	April 1, 2016	Retired, water calligraphy writer at the Taoranting Park, President of the Water Calligraphy Association Taoranting
Yao Xinran (children and parents' names anonymous)	April 30, 2018	Focus group with teacher and founder of calligraphy school Hancheng Shuyuan, four mothers of children learning calligraphy at Hancheng Shuyuan and their four children
Ye Xiaoyu	May 11, 2018	Student of Computer Design at Zhejiang University, taking extracurricular calligraphy classes at Zhejiang University School of Art
Zeng Xiang	April 28, 2018	Contemporary calligraphy artist
Zhang Rongqing	March 22, 2016	Visiting professor of China Academy of Art, Director of the Overseas Chinese Association, Vice chairman of the China International Painting and Calligraphy Society

Zhang Shijun	March 9, 2016	Calligrapher and director of the Calligraphy Association of Beijing Xicheng
Zhang Xiyue	April 10, 2018	Taking calligraphy classes at Dongfang Moyun
Zhao Bandi	May 12, 2018	Contemporary artist
Zhao Shuzeng	April 27, 2018	Artist, calligrapher, retired art professor at Beijing Communication University

List of Figures

Acknowledgments

This book is the result of the invaluable input and support from so many scholars, colleagues, informants and friends. I extend my deepest gratitude to Jeroen de Kloet, whose guidance has been instrumental. Your enthusiasm for scholarship has demonstrated that academic pursuit can be both exciting and enjoyable, and you have taught me how to approach Cultural Studies with rigor, humor and creativity. Your optimism, generosity and support—both practical and academic, and hotpots—have been profoundly motivating. I also want to thank Stefan Landsberger for his meticulous attention to my writing.

I am honored to thank Prof. Adriana Iezzi, Prof. Dr Esther Peeren, Prof. Dr Mia Lerm-Hayes, Prof. Dr Maghiel van Crevel and Prof. Dr Giselinde Kuipers for their thoughtful review of my research. The insights you provided were greatly appreciated. I am also grateful to Manya Koetse and Fresco Sam-Sin. Your work in Chinese Studies, which both of you have managed to make fun, cool and engaging, has been a continual source of inspiration. Thank you both, for your support, online and offline, for our discussions, and for your genuine interest in my research. Being part of the ChinaCreative research group has been wonderful. Rowan Parry, Arjen Nauta, Zoenie Deng, Jian Lin and Shuaishuai Wang—our shared conferences, meals and discussions are memories I will always treasure. I want to thank the extended University of Amsterdam family—YiuFai Chow, Jori Snels, Arnoud Arps, Leonie Schmidt, Penn Tsz Ting Ip and Gladys Chong. Thank you, Eloe Kingma and Esther Peeren for embodying the warm and welcoming spirit of the Amsterdam School for Cultural Analysis. Thank you, Jeroen Wiedenhof for your interest in my project. Michiel Nonnekes, thank you for introducing me to the calligraphy scene in Hangzhou, and for your inspiring views on art and fruit-soaked baijiu. I am deeply grateful to all my informants in China, too numerous to list individually, who participated in interviews, supported me via WeChat and guided me into the more obscure aspects of calligraphy. Special thanks go to Yao Xinran and her family, Huang Ruiting, Pei Randi, Wang Siqi, Lin Shujie, Qiu Zhenzhong, Wang Dongling, Zeng Xiang, Saana Virtanen, Daniele Caccin and Zhou Lesheng, my first calligraphy teacher.

And, of course, I am grateful to my family for their patience, love, support and care. Elise, thank you for being such a wonderful sister. Gareth Wakeling, your encouragement and suggestions were so helpful. Your companionship throughout this journey made me feel supported and less alone. I also extend my thanks to the readers for their interest in contemporary Chinese calligraphy. And finally, during the course of researching and writing this book, my two beautiful daughters were born. Thank you, Rosie and Noor. This book is for you.

Preface

While preparing for the research on this book, I had considered how the different writing practices that I knew existed could provide me with insights in how calligraphy is lived and experienced in Beijing today. How, for example, it is employed as a disciplining tool, or how it would allow for creative bodies to fulfill a certain potential. Then, having arrived in Beijing I soon learned that not only is calligraphy everywhere—which made distinguishing fields more complex than I had initially thought—but that those involved in calligraphy are often very passionately involved. My eclectic approach to calligraphy was not immediately appreciated everywhere. As I tried to become part of an inner circle, whatever that meant, I found out that being able to write a beautiful 横笔 *hengbi* (a lying down brushstroke) before starting a conversation, or recognizing the styles of the calligraphy masters in other people's works, helped me to be taken seriously in this complex cultural scene. With the help of connections (关系 *guanxi*), I finally met many people who were willing to take me along to their calligraphy clubs, writing spot in the park, their calligraphy schools, to lectures, exhibitions and calligraphy-loving friends and parents. This book draws on data collected during a research period of five years, with two fieldwork periods in Beijing and Hangzhou. Beijing is regarded as the center of calligraphic power and culture. It is tremendously rich in cultural and calligraphic spaces. Among them are small calligraphy schools; universities offering BA, MA and PhD tracks in Calligraphy Studies; there are hobby clubs and water calligraphers; children's contests, plays and exhibitions. There are also shops with calligraphic banners made by famous artists; calligraphy museums exhibiting modern and traditional calligraphy side by side with experimental art spaces showing avant-garde artworks that walk the blurry lines between modern calligraphy and experimental art. For a study on calligraphic practices, this means that there is a wealth of calligraphy-related activity to research—provided that you are allowed access. Such a condensed cultural space made research immensely enjoyable. I would hop on a Mobike—the (then) popular bike sharing system—in the morning to interview the manager of a small calligraphy school before visiting the Dongyue temple to see the extant stone stele of Yuan dynasty calligrapher Zhao Mengfu in the afternoon while drinking bubble tea and chatting to other visitors. To end the day, I would take a stroll around the hip art district of Caochangdi, looking around for contemporary art that might feature calligraphic strokes and lines, while in between, on the metro, I would check the talk of the day on the calligraphy WeChat groups. The fieldwork allowed me to undertake a variety of research methods: I conducted participant-observation methods, visual analysis and interviews during my period in "the field." The interviews were all done face-to-face and are in-depth, qualitative and semi-structured—recorded and transcribed afterward. Most interviews were conducted in Chinese by me, sometimes accompanied by an assistant, and translated into English by me. The quotes in this book are directly taken from the interviews and translated by me. Then, there were also many talks, random chats and serendipitous encounters with calligraphers, hobbyists, water calligraphers, taxi drivers, park visitors, students, children and parents that were not recorded and transcribed—I consider these as enormously valuable for gaining insights in the discourse as a whole. But this approach—focusing almost solely on one city, apart from a stint in Hangzhou for interviews and school visits—has resulted in a Beijing-centeredness that remains visible in this book. The people who speak throughout the book and inhabit the calligraphic spaces of Beijing, however, are rarely born in Beijing—they have moved from other provinces either for work or study and, as many people do in China, they still refer to themselves as from the province where their *laojia*, their ancestral home, is located. It is important to realize that Beijing is not representative of the People's Republic of China as a whole, and that practices of calligraphy in Beijing are not, or, following Yuehping Yen, might even be *less* representative of other parts of China. Feeling more secure as a culturally homogeneous group, she argues, Beijingers might be more willing to diverge from established traditions, allowing for a more experimental and avant-garde approach to calligraphy[1]. But I am confident that while Beijing, as the capital, might indeed have a more developed calligraphic scene, this should not be a reason to *not study* its particularities, bearing in mind that I consciously shy away from any idea of representativeness. This scene is too vast, too diverse, and, as a whole, beyond the scope of this book.

Seeing calligraphers and their brushes move, smelling the soothing scent of ink in the calligraphy studios, observing how teachers speak to their students and how students sit straight, witnessing how water calligraphers spend smoggy mornings with their homemade brushes and buckets of water in the park, was indispensable to contextualize calligraphy as a living and vibrant cultural scene. Ethnography, however, as Lily Chumley remarks, is always already history.[2] It is something in the making, forever unfinished and prone to imperfections and distortions. I thank those who were willing to take that risk and speak in this book.

Introduction

> People think that children cannot write, but that is not the case. The calligraphy of young people is actually much better than the writings of old men these days. People think that the writing of old gentlemen is so good; they think: the older the better. But in fact, the opposite is true. In China, it is now: the younger the better.
>
> —Interview with Jian Meng

My Chinese calligraphy teacher seems to embody all the rather clichéd characteristics of the archetypical Chinese scholar: a slightly absent and friendly older man, working in an atelier stacked to the ceiling with thumbed manuscripts, catalogs and rice paper covered in skillfully brushed characters. Many of us, when thinking about calligraphy, will find ourselves led by a stereotypical impression that this vast cultural field seems to inflict on all of us: Chinese calligraphy is an ancient, culturally specific and elitist form of art that is practiced by older—wise—men. Their brushed characters in black ink on white rice paper look roughly like what the word calligraphy itself promises: a type of beautiful writing. As a derivation from the Greek *kallós* (beauty) and *gráphein* (writing), the English term appears at least self-evident. But in Chinese, the immediate assumption that writing has to be aesthetically pleasing is absent: the word 书法 *shufa* is used. 书 *Shu* refers to writing while 法 *fa* should in this context be translated as method, law, rule, or principle. The reality is, as always, more complex than a simple stereotype can convey. This "method of writing" was never just beautiful. It was never exclusively reserved for the old, the male and the well educated, nor was the Chinese calligrapher solely bound to a dimly lit studio to perform their art.

China has been, famously and evidently, drenched in calligraphic shapes and forms for thousands of years. Public buildings carry signs with calligraphic captions; landscapes are adorned with inscriptions of literati from imperial times; squares, pavilions, parks, restaurants and even subway stations in Beijing boast engraved stone and plaques with calligraphy; online platforms such as *Douyin*, *Kuaishou* and *Bilibili* are full of calligraphers showing off and livestreaming their works, and the mastheads of daily newspapers feature well-known writings in calligraphy. And then I have not even mentioned the vast amount of calligraphies found on everyday objects: printed on T-shirts, kitchen magnets, mugs, wrappers and packaging, or tattooed on shins and arms. Calligraphy permeates everyday life, or more accurately: seeing calligraphy on a daily basis in China is virtually unavoidable. Its significance in China is difficult to overstate, and both discourses of theoretical and practical calligraphy should be considered a vast and rich cultural field spanning more than three thousand years, leaving very little about the practice undiscussed.

In understanding the development of calligraphy it is helpful to see its trajectory as a process of adaptation: to the needs of communication and administration but also artistic expression and the evolving demands of everyday lives. Around the beginning of the 1980s, the field of calligraphy irreversibly shifted and incorporated itself into many different domains. Now, practices of calligraphy are multi-varied in a way we have not seen before, and have also become a widespread practice. A rapidly growing number of people are now practicing calligraphy in different ways, many speaking of an ongoing 书法热 *shufare*, a calligraphy fever that shows no signs of breaking since the 1980s. Approaching calligraphy first and at its most basic as a method of writing helps in understanding its national significance as well as the pervasiveness of the earlier mentioned stereotype both in China and in the west. The written Chinese language, standardized in the third century BCE, has worked since as an effective unifying mechanism throughout the vast empire and across the long span of history, because the writing system is character-based. The meaning of the character is unaltered when pronounced in accordance with a person's local dialect. The ruling elite, therefore, used the written word more readily than speech to convey messages to its subordinates, and an intimate connection between the elite and the written word developed. As with all writing systems, Chinese writing too represents power. The ruling elite, united by writing skills, self-identified as men of words. Over time, more significance, connotations, contextual references and alleged qualities were stacked up on those skillfully written characters, which have remained remarkably similar in shape throughout the centuries. By the time the Tang dynasty (618–907 CE) ruled over the area, having good calligraphy skills formally became one of the four criteria in selecting men for office, as handwriting was considered revealing of a person's moral character.[1] This is a point of view that will frequently return in this book, as it prevails tenaciously in the present day. Writing calligraphy gradually came to signify a multitude of things: a cultural rite for the elite, a way to read one's educational background, intelligence, moral integrity and physical vigor, and it even acquired magical properties as a mediatory tool between gods and humans in Daoist rituals. But calligraphy was also very much a part of the everyday lives of people, and the deep respect for calligraphy becomes evident in a fond memory of one my interviewees. This retired man still recalls that as a child they did not light their stoves with paper with characters on it out of respect for the written word. I met him on a freezing Monday morning in Beijing in Ditan Park in the northern part of Beijing close to the Lama temple, where he writes calligraphy every day. But this calligraphy is far from what it used to be when he was young. I find him, rather vigorously, wielding a large brush made out of trash. With a piece of hard yellow foam cut out of an abandoned sofa, a plastic bottle sliced in half and an old umbrella stick, he is writing with water on the tiles of the park purely for his leisure. Concerns about whether or not to burn calligraphy out of respect for the written word have evaporated, and forgive me the poetic license, quite like the characters on the tiles: time, wind and sun have dissolved them before our eyes.

The once sacrosanct nature of calligraphy seems to have shifted somehow, and it is at this junction, characterized by a striking difference of attitude toward calligraphy, that this book inserts itself. It does so convinced by the necessity to expand ideas on what calligraphy in China does, and is today. How, I ask, is it possible that in the span of one lifetime, a rather elitist high art could morph into a carnivalesque water play in the park? Who is now making calligraphy, and how are they doing that; what does their writing afford if it is no longer a tool to climb the bureaucratic ladder? Or is it perhaps still also that? How has technology affected calligraphy? What, actually, is calligraphy now, and who decides where these conceptual boundaries lie? This book explores how calligraphy is bursting at the seams of the confined framework many people both in and outside China consider it to be in. With the increased adaptation to a globalizing world but also the current nostalgic retreat from that adaptation, the developing and increasingly international art market with its own particular desires and demands and the discourse of creativity playing a leading role in governmental policy to boost economic development, the notion of what "calligraphy" is, not clear-cut by any means. It is artistically reconsidered, creatively reimagined and digitally remediated. Moreover, what calligraphy promises to deliver to those making and consuming it has also changed drastically. It is no longer straightforward what kinds of cultural practice fall within the category of "calligraphy," and which practices should be defined otherwise. Much of the research in this book is concerned precisely with these boundaries and the rough edges of the definition of calligraphy. This is not because I aim to establish a definitive definition of calligraphy, but because it is an ongoing concern for my interlocutors in these fields: when does something stop being calligraphy and become, actually, "modern art"? Does physical exercise by way of water calligraphy automatically mean that the practitioners are calligraphers? What textures of selfhood are constructed when calligraphers deny—as they often do—that their practice is art and rather say that they are "just playing around" (只是玩儿 *zhi shi wanr*) with the brush? What happens when the calligraphy you write is ephemeral or when it is digital, and can we still consider that "writing"? Why is what is done in the past taken so much more seriously? The complexities of the expanding field of calligraphy today deserve close attention.

In this book, I aim to uncover how all these distinctions and the communities indexed by them shape the field of calligraphy—and how these communities are in turn shaped by calligraphy. It does so by magnifying five central themes that I think lie at the heart of calligraphy practice today: education; vernacular creativity; criticality; new media; and creative consumption. These themes should be read as heuristic tools that will help understand and compartmentalize the different practices observed ethnographically. They do not reflect the complexity of the field as a whole, nor do they correspond on equal par with the by now tired distinctions between "high culture" and "low culture," as this binary tends to divide artistic cultural productions of a certain educated class and leaves the rest as marginal, or "popular." The latter is a notion that I specifically aim to problematize in the context of contemporary practices of calligraphy. Although within the scenes of calligraphy such a binary conception still persists, as we shall see, this book will shed light on how calligraphy as a cultural practice has moved away from an exclusive association with high art to many spheres of cultural endeavor. In doing so, it is important to not oppose too bluntly a static and immemorial tradition of calligraphy to new, creative and modern experiments. Such a static tradition never existed, as cultural traditions in general tend to be dynamic and on the move.

This book takes up practices that in a varied range adhere to and respect calligraphic principles, yet simultaneously expand these, rebel against, poach on and reinterpret them. These calligraphies are not all written with ink and brush; a variety of surfaces and tools are used—from expensive rice paper to pavements to digital screens—through which both bodies and minds behave differently. These practices, because they venture away from ink and brush, provide exceptional case studies. They are all located on different planes in terms of skill, accessibility and visuality, and as such they allow us to ask questions specific to the medium. How does the calligrapher move, act, and how do they negotiate and interpret calligraphic rules? And how do the different visual outcomes matter when it comes to constructing new types of calligraphy, or rehabilitating old ones? The historical and national significance of calligraphy is difficult to refute and, of course, this is also not the aim of this book. Rather, I intend to carefully pry this large field apart, to then scrutinize the dismantled pieces separately. Which pieces—elements of practice or ideas—are most valued today, and by whom? And which ones have been discarded in the present? What about the emerging practices of calligraphy that are perhaps too readily labeled as "creative" today? Is "creativity" even a useful notion to apply to an art form that is firmly rooted in the practice of copying models?

Theoretically grounded in Cultural Studies, this book borrows, as Cultural Studies by its very definition borrows, from Area Studies and employs ethnographical methods. The benefit of such a heterogeneous grounding lies in the hope of creating a cross-fertilization of disciplines.[2] The main project of Cultural Studies from its inception was to take "popular" culture seriously, and to approach it as a site of struggle over power, resistance, and over individuality and hegemony. Its pitfalls stem from the same aspiration. Meaghan Morris notes that this project has led to a tendency to take any popular object or practice, and theorize it to the extent that it becomes active, resistant and creative. It does not matter which topic is taken, according to Morris, because the arguments remain the same.[3] Morris' cautionary words should be taken to heart here. Chinese calligraphy is not often seen, or indeed researched and analyzed, as part of popular culture. Doing so would already imply, from the perspective of Morris' critique, that its current popularity or everydayness renders it somehow counter-hegemonic; more active; more resistant to structures of power; and more creative. I reject this implication. Instead, I believe that by researching calligraphy today there is strength in approaching new and popular forms of calligraphy—which in various degrees are indeed theorized as marginalized, obscure, or resistant—as deeply informed by their former, and ongoing, status of high art.

Contemporary practices of calligraphy thus offer the speaking position of an elite art that is now also popular at the same time. It is produced, enacted and consumed widely in different realms of popular culture while it maintains complex relationships with both creativity and political power. By acknowledging these complexities, and by taking the traditional forms of calligraphy and its derivatives in various domains of everyday life equally seriously, this book is set on introducing new perspectives to the field of Chinese calligraphy.

A Calligraphic Timeline

The historical status of calligraphy as an elite pursuit has made sure that literature on traditional Chinese calligraphy in China abounds.[4] Discussions of traditional Chinese calligraphy in the west are mostly done by art historians.[5] These works usually start by tracing the evolution of Chinese calligraphy and explicate how the calligraphic sign has evolved from its beginnings when writing was first carved into turtle shell and bone, and held over fire to read its cracks as part of divination rituals, and then move toward the final visual outlook of the Chinese character: *kaishu* or standard script. These teleological overviews, which retrospectively create a coherent narrative of a vast and complex system spanning thousands of years, are hugely important, not to mention very practical for a student of calligraphy. This student can, for example, decide that they are in the mood for writing a neat seal script today, grab their smartphone and open the category "seal script" on their calligraphy app. They will then be presented with a list of generated model writings in that style to copy from.

Categories such as these are useful. But timelines spanning thousands of years are also, by definition, problematic. They tend to leave out discontinuities, revivals of earlier forms and parallel existing systems. In effect, they produce merely the simplified and dominant narrative of the historical development of calligraphy.

Still, an overview of how the calligraphic sign came to look the way it looks today, keeping in mind that all of these scripts are still in use, has value. It is an integral part of how calligraphy is conceptualized today. It is the leading tale that children grow up with and hear about in their calligraphy classes, and the narrative that is reproduced over and over again in lesson materials on Chinese writing. Calligraphy educators frame their lessons around the timeline presented in this account, and it features persistently in the widespread idea of the supremacy of Chinese culture, shaped around China's long and continuously united five thousand years of cultural history.

Perhaps rather unsurprisingly, this history starts often with the most emblematic of human culture: writing. The Chinese word for "culture" is made up of the characters 文 *wen* and 化 *hua* (*wen* being the carrier of meaning: writing, literature, culture; while *hua* means transformation, or "to make into," and is often placed after a noun to make a verb). The earliest meaning of *wen* is visible in the Chinese character itself, which is made up of a diagonal crossing of two strokes: 文. Xu Shen, the compiler of the first Chinese dictionary, the 说文解字 *Shuowen jiezi*, explains around 100 BCE that "*wen* is the crisscrossing of strokes; it imitates intersected patterns."[6] This patterning refers to the ordering of things that are naturally occurring in nature; the idea of the human patterning or ordering of nature is derived from there. *Wen* came to mean that which is opposite to naturalness: human culture.[7] Human ordering, writing and culture, are thus semantically linked in the Chinese language, and the origins and composition of the word *wenhua* indicate that writing is at the very core of culture.

The earliest forms of recognizable and systematic Chinese writing, or this culture making, are found in the so-called oracle bone inscriptions (甲骨文 *jiaguwen*). Inscriptions were carved on the scapulae of oxen and turtle shells with an awl, and they date back to the late Shang dynasty (1200–1045 BCE). They were meant for divination, and reveal that by that time a system of writing was already fully developed. From the beginning, the script has been morphemic: every sign stands for one morpheme. It was primarily pictographic, although this assumption is also open to debate. William Boltz, for example, argues that "hardly a single character can actually be regarded as pictographic. If by 'pictographic' we mean a graph that depicts a thing realistically enough for us to identify it without knowing what word the graph stands for."[8] With time, these recognizable representational images were progressively simplified and stylized. More abstract representations were added, such as semantic indicators and phonetic compounding, in which elements were added not for their meaning, but for their sound.

This very early carved writing continues to captivate both the academic and artistic world in China and the west. The first pictographic beginnings of the script led to the incorrect but very pervasive idea that Chinese writing is "ideographic": a word that symbolizes the idea of a thing without indicating the sequence of sounds in its name. In other words, such a writing can convey an idea directly to the mind without interference of a sound or language. This is, of course, a tantalizing hypothesis, and held sway among early western missionaries in China, as it, according to John DeFrancis: "took hold as part of the chinoiserie fad among western intellectuals that was stimulated by the generally highly laudatory writings of Catholic missionaries from the sixteenth to the eighteenth centuries."[9] Around the Zhou dynasty (1046–771 BCE) and the Spring and Autumn period (770–476 BCE), inscriptions on bronze vessels started to appear, called "bronze script" (金文 *jinwen*). In style and structure, the script is similar to the writings of the late Shang dynasty. These inscriptions are referred to as "greater seal script" (大篆 *da zhuan*), as various different styles appear in different regions. Greater seal script remained dominant until the third century BCE, while gradually the lines became simpler, and rounded shapes increasingly angular. Around the time of the Warring States (475–222 BCE), diversity among the scripts written by the peoples of different states grew as a consequence of political fragmentation. Then, in the Qin dynasty (221–206 BCE), emperor Qin Shi Huang (259–210 BCE) embarked on a wide-ranging standardizing policy aiming to homogenize various measurements, including the script. All the different systems of writing that were prevalent in the former states were now brought together, simplified and standardized. This system is referred to as "smaller seal script" (小篆 *xiao zhuan*).

Smaller seal script was difficult and time-consuming to write and, in time, was gradually simplified to a more easily written form, referred to as "clerical script" (隶书 *lishu*). The careful straight lines of the seal script were slowly replaced by more angled strokes, and while clerical script began to naturally develop from seal script already around the third century BCE, this script type was most widely used in the Han dynasty (206 BCE–220 CE), and became the official writing system during the Han dynasty. The Han clerical script styles were engraved on to steles and the rubbings of these steles have been used, and are still being used today, for the study and copying of calligraphic styles. We also find the clerical script styles on excavated wooden and bamboo strips or on silk. With the increased popularity of the brush, calligraphy evolved further. Semi-cursive or "running script" (行书 *xingshu*) developed in the Han dynasty as well, and is characterized by a more flowing style in which the strokes of the characters are visibly connected while maintaining legibility. By the end of the Han dynasty the use of the very cursive "grass script" (草书 *caoshu*) accelerated. In this expressive script type, the strokes in one character are reduced to single or several meandering lines and there is a great variety in thickness and thinness of the strokes, which can be combined, omitted or repositioned. Throughout the Western-Han dynasty (206 BCE–24 CE), a Han variety of the clerical script took shape, and by the end of the Eastern-Han dynasty (25–220 CE), the "standard script" (楷书 *kaishu*) which is still in use today grew out of the clerical script. Standard script is characterized by its square form and a balanced structure, and it became commonly used during the Wei and Jin dynasties. Calligraphy became more and more also a medium for artistic creation and creative expression, and forms of calligraphy started to be referred to as "art" and were valued as such in textual discourse.[10] This matured during the early Six Dynasties period (222–589 CE), when a culture of calligraphy took shape, including the emergence of a critical discourse on calligraphy and a flourishing art market in which calligraphy was sold as a valuable commodity.[11] The commodification of calligraphy also extended to the four tools needed to make calligraphy, which acquired much greater significance during that time. These paraphernalia started to be referred to as the "Four Treasures of the Study" (文房四宝 *wen fang si bao*): the inkbrush, inkstick, rice paper and inkstone.

A calligraphic timeline would be incomplete without mentioning the calligrapher Wang Xizhi (303–361 CE) who lived during this period, specifically, the Eastern-Jin dynasty (317–420 CE). Wang Xizhi is remembered in the collective national memory as the "sage of calligraphy"—the adulation of calligraphy started with him and his son Wang Xianzhi (344–386 CE). Wang wrote the most revered, canonical, the best-known and, for all these reasons, the most-often copied piece of calligraphy until today in China: *The Preface of the Gathering at the Orchid Pavilion* (hereafter *Orchid Pavilion*). The *Orchid Pavilion* is supposedly a commemoration of a party hosted by Wang Xizhi on a festive spring evening in the year 353 CE, when his 41 guests drank wine, composed poetry and generally enjoyed themselves. At the end of the evening, Wang Xizhi, inebriated, collected all the poems that were made and in a jolt of creative genius, wrote a commemoration of the party that would turn out to become an immortal piece of calligraphy.[12] Following the reign of Emperor Taizong, the style of Wang Xizhi and his son, who was said to be equally gifted, further gained popularity. Their style has since then dominated the canon of calligraphy. The "School of the Two Wangs," or "Two Wang Style" (二王 *erwang*), to this day, continues to be among the standards to copy from for any student of calligraphy.

By the time of the Tang dynasty, standard script, running script and grass script were the predominant ways of writing characters. With script styles fully matured, calligraphers started to develop their own unique creative styles. Among the most acclaimed calligraphers of this period were Ouyang Xun (557–641), Chu Suiliang (596–658), Yan Zhenqing (709–780) and Liu Gongquan (778–865), names that keep coming back today in calligraphy discourse, as their writings are used every day by millions of students as models for copying and, as we shall see in Chapter 1, their moral character. And while the principles of regular script gradually became the foundational rules for learning and practicing calligraphy, there was also daring work in extreme cursive script most notably by Zhang Xu (active ca. 700–750) and Huai Su (ca. 737–ca. 799) from the Tang dynasty—we will see them again in Chapter 3. Calligraphy of the Song dynasty (960–1279) is often described in commentaries as "romantic" and more liberal in style. Song calligraphers sought to break free from the more rigid models of the Tang calligraphic styles, and wanted to create unique, individual styles. The most influential Song calligraphers, such as Su Shi (1036–1101), Huang Tingjian (1045–1105), and Mi Fu (1051–1107), all have a personal style that is easily recognizable, even for a beginner calligraphy student. In the Ming dynasty (1368–1644), a nostalgic return to the old masters of the Jin and Tang dynasties, especially Wang Xizhi and Wang Xianzhi, inspired the calligraphy giants of the Ming dynasty such as Zhao Mengfu (1254–1322), Wen Zhengming (1470–1559) and Dong Qichang (1555–1636). This "return to tradition" movement became popular and soon spread nationwide. Calligraphers copied from original works as well as woodblock rubbings (帖 *tie*). Visual changes in the calligraphic sign took place, naturally, in tandem with the inventions of new methods of writing and preserving. Moreover, technical methods for reproducing characters[13] have been in use since as early as the second century BCE, with new methods appearing in the sixth, seventh and eighth centuries CE. These methods have coexisted alongside handwritten calligraphy for centuries. Commercial publishing houses started to print texts such as popular novels in the vernacular, fortune-telling handbooks and household manuals in the Mongol Yuan dynasty (1279–1368) and especially in the Ming dynasty. This meant, in effect that by that time, many people including the lower classes, craftsmen and peasants, were able to see a variety and a multitude of calligraphic characters on a daily basis, just like in China today. Brokaw and Chow note, moreover, that woodblock-printed books never broke away from the prototype of the handwritten text, as western books did. The best texts were those that managed to reproduce the appearance of a manuscript through beautiful calligraphy.[14] During the Qing dynasty (1644–1911), calligraphers slowly grew tired of learning from woodblock rubbings, and, in yet another turn of nostalgia, returned to the archaic Han steles and bronzewares. They believed that the stone inscriptions showed what calligraphy should look like in its most honest and pure form: unadorned and fresh—I discuss this further in Chapter 3.

So here we are, by means of this overview, presented with an almost too neatly fitting and rather awe-inspiring grand narrative, which takes us from bone carvings to the expressive grass script and the inevitable retelling of Wang Xizhi's drinking party. It affirms the long and continuous intellectual history of China through a skillfully brushed, rubbed, carved and printed calligraphic script. And, it also points to the fact that the script has always been subject to negotiation, trends, fads, nostalgic turns and returns, and creative deviation—we will delve further into this area in Chapters 4 and 5. From here, we can start our analysis on emerging contemporary creative practices of calligraphy.

A "Creative" Contemporary Calligraphy?

There has been a fair amount of buzz globally surrounding the word "creativity" in the last two decades. Not many words have the power to conjure up so many positive associations: to create something suggests original thinking, newness, intelligence, autonomy and an artistic *je ne sais quoi* that everybody wants to possess. Or, as Andreas Reckwitz says aptly, "Not to want to be creative . . . that would seem an absurd disposition."[15] The concept of creativity however, as appealing as it sounds, remains a slippery one. Activities associated with creativity run from a "motherhood-and-apple-pie banality" as Hesmondhalgh and Baker call it,[16] to a discourse that plays a leading role in governmental policies, aiming to boost economic development through a focus on the creative industries.[17] And then there is everything in between.

The Chinese government is not immune either to the fact that creativity is now, to add even more texture to this notion, globally seen as a marker of modernity, progress and a source of growth. It has therefore, since the early 2000s, become invested in implementing an idea of creativity in national policy, as a means to push China forward in a global production market where creative, aspirational and enterprising individuals should take the lead. The main driver of a multitude of policies to ensure such a move is the desire and necessity to transform China from a low-cost manufacturing industrial nation to a confident, creative and innovation-led economy. The slogan "From Made in China to Created in China" was rolled out in 2004, and promoted among other things the idea of the cultural and later also creative industries. Although still dominated by state-owned enterprises, and still also responsible for state propaganda, the media and cultural sector started to embrace a market economy as soon as the government legalized commercial cultural production. Since the 13th Chinese Five-Year Plan (2016–20) cultural industries are regarded as "a pillar industry of national economy." At the same time, creativity is also still a concept to be wary of. The creativity discourse not only promises prosperity and upward mobility, but also brings with it the more western ideals of individualism, self-expression, creative destruction and change that the Chinese state is hesitant to promote.[18] Creativity in such an imagined constellation is weighted toward disruptive rather than aesthetic considerations.

The appeal of anything creative has also affected the art of calligraphy today. As a highly institutionalized form of art, calligraphy seems at first sight wholly incompatible with creative aspirations. After all, calligraphy, traditionally, means by and large modeling characters after pre-existing configurations that have been transmitted from calligrapher to calligrapher over thousands of years. As Robert Harrist phrases it, there is a basic "graphic DNA" of a character,[19] on which all future arrangements are necessarily founded: they will always and forever be *re-productions*. Indeed, the art of calligraphy is often explicitly juxtaposed with claims of creativity, serving as a prime example of the familiar trope of the "Chinese tradition of copying." The idea of a copying tradition is then posited in opposition to an allegedly more creative tradition in the west. In the west, so the assumption goes, originality or creativity is often linked to individuality, and China's artistic production, based on imitative reproduction, is set against this western idea of an individual creative genius. Although scholarship on Chinese art has convincingly attempted to undo these stereotypes, the belief that there exists an essential unbridgeable difference between Chinese and western creativity persists.

However, calligraphy today is increasingly conceptualized and described as a creative endeavor, possibly riding the slipstream of the contemporary creativity discourse. Different, and sometimes opposing, claims of creativity in relation to calligraphy will be put forward in the five case studies of this book. These claims are, as we shall see, contingent upon the meanings ascribed to them by the various aesthetic communities. In the following chapters, we shall engage with different groups that have each developed a different relationship to the concept of creativity vis-à-vis calligraphy. Where calligraphy educators in Chapter 1, for example, speak of creation (创作 *chuangzuo*), they do so in the context of a political discourse that ascribes to creative or creating individuals the power to instigate nation building. In Chapter 5, the discourse of creativity takes on Marxist-like features: creative individuals are seen as central in the development of China's economy toward becoming a creative producer. Yet, in the case study of font design, creativity, rather than being equated with modernity, is dug out from an imagined Chinese past. At the same time, as I illustrate in Chapter 3, a discourse around creativity is developed not as a skill to cultivate, but as a mindset that can, and should, be inserted in the practice of calligraphy to maintain its relevance. Creativity is regarded as a skill, a tool of power, a form of knowledge and a quality of the mind. These intertwining discourses, with the various expectations of what creativity affords within, will be discussed separately in each chapter. It seems, and I say this tentatively, that a discourse is emerging in which calligraphy practitioners, in the different shapes and sizes they come in, are increasingly digging into their native practice, which has long been seen (both in China and the west) as something based on copying, and seeing this as a creative practice. This might then speak back to, and potentially open up, the notion of creativity as theorized in the humanities itself.

Let me end here with a viewpoint put forward rather frequently by my interlocuters. It suggests that, indeed, we should not necessarily look for "creativity" in calligraphy, but rather complicate that ungraspable notion of creativity itself *through* calligraphy. Young calligraphy teacher Tao, who I interviewed in Beijing, explains how the term "creativity" (创意 *chuangyi*) is not very appropriate to use in calligraphy discourse, and instead "creative work," or "creation" (创作 *chuangzuo*) is employed, with the latter morpheme meaning "to make, work, compose, write, act or perform":

> Ah, you mean creative work (创作 *chuangzuo*) and creativity (创意 *chuangyi*), right? I do not really understand this concept of "creativity," I always thought that it was one of these imported foreign concepts. Because in traditional Chinese language, we do not talk about creativity, so it must come from a western cultural category. They emphasize "ideas" much more. This is my opinion, and I have a very easy point of view. Let's first talk about creativity. If I want to do creativity (做一个创意 *zuo yige chuangyi*), a creative work, it does not surpass similar things that were made before that much, only a little bit, that is the "idea." Then, creativity is established. But creative work (创作 *chuangzuo*) is different. The creative work in calligraphy is placed in the coordinates of horizontal and vertical lines, and there we judge whether the creative work is valuable. The horizontal is the present, in which I am now writing these lines. I am doing creative work in the present. Is that not adding new research significance? Is that not something new to reflect on? On the vertical coordinates we place the ancient sages and the classic works that they left behind to compare. I have taken another step forward from the context of such a continuous inheritance. In fact, I think that in the field of Chinese calligraphy and Chinese painting, creative work (创作 *chuangzuo*) is far more difficult than creativity (创意 *chuangyi*).
>
> —Interview with Teacher Tao

If, as Tao suggests, the very act of producing a work in the present renders it creative, then a broader understanding of contemporary practices of calligraphy might help not only in further breaking down what calligraphy is today, but also deepening our understanding of the notion of creativity at large.

Contemporary Calligraphies

The case studies in this book combine the more classic genres of popular culture such as social media with the less archetypical: art and typefaces, as well as ethnographical data on parks, schools and universities. Chapter 1 starts by asking who is taking calligraphy classes, and what their motivations are for doing so. Calligraphy schools are mushrooming as calligraphy class is now compulsory at elementary schools, and many universities are starting calligraphy BA and MA tracks to meet the subsequent demand for calligraphy teachers nationwide. Chapter 1 demonstrates how the current popularity of calligraphy is indebted to a top-down emphasis on the importance of calligraphy fueled by the desire to preserve traditional culture—of which calligraphy is perceived as a chief embodiment—and the aspiration to build a quality population that can write by hand despite technological advancements that are understood to cause a serious assault on the longevity—and sheer existence—of the handwritten character. It suggests that this is an effective way of governing: calligraphy students behave like self-disciplined subjects that have internalized the productive discourses put forward by the state. These discourses offer opportunities for calligraphy practitioners to invent new modes of being, as quality citizens of a self-conscious country. It demonstrates how a moral discourse mobilizes self-cultivation, while a discourse focused on physical discipline attempts to motivate practitioners to enhance both body and mind. I show how much of what is being done in calligraphy schools is geared not toward educating new generations of talented calligraphers, but in making sure the skill is preserved.

Chapter 2 takes two public parks in Beijing as its ethnographic site, and probes the activities of water calligraphers, practicing ephemeral water calligraphy as a pastime and physical exercise. I analyze how the distinctive spatial and ephemeral characteristics of water calligraphy might be constitutive of new imaginations in calligraphy. Water calligraphy, done by elderly individuals in Beijing, challenges the idea of creativity as the domain of a young urban class, while its ephemerality contests the increasingly prevalent idea that (urban) creativity is now, or should be, always forced into structures of commodification and governmentalization. Despite several creative deviations in water calligraphy, I show how a faithful adherence to the traditional discourse of calligraphy is maintained.

Chapter 3 continues to problematize the hegemonic notion of calligraphy, presenting the works of two artists, Wang Dongling and Zeng Xiang. I show how their considerate and deliberate aberrations from traditional calligraphic practice are invested in making possible new ways of doing and thinking about calligraphy. It lays out how this is a precarious work: every line, blot and irregularity stems from a careful positioning vis-à-vis traditional calligraphy. These alternative representations are not read as critiques of calligraphy—and all that calligraphy connotes—but as a making visible of what had remained invisible in earlier configurations. This chapter shows how contemporary calligraphy artists are, by and large, concerned with how to *best serve* modern times—they employ techniques deemed most attractive for the contemporary situation in order for calligraphy to keep its relevance.

The widespread concern that calligraphy might lose its significance, or will indeed disappear altogether, is most often attributed to advancements in the digital realm. Chapter 4 demonstrates how calligraphy practices thrive there, against these odds. Building on Bolter and Grusin's notion of remediation,[20] it develops the argument that traditional practices of calligraphy are remediated to reaffirm their status, rising to the challenges of new media. It explores the impact of online and app-based calligraphy communities through learning, motivational friendships, exhibition and practice. It scrutinizes the role of internet-based platforms in developing calligraphy consumption, promoting connoisseurship, and forming appreciative communities. This chapter argues that the creation of native digital calligraphy is an opportunity for revisiting older media rather than erasing them.

Chapter 5 demonstrates how in font design, the visual outlook of the Chinese character has become based on a shared technological agreement, which is contingent upon the skill and creativity of the designer as well as market and governmental demands. It develops how this has led the hallmarks of older writing methods to increasingly reappear, and reads this as an articulation of Chineseness that ties in with the Party's directive to cultivate national and cultural self-confidence through a cultural rejuvenation of the past—a past that is mobilized as creative. This chapter analyzes how the aesthetics in Chinese type font design mobilize calligraphic aesthetics, and argues that in the search for creative input, creativity is located in a re-engagement with a Chinese past that is constructed and mobilized as a *creative* past that affords an affective production.

The coda presents concluding remarks. I explain what we have gained from combining five sets of data on calligraphic practice, and approaching these as a discursive field. The methodology has, necessarily, excluded many other calligraphic practices, and I reflect on these. I discuss the theoretical implications of my findings and argue how the questions I have engaged with throughout are not limited to calligraphy, or to China, but are relevant for wider studies on creativity and the role of everyday practices in cultural politics, nation building and governing tactics.

CHAPTER 1

Calligraphy Education: Disciplining Conduct

> We cannot let Chinese characters die out. . . . So, what is calligraphy education? It is to pass down traditional Chinese characters generation after generation. It is not to cultivate numbers of calligraphers.
>
> —Interview with Zhang Shijun

The large and chilly calligraphy classroom of Renmin University in Beijing smells of ink and is packed with rice paper when I join the early morning class: in folded bundles on the shelves, hanging on the walls, laid out to dry on desks and crumpled up in bins. Eight graduate students of calligraphy have arrived as early as seven o'clock to practice their brushstrokes. In a primary school just across the street, a group of school children practice calligraphic characters in the clean regular script of renowned calligrapher Yan Zhenqing. This has become a weekly task since the Ministry of Education (MOE) decided to make Chinese calligraphy a national compulsory course (必修课 *bixiuke*) in primary and middle schools in 2013. And in the myriad private calligraphy studios dotted around town, many more people have set themselves the task of learning how to write calligraphy with ink and brush.

Calligraphy class is on the rise: at university, in primary schools and in commercial calligraphy studios. In Beijing, numerous private calligraphy education institutes are rapidly emerging, reminiscent of the private schools (私塾 *sishu*) from the late 19th century, and akin to the resurgence of private Confucian education since the early 2000s.[1] According to my interviewees, it is near impossible to estimate just how many institutes have been set up, and how

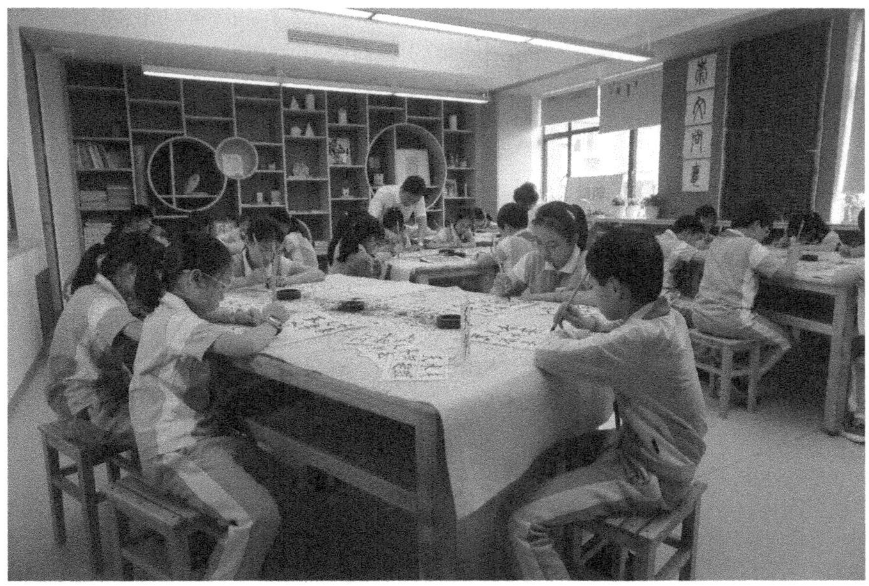

Figure 1.1: Children practicing calligraphy in an elementary school in Hangzhou. © Laura Vermeeren.

many people are following calligraphy classes—indeed, it proved impossible to crosscheck. One calligraphy teacher knew that within a one-kilometer radius from her own school, located in Beijing's university district, at least 30 other institutes have established themselves within the last five months as new calligraphy schools. An inaccurate estimation but, nevertheless, it indicates that calligraphy classes have become popular. *Calligraphy is hot* (书法很热 *shufa hen re*), interviewees declare time and again. And not only are private schools bourgeoning and an increasing number of primary schools are now able to offer calligraphy classes, but the number of universities offering calligraphy as an independent major is also substantially growing (see Figure 1.1).

What exactly does this rise of calligraphy education point toward? Calligraphy education is state-initiated within the context of the Chinese government's broader educational strategy to cultivate people by means of moral education. The goal of calligraphy education from the viewpoint of the state is to nurture talent for a confident nation, and this feeds into the marketization strategies of private schools as well. The latter similarly promote calligraphy education as an ideal tool for the general improvement of a type of "human quality" (素质 *suzhi*) through the cultivation of both traditional and national skills. What this means is that by taking calligraphy classes and behaving in the way calligraphy class steers and disciplines them, individuals commit themselves to objectives of the Chinese government. These objectives, as I will show, are postulated as an individual choice, but serve at the same time as a disciplining tool to create both an obedient and self-assured patriotic citizenry, and not necessarily a cohort of calligraphy artists.

To begin contextualizing these recent developments in calligraphy education, we must first understand the complex links between education and politics in China, along with the more recent reforms of China's intricate system of educational governance. Although the formal, millennia-old education system has suffered major blows throughout the last century, the traditional ways of thinking about education and what it should do have largely survived social and cultural changes.[2] Now, the Chinese government has made education a top priority again, to ensure the nation's progress, as declared in the 2022 National Education Conference.[3] It is specifically the idea that individuals can be trained through education to become individuals of value to society that dates back to governing practices of imperial China. This idea was largely founded on a school of thought associated with Confucius (551–479 BCE). Having lived through chaotic periods of rivaling kingdoms and warfare, Confucius' teachings place major importance on creating order and harmony to achieve a civilized and peaceful state. His teachings, disseminated through his disciples, emphasize a hierarchical system of social relations to achieve this state of order, maintained by a sense of morality. Every individual has a clearly defined position within this imagined "good society." The emperor is placed at the top, obeyed by his officials, citizens follow and accept the authority of the officials, students likewise their teachers, wives their husbands, and children their parents, referred to as filial piety (孝 *xiao*).

Within this set of hierarchies, everyone knows their place, and hence order will prevail. As an individual, one can pursue self-cultivation through learning and studying and the practice of ritual to become a better person, and attain what might be described as "a good life." This concept of achieving a good life through perseverance in learning calligraphy is re-emerging in the narratives of today's calligraphy students. In order to create a well-governed and civilized state as per Confucian philosophy, the state needs to be governed by an educated and morally upright class of scholar-officials, imbedded in a clear and comprehensible system of hierarchy. These officials, then, were selected through a system of imperial civil service examinations. Although some form of examination existed as early as the Han dynasty, the civil imperial examinations were officially implemented in the Sui dynasty (581–618 CE) and developed further in the Tang dynasty. They were only abolished in 1905 along with a wave of other modernizations, which means that a highly developed system of moral education serving primarily as a technology of governing had been in place for over a millennium.[4] These examinations were extremely challenging, and required years of dedicated full-time education and preparation. This meant that although in principle the examination, and thus a chance to serve in the government, was open to every man, only those with the financial means to spend years of studying and away from the labor market realistically had a chance to succeed. The idea that this system was based on meritocracy and led to an upper ruling class made up from all layers of society has been debunked as a myth.[5] Subjects of the examination included the Confucian classics annotated with extensive commentaries from Buddhist and Daoist strands of philosophy, mathematics, calligraphy and legal knowledge. The student was expected to memorize vast amounts of information, internalize the moral messages with which the Confucian classics and annotations are permeated and produce highly formalized calligraphic writing. An essential part of the examinations since the Ming dynasty was the so-called eight-legged essay (八股文 *baguwen*): a highly formulaic and rigidly structured set of answers on questions about Confucian thought. Not only were the structure and format limited, even word selection and calligraphic handwriting style were restricted. One misplaced character could result in a fail and because of the tens of thousands of candidates participating every year, this was considered an impartial way to separate the wheat from the chaff. This essay later became a target of critique for modernizers: repressive of creative thought and writing, it restricted the imaginative ability of the literati in late imperial China. Janette Ryan notes how in China today the emphasis on acquiring knowledge through memorization and repeated reading endures,[6] while others remark how this dedication to education still persists in China today.[7]

Foreign encroachments, military defeats by Japan and the west, as well as internal uprisings from the second half of the 19th century, forced Chinese intellectuals—because of the association of education with the politics they stood at the forefront of restructuring—to reform their ways of thinking. These reforms stemmed from the desire to comprehend how and why western technology, science and ideas had resulted in these humiliating military defeats, with the aim of potentially avoiding such outcomes in the future. From the late 1800s, the Confucian academies closed or were rearranged, and began to be replaced by new educational institutes modeled on the three-tier system of elementary, secondary and higher education found in Germany and Japan. The imperial examinations became a hindrance to the smooth development of these schools, which could not freely compete for funds or students and the imperial examinations were finally abolished in 1905.[8] The link between education and bureaucratic power was officially broken, and six years later the last dynasty also came to an end.

The following years were marked by a quest to find the right models and methods for a new Chinese school system: how to combine Chinese and western traditions of acquiring knowledge, how to incorporate western science, and what to do with the Chinese classics and theories on education and morality? Suzanne Pepper elucidates at this point that although new models of schooling were based on systems from Japan, Europe and the US, these were set up and co-opted by the educated classes "whose support had only been won by abolishing its main traditional source of authority and status."[9] This meant that the newly set-up modern universities were predominantly oriented toward the legal and liberal arts, and university examinations were organized and managed in much the same way as the old imperial exams were set up. During these reforms, and up until 1962, calligraphy was not recognized as an independent artistic skill to be developed at universities. Instead, it was viewed as a necessary ability for reading and writing, and therefore an essential part of the life of the educated class. Those at the universities particularly excelling in calligraphy could be found in the departments of Chinese literature or history.[10]

Another important shift in thinking about education occurred after the establishment of the People's Republic of China (PRC) in 1949. Now even more, Confucian views were seen as feudal, backward and hindering the country's progress toward modernization. Students were encouraged to learn socialist theory and the ideology of Mao Zedong. While the early period witnessed great expansion in literacy rates and school enrollment, this was severely disrupted by a series of campaigns attacking intellectuals and teachers. This culminated in the Cultural Revolution (1966–76). These disruptions included, but were not limited to, the disappearance of faculty members as they were sent away to reform themselves in rural areas; a quickly changing and increasingly elite student body of cadre family members; and finally the complete shutdown and occupation of all faculties by squads of Red Guards. Consequently, an entire generation were not educated in schools in these years. This might well explain the heightened interest in education and the desire for their children and grandchildren to receive a proper education today.

While calligraphy was not banned during this time, it had been restricted in content, style and purpose since the early 1940s. Revolutionary slogans could be written in calligraphy, but they had to be written clearly, and grass script was to be avoided.[11] Primary and secondary schools that closed down in 1966 reopened in the early 1970s with a shortened curriculum dominated by political propaganda. The student base in higher education was, until the reforms in the late 1970s, almost solely selected based on political loyalty and revolutionary fervor.[12] Deng Xiaoping famously stated that the closing of schools and academies during that period "created an entire generation of mental cripples" and he called for "expertise" again at the end of the 1970s when universities reopened.[13]

The 高考 *gaokao*—the National Higher Education Entrance Examination, set up in 1952—was re-established. The *gaokao*, still in full swing today, is reminiscent of the abolished imperial examination system: it is large in scale, organized on national level and successfully mastering the curriculum requires tremendous effort and memorization. Again, it is an examination with high stakes: it determines educational and career opportunities as well as social status. Three other relevant reforms were implemented at the higher educational level: universities were given more freedom over the content of existing programs; they were permitted to establish new content; and the central mission of the university, a renewed focus on research, was restored.[14] With this increased autonomy, a series of curricular changes was introduced, and it was at that point that calligraphy emerged among the newly established subjects. The first university to offer specialized courses in calligraphy was the Zhejiang Academy of Art in Hangzhou, starting already before the late 1970s reforms, in 1963, and finally establishing a major in 2001. Universities throughout the country followed suit. Since then, 23 universities offer doctoral graduate programs in calligraphy, 80 universities offer a master's degree in calligraphy, 130 universities offer bachelor's courses and another 141 universities provide optional undergraduate courses nationwide, and this number is rising fast, especially in the last five years.[15]

The more recent explosion of both university and private training opportunities in calligraphy links back directly to the decision of the MOE in 2013, which decided to turn Chinese calligraphy into a national compulsory course (必修课 *bixiuke*) in primary and middle schools. This was done in an attempt to improve the "writing ability, aesthetic ability and cultural quality" of young children.[16] The MOE declared again in 2018 that it will further intensify its focus on calligraphy education, stating that calligraphy education has a strong necessity in today's "'keyboard' era":[17] technological advancements are understood to cause a serious assault on the longevity—and sheer existence—of the handwritten character. More supervision, new standardized calligraphy text books, online education platforms and stimulating a society-based learning environment for everyone should ensure that calligraphy will be widely practiced by youths. Another more recent measure taken to stimulate calligraphy classes nationwide is through another three steering committees on calligraphy, martial arts and opera, set up to promote these activities in all primary and high schools throughout the country.[18] The fundamental goal set for these committees is "cultivating morality and improving the overall quality of students."[19]

As a result of the increased focus on calligraphy education, a huge demand for qualified calligraphy teachers to work in all primary and high schools nationwide was generated. Since 2018, calligraphy education is secured in only half of the primary schools, and even fewer high schools. There are about 160 million students in the country whose calligraphy education is compulsory, and generously calculating that one calligraphy teacher can teach 300 students, it would require over half a million calligraphy teachers to teach the whole nation.[20] Clearly, this is a problem, and COVID-19 class attendance restrictions have not helped matters either. The current shortage of professional calligraphy teachers has already caused a situation where, especially in the more rural areas, primary school teachers who might not necessarily be skilled in calligraphy are forced to teach their pupils. Alternatively, no calligraphy class is offered at all. This is cause for worry, and discussed often in calligraphy education discourse: if the principles of calligraphy are being passed on incorrectly to the new generation—or not passed on at all—what will become of the tradition of calligraphy and, as is always the subtext, of our national essence? The decision has also widely impacted urban areas, where the calligraphy education of children is increasingly being pursued outside the state-led classroom, and private calligraphy studios have established themselves as a convenient alternative for the calligraphy classes in primary and middle schools that are often still lacking either in quality or mere existence. Several measures have been taken to incentivize students to opt for a calligraphy major and a career as a calligraphy teacher. Compared to other art majors, the *gaokao* requirements for entering a calligraphy major have the lowest minimum required score, and the highest enrollment number. A score between 640 and 680 is required for high-ranking universities in China—this is only 460 for a calligraphy major and even 380 for a major at a medium-ranked university. And on top of that, while the government restricts enrollment number in the arts, sports and music fields of study, no such enrollment restriction is put in place for calligraphy—although the MOE is restructuring this system with a view to balance *gaokao* admission scores in 2024. University training in calligraphy is, in many universities, geared toward preparing students for a professional career, as it includes teacher training and pedagogy.

Jiao, a graduate student at Renmin University, states pragmatically in our interview that her main reason for pursuing a bachelor's degree in Calligraphy at Jiangsu Normal University lies in the more lenient *gaokao* requirements for calligraphy majors: "I had already practiced with my grandfather, and later I went to a weekly class, so we thought, with the issue of the *gaokao*, that this was a good way to do it." Because the *gaokao* scores that are necessary to enter art school are lower than those required for other schools, those entering art school are often suspected of circumventing a difficult *gaokao* requirement to get into a (good) university, rather than out of a genuine interest in art. Lily Chumley describes how this "loophole," as she calls it, became increasingly irrational as huge numbers of students started doing the same, and the preparatory art tests that popped up as a way to prepare for the art *gaokao* turned into "grueling, expensive years of preparation."[21]

Chumley's observation is mirrored in the experience of graduate calligraphy student Peng Houjian at Renmin University, who told me he had no interest in studying at all during high school and felt education was useless (as he phrased it: "You can go to Beida and still end up selling pork"). He was subsequently sent to a class in Changsha for six months to prepare for the additional calligraphy test required for university admission. Peng recalls that he and the other students in the preparatory school were expected to write every day from 8 o'clock in the morning until 10 o'clock at night, all writing the same clerical script and regular script in *Weibei* style.[22] This type of training camp, set up specifically to guide subjects in all learning the same model calligraphy under strict surveillance, brings to mind the aforementioned imperial examination system. Disciplinary power, as Michel Foucault reminds us, becomes effective through correct training: "hierarchical observation, normalizing judgement and their combination in a procedure that is specific to it, the examination."[23]

All of these measures can partly account for the current surge in people subscribing to calligraphy education nationwide at the levels of primary and secondary school education, university and the private studio. In the remainder of this chapter, I probe how a complex web of incentives is emerging, and, simply put, what calligraphy education *does* to its students: how calligraphy imposes self-discipline, guides conduct, empowers and gives opportunities both financially and for personal and physical improvement.

"Calligraphy Is Hot"

In conversations with calligraphy students and teachers who are engaged with calligraphy both as a hobby and a major at university in Beijing and Hangzhou, many reasons to learn calligraphy came to the fore. They acutely show the entanglement of the personal with the political: reasons vary from hopes of becoming a famous calligrapher; the desire to enter a university without necessarily having obtained very high *gaokao* grades; the wish to impress at the workplace with beautiful handwriting; as a way to increase their own or their children's groundedness and connection with an imagined Chinese cultural heritage; to calm down; or to find a steady job. Teacher Tao teaches at a large private studio where calligraphy and other "traditional" arts such as the traditional Chinese musical string instrument *guqin* and Chinese ink painting (国画 *guohua*) are taught. He tells me that his student base is becoming increasingly diverse:

> Calligraphy art is definitely an essential art, and the whole society is now slowly getting conscious of that. However, although our society in general is more self-conscious, there are still typical groups that take classes. The most obvious ones are younger ones, such as college students, urban white-collar workers, and employees in enterprises and institutions, because they have good jobs. But in general, the group is not as uniform as it used to be, and it begins to present a universal character. I think the main reason is that calligraphy is the root of all Chinese culture. . . . I think that with the development of our national strength and our economic development in the past 30 years, now the basic needs of ordinary people are satisfied and there is now time for their spiritual needs.
>
> —Interview with Teacher Tao

Teacher He, from Inner Mongolia, likewise relates how calligraphy has become popular and is now something everyone, from any layer of society, is able to do:

> In my hometown, my family wrote characters for the Spring Festival for the entire village. We would write couplets on the sheds of the sheep. I wanted to study calligraphy, but you couldn't do that then in Inner Mongolia. Now, it is different. The whole society is now paying attention to calligraphy. . . . Before, we were all learning English for the Olympics, and we were all learning computer skills. Now, we finally pay attention to our own traditional culture.
>
> —Interview with He Ruile

The time to pursue a career in calligraphy is the *now*. Calligraphy is referred to as "hot," "booming," or informants stated that "the Ministry of Education is finally pushing calligraphy," there is "now a growing prosperity of calligraphy" and "the government is now advocating the restoration of China's excellent traditional culture." Peng, mentioned before, states how there were other artistic majors in his province open for him via the prep school route, but he felt that calligraphy, as opposed to music or drama, is more "fun and interesting": "Since the 1980s, we have a calligraphy fever (书法热 *shufare*), and although it may not be as hot as it was in the eighties and nineties, we feel that calligraphy is now even better, even more interesting, and even more popular" (interview with Peng Houjian).

Peng voices an idea that many informants share: the feeling that, after the passionate and indeed feverish reopening of the arts and calligraphy in the 1980s, calligraphy has now reached a state of a certain maturity. With that, calligraphy has managed to seep into all layers of society, resulting in the boom of private calligraphy schools. "Calligraphy fever" (书法热 *shufare*), has been more readily mentioned by interviewees than the more generally referred to "tradition fever" (传统热 *chuantongre*) that has been around for over two decades. The latter notion seems to share similarities with the more widely researched "national learning fever" (国学热 *guoxuere*).[24] This "fever" is an ambiguous and undefined concept, and as such, as Shaobo Xie argues, can be stretched out to serve a range of purposes, from educational, commercial and political.[25] "In all these pursuits," he argues, "one sees an unmistakable collusion among Chinese academia, the market, and the ruling regime: what is at stake is a kind of simulacrum of something long lost, which is desired by state-officials, designed by academics, and produced by market promoters."[26]

This convincingly captures how the discourse on "national learning" allows different parties to benefit from the idea of a national intellectual heritage, but leaves out the practitioners, who are often simultaneously consumers of the practices that are associated with these fevers. While my interlocutors often spoke of the "tradition fever," "national learning fever" was never mentioned. I suspect that the first is employed more easily in the vernacular, since it implies a focus on a non-specified but nevertheless traditional activity—such as calligraphy—rather than on thought or learning. Calligraphy teacher Jian explains what this calligraphy fever, according to her, entails:

> I think the calligraphy fever reflects who we, Chinese, now are. There is now a demand from the people to promote culture, right? Because when we were young, China was very poor. They didn't have the right conditions to think about these problems. This shows already the overall level of people now, because calligraphy is a high art and people pay a lot of attention to it, right? I think this will enhance our Chinese people's understanding of calligraphy and of traditional culture, because calligraphy is the core of Chinese traditional culture. But I think the current calligraphy fever is not very balanced yet. Parents now think that the state promotes it and their children should all learn calligraphy. I think that is irrational and short-sighted. Because some children are not necessarily suited to learn calligraphy. Because they didn't choose it themselves, and the parents just think for them. . . . So,

> I think that calligraphy is now very popular, but it will slowly return to rationality. Maybe this process will take ten years or so.
>
> —Interview with Jian Meng

In Jian's view, the generally increased interest in calligraphy—although she disagrees with the undesirable excesses of the fever—will lead to an overall qualitatively better society. Her account also clearly showcases the diffusion, or entanglement, of the top-down flow of cultural policies with the bottom-up desire to reconnect with traditional culture, of which calligraphy is perceived as the embodiment. Does national policy want us to write, or do we want it ourselves? The fact that this question can be asked shows that whichever tactics of power are at work, they are highly effective. Instead of a disciplinary top-down policy, its mechanisms are dispersed and fragmented across the entire population. It seeks to discipline children, and adults, and controls the nation by preserving its heritage and thereby protecting and ensuring a quality of life, as well as the quality of the nation as a whole—these two become intertwined. Tradition and cultural heritage become discourses to exert such power. As a result, the laboring bodies in calligraphy class are subjugated to a national project to preserve and protect China and its heritage, in an earnest attempt to ensure its future.

In the next three sections I examine more closely these intertwined impetuses of calligraphy students. These impetuses can be subsumed under three interrelated discourses: (1) Chinese traditional culture, (2) moral rectitude and (3) bodily discipline.

Chinese Traditional Culture

Chiang Yee maintains that calligraphy should be seen as "the most fundamental artistic manifestation of the national mind."[27] This idea is so widely recognized that today "calligraphy" is almost always mentioned in the context of "traditional culture" (传统文化 *chuantong wenhua*). The connection between "culture" and calligraphy is so deeply intertwined that calligraphy embodies, connotes, and even *gives* one culture: in colloquial speech, culture is something that you can possess (有文化 *you wenhua*), through education, objects and practices that reinforce social hierarchies.[28] To "be cultured," or have (*you*) *wenhua* often refers to the level of schooling a person has achieved, while saying that someone has "no culture" (没有文化 *meiyou wenhua*) implies that someone has crude manners, has not had a proper education or is misbehaving (like spitting on the floor or jumping the queue). It shows how, in the everyday colloquial, conduct, culture and education are linked.

The term *wenhua*, culture, is now widely used to mean refinement, cultivation, literary competence, and sophistication.[29] Yen has further argued that by "practicing *wen*," through making calligraphy, writing poetry and the like, a person is transformed, and will "'embody' all the qualities associated with *wen*—gentility and self-control."[30] The discourse of a "Chinese traditional culture" so relevant to calligraphy practice today is built around this perceived essence. Through the act of writing, a type of self-cultivation, a calligrapher will, in time, start to possess admirable qualities. The idea that people in the past effortlessly possessed these qualities is pervasive. Calligraphy was a necessity—any writing was simply done with the tools available at the time: brush, paper and ink. There were no ballpoint pens, no computer, and none of the temptations and distractions of modern life. Those in the past who were able to spend their time writing, goes the assumption, naturally also possessed desirable character traits such as serenity and self-control. My interviewee Hong Liang, a young calligraphy teacher at an elementary school in Beijing puts it like this:

> Then, calligraphy did not exist in isolation, and was closely related to Chinese culture. Nowadays however, many calligraphers are famous and their works are very expensive. Some of them are actually not well educated. They only write, and the words they write are no more than the words of their predecessors. Nor are they particularly well written, unlike the ancient calligraphers, who were well educated in Chinese culture, were taught in private schools, and wrote their own poems about their own feelings and endeavors. Now, calligraphers just create their own style to catch up with the trend of the time.
>
> —Interview with Hong Liang

His statement evokes an idealized nostalgia for the times when calligraphy was well written, and the calligraphic brush lines expressed pure and real sentiments. Today, however, is a superficial time, a modern and trendy era, and we will never be as good as those who lived in the past. The idea that calligraphers in the past were somehow better—both in skill and character—than they are today comes back in many reiterations. A young couple that recently opened a calligraphy training center in the university district in Beijing believes that "calligraphy is the core of the core of Chinese traditional culture. If there was anything to represent Chinese traditional culture, it should be calligraphy." The content of what you write in their calligraphy lessons, they say, should also be "traditionally Chinese," such as ancient poems or the classics.

The past that is imagined and constructed in these rather typical accounts is by and large a positive and desirable past to nostalgically look back on, and seems to function as a cure to dystopian ideas of the present: in the present, our songs lack depth, our calligraphers lack integrity, and young people lack self-discipline and skill. In 1983, Hobsbawm and Ranger already put the idea forward that traditions might be conceived to deal with anxieties in the present, arguing that an invented tradition is "a set of practices . . . which seek to inculcate certain values and norms of behaviour by repetition, which automatically implies continuity with the past."[31] The present, with its uncertainties and fast pace could thus be overcome by inculcating behavior that links to a past in which people were skilled at writing calligraphy—were therefore cultured—and consequently behaved in a composed and all together much better way.

Like all the other commercial studios I visited during my research, the school in the center of Beijing that I frequented for eight months also stresses that practical skill is only one part of what they are attempting with their schooling. Their mission, one that largely resembles the mission statements of the many other schools in Beijing, states:

> Against the background of a Chinese traditional cultural revival, and the intensifying of popular culture, entertainment and consumerism, we use the current education of children, Internet skills as well as contemporary entertainment to renew the practice of calligraphy education for both children and adults. We do not only teach calligraphy, we teach the principles of writing and culture. We aim to pass on the essential meanings that lay behind our characters: etiquette, rules, and oriental beauty and wisdom.[32]

The idea that the past can be excavated through the study of characters is clearly articulated here. This is, of course, not really a very far-fetched idea, as the characters that are practiced in calligraphy class all appear in canonical and classical texts, and logically carry meaning: they are the bearers of these texts. Although the visual form of calligraphy is given priority over the content, the idea holds sway that the content of the copied treaties and couplets *do something* to the calligrapher who is writing them. At the same time, the calligraphy practitioner adds meaning to the historical texts by reproducing and interpreting them. Through understanding what is written, calligrapher Qiu Zhenzhong explains in our interview, the process of meaning-making within calligraphy can be continued. Throughout history, he argues, we need people to read and construe calligraphic texts, and add their interpretations to them, to be able to understand Chinese culture, and to pass it on. Most schools perpetuate this view in their calligraphy classes: while the form and line of a character or sentence is taught, information on the author, the usage of the words and its historical background are passed on as well. It is, simultaneously, the critique I came across most often from calligraphy teachers about other schools they saw as inferior: they might teach their students how to hold the brush, but they forget about the content and historical backgrounds of the calligraphy, and as such they lack depth, and are bad and superficial schools.

This imagined past within calligraphy educational settings is enacted through objects as well. Especially commercial studios go through great efforts to portray a tranquil and cultured past through objects of *wen*, or culture. A studio in the center of Beijing, for example, opens in a big hallway with antique chairs and glass display cases exhibiting antique inkstones, ivory-stemmed brushes, and seals made from semi-precious stones. A luxurious tea table is always prepared for guests, and employees wear serene smiles and humble simple clothing. Calligraphy teacher Lin, at an elementary school in Hangzhou, chooses to play traditional *guqin* music to the children during their hour of practice. Other studios similarly exude a vague generic sense of traditional Chineseness, and construct a fantasy of an ideal traditional China located in an undefinable point in the past. This recreation of the past through objects is not meant to be an accurate historical reconstruction: Qing dynasty calligraphy scrolls hang side by side with imitation Ming vases and plastic, ancient-looking tea cups.

These tactics evoke Svetlana Boym's ideas on restorative and reflective nostalgia. While restorative nostalgia, she argues, attempts a historical reconstruction of a lost home or time, and "protects the absolute truth,"[33] reflective nostalgia on the other hand "does not follow a single plot but explores ways of inhabiting many places at once and imagining different time zones; it loves details, not symbols."[34] It is this latter type of nostalgia that we find in these educational institutes: they do not aim to precisely recreate a specific historical period but instead seek to capture an essence of it that aligns with their school's vision and profile.

In one small calligraphy school in Beijing, students are asked to wear a traditional Chinese scholarly dress over their regular clothes before entering the classroom, by doing so literally stepping from the inferior present into the preferable imagined past. The teachers also wear traditional clothing without seams and have decorated the studio as accurately as possible in "Ming style." This, the owner asserts, is all part of "restoring antiquity" (复古 *fugu*):

> When I was still working in the work unit, my colleague told me that you should pass through the ancients (穿越到古代去 *chuanyue dao gudai qu*). So, the clothes that I am wearing and everything, is all a bit *fugu*. It shows that I am not like modern people. . . . We, people who like calligraphy, like old objects. For example, we like buying ancient inkstones, old paper, and we like fiddling with a piece of wood. To be frank, I think that this type of *fugu*

> is a nostalgia for traditional Chinese culture. . . . I think everybody in China has this complex, but we, who like calligraphy, definitely have this complex.
>
> —Interview with anonymous informant

Restoring antiquity or *fugu* is now often used in terms of housing or clothing style, in the way in which "retro" is employed in English. The philosophy of *fugu*, however, dates back to the Sui and early Tang dynasties, gaining full momentum in the neo-Confucian movement during the Northern Song dynasty and is built around the Confucian idea that mishaps in the present can be overcome through restoring the ideal past.[35] To be able to restore the past, antiquity has to be understood through learning, and through collecting ancient objects. It is thus not merely a melancholic longing for a romanticized past, but an actual effort to reconstruct that past, similar to what Svetlana Boym's notion of "restorative nostalgia," which "does not think of itself as nostalgia, but rather as truth and tradition."[36]

Although the abovementioned discourse of idealizing the past is pervasive in calligraphy education, a not-so ideal past is often talked about as well: the more recent history in which writing calligraphy was restricted and controlled. The generation of young people in China today, starting with those born in 1980–89, referred to as the 八零后 *balinghou*, are the first generation that benefited from economic reforms in the 1970s, while the digitally native post-1990 and 2000s generations (the 九零后 *jiulinghou* and 零零后 *linglinghou*) have been raised in a time of constant economic growth and rapid social and technological change. Unlike their parents, they have not experienced obvious hardship imposed by the government, political upheaval or strong social unrest.[37] These upheavals, which I briefly introduced at the beginning of this chapter and will explain in more detail in Chapter 3, had made it difficult—if not impossible—to receive proper training in calligraphy for the older generations. The parents of the children and young adults today—those who are the motivators, the financiers and often the decision-makers—make up this "lost generation," and while they recall how their parents and grandparents wrote calligraphy, they have often not received any training themselves. This fact is often lamented and gives reason for embarrassment. A grandmother who brings her grandson to calligraphy class every week remembers:

> We had classes every week when we were young, and then there was a period in which nobody studied it. Now, we encourage it again. My daughter is very busy, and does not have a lot of time to take care of her son, so we give him this kind of intellectual environment. The inheritance of the Chinese character is the most important, but there are many other benefits. He will

> be able to write well, he will have a good character, and he will be able to sit still. And the child will not feel like fighting. He exercises his arm strength and his moral strength at the same time.
>
> —Interview with Miss Deng

Calligraphy education, in her view, allows the nation as a whole to return to its—briefly ignored—essence, while simultaneously bringing personal benefits to those practicing it: a good moral character and a calm body. In the next section, I analyze how calligraphy education is believed to indeed shape the moral character, and I will zoom in on the practicalities of the learning process, showing how the correct usage of the brush is believed to mold and improve the inner self of the practitioner.

Moral Rectitude

Calligraphy is permeated with moral implications. There is a vast amount of literature, both western and Chinese, classic and more contemporary, describing the enmeshing of aesthetic, physical and moral judgments within the discourse of Chinese calligraphy practice over the course of centuries.[38] The addition this book offers to these accounts is ethnographic: it lets the lived reality of everyday calligraphy practices in educational settings speak. In the previous sections, I suggested that calligraphy schools are spaces where a positive Chinese past—either restoratively or reflexively—is imagined and enacted. Stepping into these spaces, the real world is kept at a distance, while at the same time, the real world is believed to be improved by what happens in calligraphy schools. There is thus a *circulus in probando*: calligraphy improves the moral character of people, while vice versa, calligraphy can only be good calligraphy when made by people with a high moral standing. This section starts with a short introduction on how the connection between calligraphy and morality is historically constructed, and then moves on to the present, showing how the idea of morality through calligraphy education is imparted.

A famous tale describes how during the Tang dynasty, Emperor Muzong (r. 821–824) asked his minister—a very skilled calligrapher—how one should hold the calligraphy brush. The minister, Liu Gongquan (778–865), answered: "The use of the brush is in the heart. If your heart is upright, your brush will be upright" (用筆在 心, 心正則筆正 *yong bi zai xin, xin zheng ze bi zheng*).[39] This well-known anecdote illustrates how the *xin* (心), the heart/mind, is believed to stand in close relation to the brush. Amy McNair mentions that the idea that writing and personhood are linked together has been documented from the

Han dynasty onward. It is part of a broader theory, according to McNair, of characterology, which is founded on the idea that the inner person and its outward expressions are united. The moral character of the person is manifested in external expressions such as "appearance, behavior, and aesthetic endeavor," and characterology has been widely applied in matters of government since the Han dynasty.[40] When choosing the right men who were fit to govern, the belief in characterology allowed for the assessment of their handwriting, looks and behavior in order to find a man of moral standing—the imperial exams served as the vehicle to make such an assessment.

One of the implications of this aesthetic attitude was that, according to Ledderose, "handwriting itself could replace content as the main criterion by which to judge a written piece."[41] Calligraphy, therefore, and not the content of the written words, became a way to measure someone's inward qualities, and moral significance became attached to the practice of calligraphy. Elsewhere, McNair develops the idea that this widespread belief is an act of imagination: "To see the trace of someone you know in his handwriting is largely an act of memory and association, but to take that 'seeing' a degree further, into the realm of graphology—that is, to see a man you never knew in his writing—that becomes an act of imagination."[42]

This act of imagination, following McNair, developed into a deeply ingrained conviction, one that is still alive in different reincarnations in the present with powerful and productive implications. In the colloquial, the idea of characterology is most often mobilized using the phrase 字如其人 *zi ru qi ren*, "the writing is like the man." The phrase is thrown around often and would typically be used along the lines of what 18-year-old student Li states when I drink a matcha latte with her in a cat café in Beijing:

> Yes, from writing you can see someone's character. You can see that some girls write very cute, and some boys write very messy. I can really see it among my classmates. . . . If someone writes earnestly, he is an earnest person. Maybe because Chinese characters are made up from brush strokes, so the structure shows a stronger personality. In comparison to English letters, there is more character and you can see if this person is serious or relaxed. It's the truth!
>
> —Interview with Li Yuqi

Li extends the idea of morality in handwriting to character traits more generally. What remains is the conviction that something about the person can be deduced from their handwriting. This serves as a powerful incentive to go to calligraphy class and to keep practicing. In conversations on the notion of *zi ru qi ren*, the example of Tang dynasty calligrapher Yan Zhenqing is regularly brought up. Yan Zhenqing (709–780) is remembered as a loved leading calligrapher of his time, and a dedicated and trustworthy martyr of the Tang dynasty. His script stands out first because it differs from the early Tang masters, whose calligraphy was slim, beautiful and elegant. Yan Zhenqing's characters, in contrast, are straight, clear, muscular and bold: adjectives that are of course readily applicable to moral character as well. His calligraphy, instead of being overly crafted and therefore considered artificial, was unpretentious and clear, and this is widely thought to reflect his equally unpretentious, honest and upright character.[43] Today, his regular script-calligraphy style, called 颜体 *yanti*, is the first and standard model for calligraphy learning in primary schools throughout China. This means, in effect, that every schoolchild in China is familiar with Yan Zhenqing and has likely practiced copying his handwriting—a likelihood that is set to grow as calligraphy education becomes more intensified in the coming years. The linkage between moral character and calligraphy is, perhaps surprisingly, seldom as explicitly employed by teachers as a didactic tool to motivate students to practice more, or work harder. Instead, it is mobilized more ambiguously through the use of historical models such as Yan Zhenqing: the moral virtue of exemplary calligraphers in the past is mentioned in relation to their exquisite calligraphy. What the student has to do is manually copy the characters of this virtuous model as accurately as possible. Morality and copying are therefore intricately linked. The fact that teachers do not openly equate their student's morality with their calligraphy can be explained by thinking of this belief as an already normalized principle that is ascribed the notion of truth—and thus does not need to be voiced. Foucault asserts that: "Each society has its regime of truth, its 'general politics' of truth: that is, the types of discourse which it accepts and makes function as true."[44] This regime of truth, as Foucault reminds us, is always linked to power, which produces reality and rituals of truth. The account of morality in relation to calligraphy is a powerful narrative that is able to shape and guide the actions of students of calligraphy, not by being stated explicitly or forced, but through tactics of normalization.

If the brush and the mind are believed to be so intricately connected, what happens to your own mind when you copy calligraphy from a model—which is really the only way toward mastering calligraphy? Calligraphy is believed to have many benefits, physical, moral and spiritual, that are instilled in the student through the learning process. Importantly, this process is wholly founded on the emulation and copying of exemplary past calligraphers. What is calligraphy class then supposed to do—ensure that the student inherits the moral

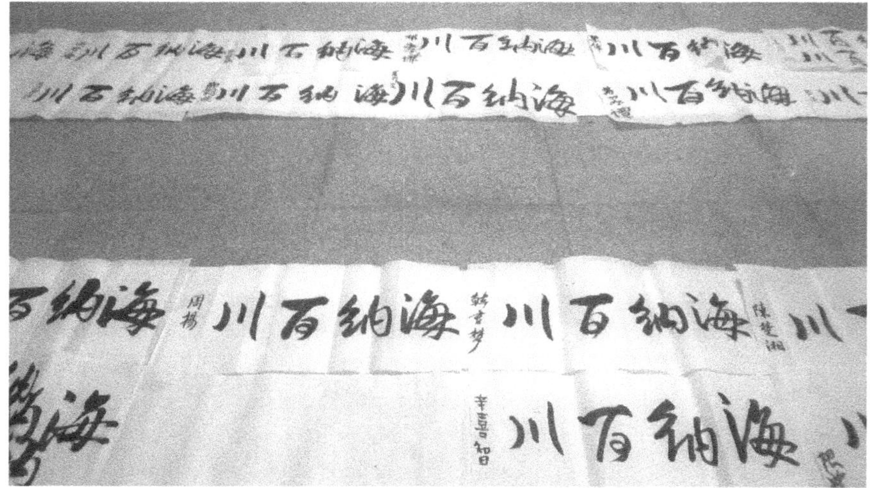

Figure 1.2: The results of the class laid out on the floor. © Laura Vermeeren.

qualities of the model? Does the student need to *become like* the model, or is it enough to copy the shape and contours of the character?

Calligraphic techniques, according to Francesca Bray, like other types of technology, "create material forms that embody shared values and beliefs, tying people into orthodoxy through their everyday practices."[45] This is the case in calligraphy class, where techniques are being taught in a way that has not changed much since antiquity. In what follows, I will describe a typical calligraphy class taught in Beijing, zooming in on how the skill of calligraphy is imparted through copying. I provide a full description of a class rather than a summary of its highlights, to provide an accurate account that allows for the repetitive aspects that come to the fore with exact copying and writing. As will become clear, observation and imitation form the core elements of the didactic strategy, and few rules are directly voiced.

Figure 1.2 shows the results of a two-hour optional undergraduate university calligraphy class, laid out on the floor of the hallway to be publicly compared and examined by the teacher and the students—aptly reiterating Foucault's statement that disciplinary power works through simple instruments: hierarchical observation, normalizing judgment and their combination.[46] Prior to arranging these calligraphies on the floor, the classroom was filled with around 25 people. The professor sits at the front of the class, his hand and brush visible for the group of students through an overhead projector that projects his hand and the paper he writes on. He announces that today the class will have to copy a four-character *chengyu*, a traditional type of idiomatic expression, most of which consist of four characters, in the style of famous Song painter and calligrapher Mi Fu (1051–1107): 海纳百川 *hai na bai chuan*. This idiomatic expression carries a moral message, as it means "all rivers run to the sea" and is used to describe a tolerant society or people. The four characters are written in running script, and the professor clarifies his choice by explaining that they "are a fairly standard running script, because none of the character strokes are omitted, but they are linked together." The characters are therefore well-defined enough for beginners to be able to copy them. The professor explains how Mi Fu has linked up the brushstrokes within the four characters:

> You see how this character is built up out of two strokes? First there is this little dot. Then, the rest of the character is completely joined together. And 纳 is altogether made up out of one single brush stroke. This is the main characteristic of running script: the brush strokes have been completely preserved, but are linked together. How much should we link them together? And on which spot should we link them? That you will have to decide for yourself. But, there is an order to these linkages, and this order has been shaped throughout history. The calligraphers of the past have all abided by these rules.
>
> —Observation of Zheng Xiaohua's calligraphy class

The discourse of "traditional calligraphy" is mobilized by suggesting that all past calligraphers managed to write these characters as such. He then switches on the overhead projector, making his hand, his brush and the paper visible for the entire class, and begins to precisely copy the characters on the paper next to him, looking back and forth from the example to his hand. While he simultaneously writes and explains, some students are filming him with their mobile phones, while others write the character with their index finger in the air. Professor Zheng is extremely detailed in his explanation:

> Watch out for this, for this shape; look closely at this knot here. Where is it placed? It connects at around one-third, two-third. And then it continues again, like this. Not too much right here, this fits with this here, and only then you go on, like this. Like this. It could be that you have to go back and redraw the basic structure of this character, make sure to master the grip of the hand first. If your grip is not correct, just write this knot according the basic structure, it cannot be ugly, eh.
>
> —Observation of Zheng Xiaohua's calligraphy class

As soon as the professor has finished writing and explaining the structure of the four characters and has meticulously copied them, the verbalized explanatory part of the lesson is over and now the students have to copy, so to speak, the copying of the teacher. Most students stand up straight while writing to be "more in control of the brush." Every now and then a student writes with his brush in the air instead of on the paper, practicing the exact movement that they want to make before making them with the brush on the paper. The professor is walking around, as are his two student assistants. They correct, comment and show the students how to turn and twist the brush.

When one of his student assistants comes over to help me, she holds my wrist and says: "This is how Mi Fu would have turned his wrist. Try and do it exactly." The physicality of the instruction adds another layer of intimacy to the copying. Not only the mind has to understand how the strokes are linked, the wrist and hand should move exactly like Mi Fu's hand would have moved to be able to achieve the same result. After an hour, the students choose one of their own copies and they lay it out on the floor outside for public scrutinization and arrange themselves in a circle around the works on the floor to discuss with the teacher whose characters look the most like the original. What Professor Zheng has asked his students to do, is called 临摹 *linmo*, which can be broadly translated as "free hand copying." This is, in the vast majority of schools, studios and universities that I visited, the first and only way to start learning calligraphy. This method is, however, often preceded by *looking*: taking the model in with your eyes, while imagining how the brush has moved in the original, to create a mental image of the route that your own brush will have to take to prepare oneself for the copying. Song dynasty calligrapher Huang Tingjian said about this: "When the ancients studied calligraphy, they did not copy exactly. They spread out the writing of a predecessor on the wall and looked at it in complete absorption. Then, when they put brush to paper, it was in accordance with the writer's ideas." Huang Tingjian, remarks Susan Bush, might have been the first literati critic to emphasize the spiritual aspect of connoisseurship.[47]

Calligraphy practice, then, starts with copying, in two ways, *mo* and *lin*. *Mo* means the exact copying of the model by putting a piece of paper on top of the model, and tracing its shapes. *Lin* is the next stage after *mo*: the paper is placed next, or in front of the model, and the practitioner copies the brushstrokes of the model as accurately as possible. Because the eyes now have to move from model to their own creation, the copying is no longer exact, but a mental image of the model work steps in while writing. At this point, as informants have noticed, the lines between copying and creating become blurry. Lin Shujie, Postdoctoral fellow at Tsinghua University in Beijing, notes:

> When I copy Yan Zhenqing, you ask me: are these Yan Zhenqing's characters, or are they yours? It is an interesting question, but it has been answered already. We Chinese don't ask this question, perhaps because we are used to it: learning calligraphy is copying. But not just calligraphy, even reading a book is *linmo*; I read a sentence, or a teacher reads it out loud, and I copy. I use my ears, and my brain. This is copying, I just don't use my hands. Calligraphy is just copying using your hands.
>
> —Interview with Lin Shujie

Lin Shujie's remark that copying is not necessarily that far removed from a creative act—or that creative expression remains always unoriginal to some extent—is reminiscent of Roland Barthes' famous claim in his essay "The Death of the Author": "the text is a tissue of quotations drawn from the innumerable centres of culture . . . the writer can only imitate a gesture that is always anterior, never original. His only power is to mix writings, to counter the ones with the others in such a way never to rest on any one of them."[48] Similarly, Walter Benjamin's ambition as a writer, according to Hannah Arendt, is to produce a work consisting entirely of quotations:

> [H]is method [was] drilling to obtain the essential in the form of quotations—as one obtains water by drilling for it from a source concealed in the depths of the earth. This method is like the modern equivalent of ritual invocations, and the spirits that now arise invariably are those spiritual essences from a past that have suffered the Shakespearean "sea-change" from living eyes to pearls, from living bones to coral.[49]

What most of my interviewees in Beijing and Hangzhou are in agreement on, in different phrasings, is that what ultimately needs to happen through this process of *linmo* is acquiring a "spiritual likeness," after the initial likeness in form. The final aim of *linmo* is capturing the essence, spirit or intention of the copied work. It is not enough to just mimic the form as accurately as possible, but, eventually, you want to "enter its spirit" 入神 *rushen*. Susan Bush adds about *rushen*: "One could enter a state of absolute concentration in which an object was grasped through total identification (ju-shen) and then arrive at a fusion of the subject and the object – the artist, or viewer, and the work of art (shen-hui)."[50] When a student manages to capture the essence of a copied piece, a transformation or creation takes place. A new work is created that inevitably differs from the original, in time and place, but with likeness in essence. This is not an easy task, as Liang Qichao noted in 1926: "Even though you can make copies, you can only imitate the form, and cannot emulate the strength or force in the brushstrokes. It can be said that a copy nearly reproduces [the original work], but it is not easy for one's copy to be as powerful as the original."[51]

I have heard this narrative repeatedly in conversations with established calligraphers and university educators of calligraphy, but I have not encountered it during calligraphy training in private studios or elementary schools, where the first phase of trying to make students physically capable of copying correctly is paramount. In later stages of the learning process, however, the aim becomes to enter the spirit of the model, which, we can now understand, should be a lofty and morally upright spirit. Throughout the first phases of acquiring brush techniques by copying, creative brushwork, or 创作 *chuangzuo*, is not part of the lessons. While there will be discussions on how the work of ancient calligraphers is creative, innovative or different in style from other calligraphers, deviation of the norms by the students is not encouraged in private studios, nor in university and elementary schools. In calligraphy education at Renmin University, as a general rule, Professor Zheng Xiaohua only allows "5% of creativity," meaning that he only tolerates a very small deviation from the original model. Teacher Lin of Tsinghua University holds the same view:

> You must not create. Or; you don't *need* to create. If you would want to be creative, I would let you do non-calligraphy (非书法 *fei shufa*), or borrow elements of calligraphy to create something else, and of course that is perfectly fine, but I think it is a waste . . . because calligraphy in itself is already a good thing.
>
> —Interview with Lin Shujie

Chapter 3 will further unpack the tensions and assumptions surrounding creativity and creative brushwork within alternative scenes of calligraphy. In the context of calligraphy education, creative brushwork is considered a skill that can be developed through sufficient copying and practice. However, it is regarded as a future goal to aim for, while emphasizing that the initial process of copying should not be rushed or overlooked. This makes calligraphy education necessarily a slow and laborious process, demanding a physical process of reiteration. Wrist, eye–hand coordination, brain and posture all work together to make sure that the characters produced by the learner will take on the shape of the model. Correct training and discipline thus focus by and large on the physical aspect of the practice, as the next section will show.

Bodily Discipline

In the previous sections, I suggested that the powerful discourse of "traditional culture" serves as a disciplinary motivator to enter calligraphy education, while the perceived moral uprightness of calligraphers in the past further shapes calligraphy education today through copying. The training is focused on copying their model through exact and freehand copying with the aim to approach a likeness of the original form as well as a shaping of moral character. It is hard to underestimate the physical aspect of this type of training, and the role of the body in calligraphy learning. Calligraphy theory traditionally is permeated with bodily metaphors of movement, force and body parts that serve as allegories to describe the calligraphic line. One teacher repeatedly compared the unbalanced characters written by her students to two bodies leaning uncomfortably against each other, instead of being balanced and able to stand on two feet. While the next chapter will address this in more depth, along with the many health benefits that calligraphy is believed to bring—which also served as an impetus to enroll in calligraphy class among my informants—in this section I analyze how the body is disciplined in the training of calligraphy today. During our interview, calligraphy teacher Hong recalls his initial discomfort with sitting still to learn calligraphy: "When I was a child, I was forced to learn calligraphy, but I didn't like learning it . . . Why? Because I was four years old, and I had to sit down and write and I didn't want to. In fact, now that I teach calligraphy, I believe that calligraphy goes against one's natural tendencies."

Observing a class full of children sitting with a straight back, attempting to hold their brush straight, while trying to move fingers, eyes, wrist and hand in order to create the flowing lines that should—ideally—form a legible character on paper, Liang's experience of unnaturalness is palpable. Both the body and mind need to go through a considerable amount of disciplining before it is able to write coherently, for which the body in its entirety is mobilized. First, the tools of calligraphy demand a poised body, as they require a delicate treatment: the soft-haired brush is supple and bends very easily. A steady grip is therefore paramount, and the way the brush is supposed to be held (执笔 *zhibi*) can initially cause cramps and wrist pain. It takes time and practice to be able to understand how the brush reacts to pressure, speed and grip, and with that comes the added difficulty of ink: it is runny and can easily drop on the very absorbent *xuan* paper if the brush is dipped in the ink too enthusiastically.

Part of the training I have observed in several private calligraphy studios and at elementary school, but not at the universities, involves the teacher

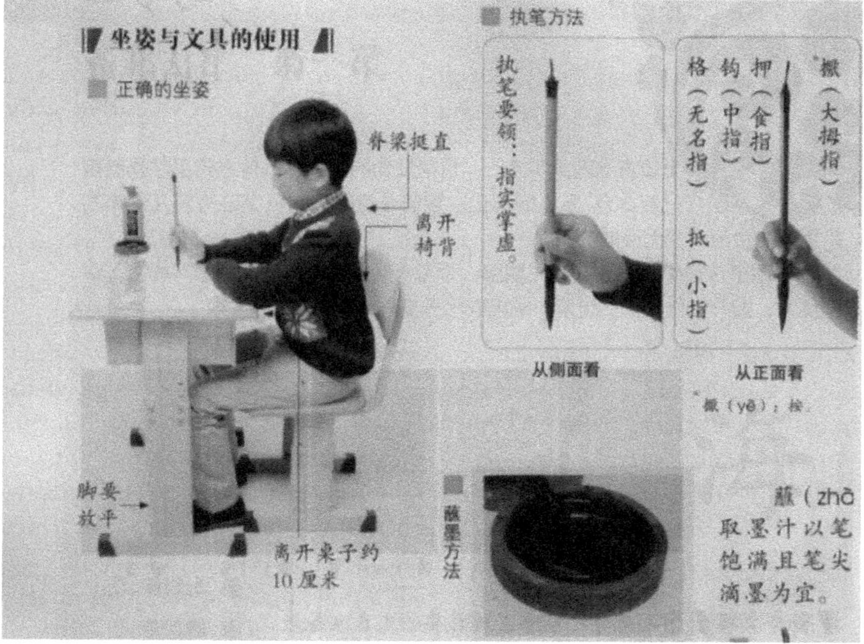

Figure 1.3: The introduction on physical training in one of the guides used in elementary schools throughout China: *Shufa lianxi zidao* 书法练习指导 [Guidance for Calligraphy Practice] (Qingdao Cubanshe). Courtesy of Liu Shaogang 2014. © Liu Shaogang.

holding the wrist or the entire hand of the student; then guiding the hand with the brush on the paper. This way, the student has made the movement once with his hand, and can proceed further from memory. Special attention is given to the hand holding the brush: the thumb, index finger, middle finger should be naturally bent, holding the pen from three sides; the palm of the hand should be empty when holding the brush, like holding a small egg.[52] Posture is similarly important. Children are often told to sit still, sit up, not slouch or if they cannot sit anymore, to stand up straight. The entire body is supposed to be mobilized in a straight and alert position, which is illustrated clearly in Figure 1.3, which shows lesson material approved by the MOE and used in elementary schools in 2018 for the third grade.[53] We can see how the child is instructed to first, straighten their spine. Sitting up straight creates an alert mind and more tranquility in the body. Second, their back should not touch the back of the chair, to make sure the pupil will not slouch and their body will stay straight. Third, the child should sit approximately 10 centimeters away from his table. This way, a perfect distance is established between the brush and the paper on the table in front of the student to create better control of how the brush will land on the paper. Fourth, their feet should be placed flat on the ground to ensure the body is grounded and stays connected to the floor. In this position, the body is brought in a physical state of preparedness, and as such, all the attention (sometimes referred to as energy) should flow through the spine, the shoulders, the arm and the hand to, finally, the brush on the paper.

One informant commented that, ideally, one should no longer be aware that the brush is not part of your hand. The initial process of learning to control the body is uncomfortable, painful and tiring (although some of my informants noted they never felt it was uncomfortable, if only you take enough breaks). Jia, a student at Peking University, mentions how her training is physically tiring:

> Then this semester I went to the classes at an art school, and the teacher let us choose between *Yanti* or *Liuti* not *Outi*.[54] I could only choose *Liuti*, because I cannot really write *Yanti*. But I found that *Liuti* was so thin and hard, or as we say, *Yan* is muscled, and *Liu* is bony. And the tip of his brush is so exposed; these characters really require a stable brush. After I was done writing, I felt incredibly tired, this writing demands a lot of the wrist.
>
> —Interview with Jia Ruoceng

The almost military precision with which the body is instructed to behave reveals its links with disciplinary power: "A well-disciplined body forms the operational context of the slightest gesture. Good handwriting, for example, presupposes gymnastics—a whole routine whose rigorous code invests the body in its entirety, from the points of the feet to the tip of the index finger."[55] With what we know about the popularity of calligraphy education, we can visualize troops—to continue the military analogy—of hundreds of thousands of individuals today subjecting themselves to this rigid training, and many enjoying it. Now, of course, more forms of art such as painting, dance or playing a musical instrument involve the body and a physical disciplining of that body. In calligraphy, however, a physical disciplining concentrating on straightness and uprightness overlaps curiously with the uprightness of one's personal character. The body is therefore not just an instrument for holding a brush, but works together as a whole: while the brain creates a visual interpretation of the master copy, the feet, the spine, the shoulders, the arm and the hand all join forces to achieve the desired control of the brush, while simultaneously cultivating one's moral being. This control, importantly, allows us to approach these disciplinary techniques not as subduing or repressive, but as one that ultimately gives power; rendering the trained body in control.

This chapter has illustrated how the growing popularity of calligraphy education is in part indebted to a top-down intensification of calligraphy to preserve traditional culture—of which calligraphy is perceived as the embodiment; the desire to build a quality population; and the desire to make people write by hand again in the digital age. This is done through mandatory calligraphy classes in all primary and high schools and lenient *gaokao* scores for those entering calligraphy education, which has further incentivized people to start learning the skill—or parents to send their children to private calligraphy schools.

The proliferation of calligraphy education nationwide at the levels of primary and secondary school education, university and the private studio, are mutually constructed and sustained as a direct result of national policy. This can be seen as a highly successful form of governing in Foucauldian parlance: instead of citizens being and feeling forced to behave in a certain way, power has been distributed to the family, the self and the market and it has created self-disciplined subjects that have internalized the discourses employed by the state. Yet, this does not imply that they are oblivious subjects, deftly being coerced into a repressive regime of power. To the contrary, as Foucault notes: "what makes power hold good, what makes it accepted, is simply the fact that it not only weighs on us as a force that says no, but that it traverses and produces things, it induces pleasure, forms knowledge, produces discourses. It needs to be considered as a productive network which runs through the whole social body, much more than as a negative instance whose function is repression."[56]

Calligraphy, and the three discourses that this chapter identified—traditional culture, moral rectitude and bodily discipline—impose self-discipline and guide conduct as much as they empower and give opportunities. The discourse of traditional culture offers new opportunities for calligraphy practitioners to invent new modes of being: as a citizen that possesses culture; it gives possibilities to correct the errors of the recent past when calligraphy education was halted; and it allows for performing an identity as a citizen from a self-conscious country, populated with proud citizens who are aware of their glorious heritage. The discourse of morality similarly mobilizes people and gives opportunities for self-cultivation, to identify with, and become like exemplary calligraphers of the past: composed, calm and patient. The discourse of physical discipline empowers in such a way that people undergoing this training cultivate—along with their body—their mind, which is believed to be disciplined, but also to be transformed through training. More practically, calligraphy as it is lived, performed and marketed today, presents calligraphy graduates with career prospects, allows students to enter a university with only average *gaokao* scores, and gives opportunities to entrepreneurs for entering the booming market of private calligraphy schools.

Power is thus distributed everywhere, in and through calligraphy practice. But as Foucault reminds us, where power is, there is also always the potential of resistance. If calligraphy education is popular, allows for self-cultivation and thus strengthens the self while simultaneously strengthening the nation and honoring the past of that nation, where then would potential resistance depart from? Not taking calligraphy class, perhaps? Or, as a tactic of self-technology, *not enjoying* calligraphy class? Writing badly, not complying with, or resisting the rules and strategies laid out by calligraphy training? Would it be to write with a different intention, or with different techniques—to use the body differently, or to not copy? These questions urge us to examine calligraphy practice beyond the classroom in order to contextualize better what occurs within it.

In the next chapter, I propose how the practice of water calligraphy allows for new imaginations in calligraphy practice. Water calligraphy contests the dominant structures of how calligraphy is experienced by providing an alternative aesthetics, and concurrently builds on the structure of calligraphy education that this chapter has laid out.

CHAPTER 2

Water Calligraphy: The Ephemeral Everyday

> We wrote characters on oracle bones—the immortal oracle script
> We wrote characters on magnificent bronzes
> We wrote on glorious paper
> Today we boldly dip our brushes in clear water for our leisure
> Reside with poetic exuberance on the earth[1]

"We are just having fun!" a pensioner smiles at me when he sees I am observing him one early morning in a public park in Beijing. He is wielding a large foam brush half his size, and is busy writing a beautiful running-style calligraphy with it, using water for ink, and tiles for paper. He is doing his daily practice of 地书 *dishu*, which translates as "script of the ground." It is most often translated into English as "water calligraphy." In the early mornings, the park belongs to the elderly. They convene there in large groups to dance, exercise, to sing, make music or to meditate. Amid them are the ground writers (地书人 *dishuren*)[2] or, as I will refer to them here, water calligraphers: mostly men but also women who have brought their own hand-cut brushes from home, made out of sponges, foam and broomsticks or umbrella sticks, to fill the paved areas of the public park with calligraphy written with water. It is simply beautiful to see: the agile and disciplined movements of body and brush create beautiful characters, shining bright when they catch rays of sunlight (see Figures 2.1 and 2.2). The characters dissolve again within seconds or minutes depending on the weather, transforming the park's gray tile stones into fleeting pockets of poetry and literacy. Water calligraphers and passersby admire and discuss the written characters, comment on style, meaning and references for that brief ephemeral

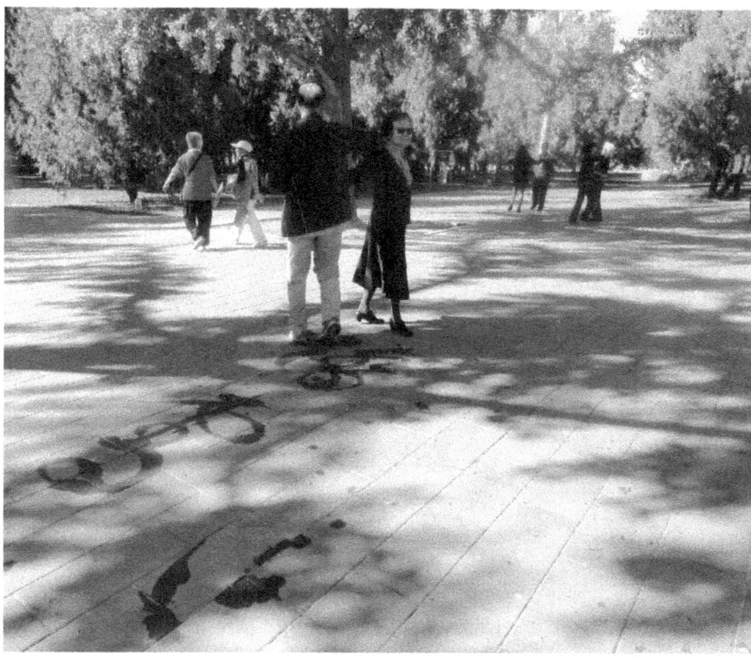

Figure 2.1: Dancing on water calligraphy in Ditan Park. © Laura Vermeeren.

moment. And then start over. Xue Fengli, an enthusiastic female water calligrapher, provides me her version of how this practice originated:

> As for me, I started doing it in 1992 or 1993. Back then, we did not have a special water calligraphy brush yet. We just used a small wooden rod and we attached some sponge to it, we didn't use scissors to shape it, we just tied it up in a bun, and then you can just write. At that time, there were only four or five people writing in Taoranting Park. We are considered one of the early groups. Then some people went away, and other people came. And then more people came here from other parks. That's how, slowly, we started to be a team here. A single spark can start a prairie fire!
>
> —Interview with Xue Fengli

Ever since the alleged humble beginnings of this practice—the story goes that these beginnings should be situated already thousands of years earlier, when people gathered wooden twigs and dipped them in water for writing purposes—the water calligraphy movement has been expanding steadily. Water

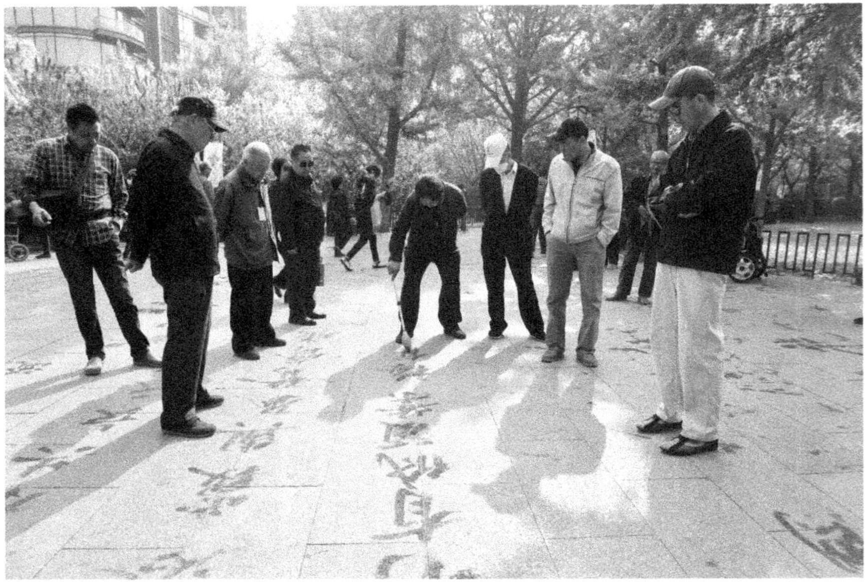

Figure 2.2: A man writing water calligraphy in Ditan Park. © Laura Vermeeren.

calligraphers can now be found in almost every public park in every large Chinese city. To include this scene in a book on contemporary Chinese calligraphic practices suggests, perhaps, that water calligraphy can be unproblematically categorized under the umbrella term of Chinese calligraphy. But let me nuance that here: the direct association with calligraphy is partly due to the English term "water calligraphy," which implies a straightforward correlation with brush, ink and paper calligraphy. The Chinese word for water calligraphy 地书 *dishu*, however, conveys a less obvious relationship: the character 地 *di* translates as ground, referring to the surface on which the characters are written, and 书 *shu* translates as book or writing. 地书 *dishu* thus points at the surface on which the characters are written, and the close link with calligraphy that the English translation suggests is not there.[3]

In order to see how water calligraphy might be part of a larger calligraphy discourse, this chapter provides an ethnography of water calligraphers' daily life in the park—moving, creating and affectively interacting within the urban space. Who are these water calligraphers, and why do they write in water? How do the water calligraphers self-identify, and why do they choose public parks to gather in? Is it a gendered practice, and how does it relate to the other activities—

dance, calisthenics, singing, birding—that are taking place in the public parks? And how do they claim their space in the highly condensed and planned cityscape of Beijing? Then, this chapter directs its focus to a visual analysis of the ephemeral calligraphic works that are created on the tiles of the park. This aspect—its aesthetics—has been largely overlooked by the already limited scholarship on the practice, contributing to the misconception that it is primarily a physical activity. Academic literature in the Chinese context on water calligraphy is scarce indeed, and is found mainly in literature on geriatric health, where the focus lies on the physical benefits the practice is expected to bring. It does not cover how this practice might then also relate to or impact a discourse of calligraphy at large.[4] Literatures on urban space and public park life in China often mention the practice in passing while describing leisurely activity in the parks. Judith Farquhar[5] and Piper Gaubatz[6] both categorize water calligraphy as a form of exercise in the context of life-nurturing 养生 *yangsheng* practices, but its calligraphic component is not further theorized. The body—how it moves, behaves and manipulates the brush—is important to take into account when unpacking and analyzing the practice. And that might explain why water calligraphy has not received more scholarly attention from the arts or humanities. It seems that the curious combination of calisthenic training and an ephemeral form of writing, done almost exclusively by the elderly, makes the practice an awkward match for either calligraphy or art criticism, sinology or urban studies.

In an effort to address this lacuna, this book expands on current scholarship concerning both contemporary calligraphy practices and studies on urban creative practices in China. This exploration aims to provide a more nuanced understanding and context for contemporary calligraphy practices today. To begin such an exploration, I approach water calligraphy as a mode of urban vernacular creativity.[7] The term "vernacular" has traveled from denoting daily speech to different areas such as architecture, music and art, describing practices that somehow take place outside or alongside traditional and hegemonic frameworks. Jean Burgess first mentioned the term "vernacular creativity" in 2006, and defined it a year later as "ordinary": "Vernacular creativity, in being ordinary, is not elite or institutionalized; nor is it extraordinary or spectacular, but rather it is defined on the basis of its commonness."[8] The idea developed from that premise is that in these vernacular practices a type of creativity can take place that offers a counterclaim to commodifiable, productive and copyrighted modes of creativity. As such, it poses a forceful counterargument to the idea that creativity should (only) be seen as contributing to economic and urban development. But also, to the still remarkably pervasive idea that creativity is a trait exclusively belonging to individual geniuses, who make their works in erratic bouts of divine inspiration. Burgess demarcates a discursive field of creative production that is not claiming to be located completely outside of artistic institutions or commercial popular production, as the boundaries between them continue to be blurry, but that invests exactly in the ordinariness of everyday life.

"Urban" then, as I am contextualizing water calligraphy as an urban vernacular creative practice, is a term now readily associated with creativity thanks to Richard Florida's work *The Rise of the Creative Class*.[9] Florida's influential theory argues that we are living in the age of creativity. The drivers of this new age are the so-called creative class, conceptualized as a group of young, agile and mobile creative workers. These professional creators, per Florida, will flock to any urban area if this area offers them the right conditions that allow for a vibrant city life and an exciting workplace.[10] This would then turn declined cities into vibrant inclusive cultural hubs, and boost economic development and urban renewal; a tantalizing, but overly simplistic idea that has been heavily criticized since its inception. Not only is his idea of a creative class too narrowly focused on a privileged group of people, which only reinforces social class biases and exacerbates gentrification and inequality:[11] it also fails to take into account how with mobility often comes precarity.[12] Moreover, because Florida's theory has become so pervasive, everything and everybody is now termed "creative," from plumbing work, to code writing and management jobs, muddying what is actually constitutive of creativity.[13] Those who are creative are now conjured as professionals, instrumentalized as urban renewers and drivers of the creative industries. The artist, argues Christoph Lindner, becomes a gentrifier.[14]

So where in this constellation might we place clusters of creatives who are neither young nor footloose, and whose convivial creative output disappears within minutes? The contrast here unsettles and excites. We have the young and productively creative people, whose place in the city is cemented into the urban design, coexisting with older creative bodies in this same city. But their creativity is neither planned nor designed and their creative output is convivial and temporary. When I walked around in the center of Beijing, I saw the streetscapes filled with exactly the spaces Richard Florida had in mind: startups, hipster joints and cafés, where self-identified creatives work on their laptops and drink expensive cappuccinos. I actually behaved like one myself when I would come back from the park for my fieldwork, thirstily looking for a café with free Wi-Fi to transcribe my fieldnotes. Afterward, I would sit in these air-conditioned cool places with my matcha latte, and the older people I talked to minutes earlier in the parks faded away from my mind. Angela McRobbie observed how quickly this "fading" happens in scholarship on the creative city: "Few urban creative economy writers focus on mothers and children, on grandmothers and older women, on play parks or on local amenities such as swimming pools or public libraries. Old people seem to fade out of view, as do aggressive youths or young teenage mums pushing prams."[15] This chapter investigates how we might begin with a making visible of ephemeral urban creative practice.

In the subsequent sections, I will provide a comprehensive ethnography of water calligraphy in public parks following four interrelated themes: (1) space: the public park; (2) body: its physical component; (3) time: the affordances of its ephemerality; and (4) the aesthetics of the written characters and their content. The practice of water calligraphy has, even in the course of this research, already evolved and expanded into heterogeneous spaces outside the park: contemporary art, film and (inter)national propaganda. This complicates the hypothesis that water calligraphy is an alternative and quotidian practice that operates completely outside the context of creative output taking place within the constraints and demands of a creative market economy. The last section will thus heuristically take up these diversions, questioning whether, as a living, growing and society-based practice, these developments should be seen either as a result of its relevancy and longevity in the context of the popularizing of calligraphy; or rather as tactics of assimilation into the mainstream of calligraphy discourse.

The Park

Most of my interviewees conveyed simply that, after retirement, you need to find an activity to keep your mind and body occupied. This activity happens for many Beijing-bound retirees in the city's large public parks, where one can indulge in almost any type of hobby activity. We find colorful groups of female fan dancers; 太极拳 *taijiquan* practitioners; choral singers and ballroom dancers; kite-fliers and crocheting groups; chess and mahjong players; and water calligraphy writers. These distinctive groups all convene in their own corners, sometimes cheerfully overlapping, producing a cacophony of sound, movement and creativity in the early hours of the day. Most of them will have left by noon, leaving the park to casual strollers and tourists. But in these early mornings, the public park shapes and produces their creative expressions by transforming into a temporary "creative cluster"; invented and maintained by retirees.

The parks in Beijing are referred to as public parks (公园 *gongyuan*), but a small entrance fee is actually required, with discounts for soldiers, students and retirees. Local retired residents who go every day have often invested in an annual park pass which offers unlimited access to the city's parks.[16] Urban public parks in China have been around since the late Qing dynasty and early Republican era. Both the municipal government and the local gentry at that time joined efforts to transform the old imperial spaces into public areas. Inclusive public urban space for all citizens did not exist as such before, as imperial gardens and green areas were exclusively used by the Manchu ruling class, high ranked officials and noblemen. But while ordinary residents were not allowed in these areas, they were able to enjoy public entertainment in the form of temple fairs and festivals, and were accustomed to occupying the streets for recreation, especially in the hot Beijing summer months.[17] The public park in China today, according to Mingzheng Shi, is taken from western examples. Around the 1830s, urban planners came up with the idea of green leisure spaces in the middle of the city for tired and unhealthy city workers to use, in an attempt to stimulate public health during the heyday of industrialization. For similar motives of health management, as well as the desire to keep up with Europe and Japan, local gentry-merchant organizations started building public parks in China around the turn of the century. In 1914, a campaign to improve the city's physical environment led to the opening up of abandoned imperial places, turning them into public parks.[18] These public parks proliferated and flourished, and concomitant with the rise of the public park came the decline of the public space of the temple. The public parks became places of leisure, as well as spaces to enjoy the type of entertainment previously available to people through the temple fair. Shi also notes that urban intellectuals enjoyed the "poetic flavor" of the picturesque surroundings; urban women started to get out of the house to meet up in the parks; and as such the Beijing parks "played a pioneering role in mixing visitors of the opposite sex."[19] But these developments were all brought to a halt when the Japanese invasion and then the formation of the People's Republic diverted attention away from urban health management. The internationally oriented approach to creating modern public urban spaces changed when Mao seized power, and while the parks were still very much in use, they now took on a rather utilitarian identity. Well before the Cultural Revolution, the length, forms and content of leisure were highly controlled and managed through the so-called work unit (单位 *danwei*). Neighborhood communities were placed under the work unit which came to control every minute aspect of an individual's life: outside of it there was no space for leisure. Shaoguang Wang notes here that "in the name of 'collectivism,' it became an unwritten rule that leisure activities should take the form of group action."[20]

These rigid routines that were forced on the people—and indeed on the spaces they were allowed to occupy—declined in intensity with the move to a market-based economy through the reforms of Deng Xiaoping in 1978.[21] An improved standard of living as a result of the flourishing economy, as well as the loosening of state control over the what, how, when and where of people's everyday lives, significantly changed the lives of urban residents. Among many other things, it also allowed for park life to re-emerge.[22] Today, the large parks in Beijing within the second ring road are very well maintained and are brimming with life: many people come through their gates daily to enjoy the ponds and boats, kiosks, broad streets, birdsong and well-kept foliage. In contrast, houses in the traditional alleys in these districts (胡同 *hutong*)—although they are disappearing fast as a result of municipal sanitizing campaigns—are often small, damp and cramped together.

The setting described above is imperative to start contextualizing what happens in the parks today. When Shi notes that the Chinese public parks are drawn from typically western plans, it might conjure up a picture of a public park in the way it is experienced and enjoyed in western contexts. They are in fact quite different. First of all, the parks are generally not quiet spaces, but loud and eclectic sonic environments. Especially in the early mornings, before mothers with children, office workers on their lunch break and tourists will stroll the parks, the space belongs to retirees and is permeated with sounds. All the different hobby groups bring their own echoes, in the shape of transistor radios exuding loud and tinny popular music and opera arias, musical instruments such as the 二胡 *erhu*, drums, cymbals and saxophones, or their voices joined in fervently singing choirs. The layout of the parks also differs from their western twin: while the parks do have green spaces, there are no grassy areas visitors can walk on, or use for a picnic or sunbathing. Instead, the green areas have wooden signs telling people they should not access the grass, and the broad pavements and squares of the park, or the little pavilions dotted around, are meant for park activity. The parks are surrounded by high walls and are accessed through large gates, often four of them and named after the four cardinal directions. And although this study does not necessarily benefit much from east versus west comparisons, these three differences in how green urban space is appropriated help to contextualize the urban park as a noisy place full of life and activity. Older people meet their friends here to sing, dance and play together, and not to find quiet place to read, lounge or nap.

The aim of creating public parks in its inception was to provide health benefits for a growing urban population. The groups in the park conform neatly to that purpose, yet in unexpected and creative ways. As for the predominantly collective nature of their hobby practices, Farquhar has theorized this might be a remnant of the times in which public life was controlled by the *danwei*. The elderly, Farquhar argues, have spent as much as half their lives in a political climate that demanded their lives to be fully submerged in collective mobilization: "the depoliticized but still committed actors in their daily practice act on a political habitus inculcated several decades ago but not yet really forgotten."[23] We should be mindful, she continues, of the fact that this generation are "veterans of the continuing revolution of Maoism, [are] experts at making politics out of the personal, and vice versa. Nationalism and the socialist collective are, as it were, in their bones."[24] How the park is used and what people are allowed to do within that space continues to be contingent on the political climate. One interviewee tells me, for example, that she is so grateful for the fact that now she can do whatever she wants in the park: "Society is getting more stable and is improving, otherwise water calligraphy could not become so popular. Xi Jinping is honest and did some very useful things for ordinary people" (interview with anonymous informant). The relatively young retirement age in China (50–55 for women and 55–60 for men) might further explain why so many retirees have the time to spend their mornings in the parks. With an average life expectancy of 75 years, there is, roughly speaking, 20 years of unemployed life to enjoy.[25] What does it signify when this pleasure is derived from writing something transient?

Ephemeral Movement

Every morning when I entered Ditan Park with my water calligraphy brush, a gift given to me when I first joined their group—a symbol of their openness and generosity—I felt as though I was participating in a celebration. Participants appear to derive genuine enjoyment from their activities. Smiles are abundant, clothes are carefully chosen, and their movements in dance, writing or martial arts convey a sense of bodily liberation and celebration. These older bodies that I unconsciously thought of as perhaps somewhat vulnerable or dignified, looked empowered and free. All in all, I could not help, as both Angela Zito[26] and Farquhar[27] have experienced as well, to be enchanted by the scene. But to proceed from mere enchantment to heuristic analysis requires a careful reading of what actually is going on here. In Chapter 1, I showed how the skill of calligraphy is largely inculcated through rigorous physical discipline: exact copying of brush movements through a meticulously poised body. The glaring contrast between those movements and the way water calligraphers move is thought-provoking. There are water calligraphers who stand very still, only bending their wrist to move the large brush. I vividly recall an ex-soldier who would come to the park every morning, no matter the weather, and would stand very still for hours, deeply concentrating on the work to be done. His characters were perfectly executed. But more often, I observed men and women bending and moving their backs, their knees and arms back and forth while moving the large brush, as if it were a writing and calisthenic exercise all in one.

They pause in between characters to stretch their arms, sway to the beat of the music or even slow waltz over the evaporating characters.

It begs analysis: what kind of recognizable poses are assumed and are they still recognizable as "calligraphic"? How do the perceived health benefits of calligraphy affect and inform these poses? The body can be molded and disciplined by external discourses of power, as I laid out in Chapter 1. Do the movements made in water calligraphy then similarly induce a type of discipline, or does the practice allow for new movements, new imaginations facilitated by the space of the park, the size of the brush, the ephemerality of water or the convivial atmosphere? How to move as a water calligrapher is intricately related to discourses of health.

Xue Fengli is a retired jade carver, and writes her characters in Taoranting Park. She is one of the few female calligraphers that I have met so far here after a few weeks of daily visits. Now in her late sixties, she has been practicing water calligraphy for ten years after she had to give up dancing because, she discloses, her partner became too old and could not come with her anymore:

> At first, when you retire, you have a feeling of loss, and don't know how to spend your time. You feel useless, and you don't have any important position in your *danwei* anymore. But now, we all feel different. There are people here with bad health, with a bad back and they ask, can writing cure me? Lower my head and write characters, can it influence my health? And then I say: writing is energy (*qi* 气). It is using the power of your body. It is "essence, qi, and spirit" (精气神 *jing, qi, shen*).[28] You let your spirit guide your brush. It's like *taijii*. The moving your spirit is the exercise.
>
> —Interview with Xue Fengli

Many water calligraphers I spoke to readily used such rhetoric—it is part of their colloquial and their everyday tactics to stay hale and hearty. Another water calligrapher simply pointed with his brush to the dancers a few meters away: "Look, it is the same as they are doing over there, but I move my arms slowly. It makes me healthy!" The overarching idea is that it is simply good practice for older people to keep the body moving. Water calligraphy specifically moves both the brain and the body. Farquhar and Zhang describe this as "养生 *yangsheng* wisdom" in their important work on life-nurturing practices in contemporary Beijing.[29] *Yangsheng* or "nurturing life" are self-care practices that have become popular among retirees over the last two decades. They are however embedded in ancient Chinese cosmology and metaphysics. Nurturing life "hinges almost entirely on the quotidian," as Farquhar and Zhang argue, and includes activities such as dancing, fan dancing, writing or qigong.[30] This holistic take on cultivating a good life also includes the ostensibly mundane habits of eating well, drinking enough tea, dressing appropriately for the weather, taking walks, being sociable, and engaging in artistic practices.[31]

Yangsheng practices are thus very diverse, and not particularly difficult to get used to or incorporate in one's daily routine. Their perceived health benefits strike a chord particularly with the older population, as one of the benefits of nurturing life is the potential of living a long healthy life. This idea of longevity (长寿 *changshou*), is a benefit also famously accredited to the practice of calligraphy. Self-help books on health have cleverly stepped in to promote certain exercises and behaviors as a means to prolong (a good and healthy) life, by revisiting and interpreting ancient Chinese medical classics. As such, as Farquhar and Zhang have noted, the movement of nurturing life ties in with the cultural fever discussed in Chapter 1, and "the centrality of health books in this broader movement suggests a certain bodily engagement in being Chinese and in having a Chinese past."[32]

Yangsheng mirrors the idea of Foucault's "art of existence," which he sees as "those reflective and voluntary practices by which men not only set themselves rules of conduct, but seek to transform themselves, to change themselves in their singular being, and to make their life into an oeuvre that carries certain aesthetic values and meets certain stylistic criteria."[33] Farquhar and Zhang add that their interlocutors, *yangsheng* practitioners, "seemed committed to making a project out of life, to carrying life to a higher level, both more disciplined and more joyful. Just being able to move is not enough: one should dance and sing. Just being able to read and write is not enough: one should read culture and write calligraphy."[34] Water calligraphy in the park combines several *yangsheng* practices, and nurtures life in several ways: it moves the entire body; it trains the brain; it is sociable, done in the fresh air; and, importantly, it is something beautiful to look at. Nurturing life is intrinsically aesthetic.

In trying to understand how to exactly move the body, similar to how it occurs in calligraphy class, few verbal rules are voiced, and the focus is very much on "just trying," an attitude perhaps easily facilitated by the ephemeral nature of the practice. Many calligraphers talked, like the students did in Chapter 1, about seeing the brush as an extension of the arm. The brush is generally not moved by the wrist due to its large size, but mobilized by the entire arm and shoulders. Those writing in large grass script generally move more than those writing smaller clerical or regular script; and the writing, especially of longer verses, is often interspersed with remoistening the brush, circling the arms in the air, walking to someone else to look at their characters, or doing some stretching. Thus, the whole body is engaged, and performs an ongoing flow of different movements.

Hiding in the tissues of these sensuous movements is the master narrative of traditional calligraphy that explicitly demands a disciplined body. By this I mean that the shape of the character is perhaps the most leading factor in how the calligrapher will move, and their moves are to a large extent predetermined by the fixed shapes of conventional calligraphy. Are there many brushstrokes in the character? Then the hand will have to make more movements. Is the practitioner making a copy of eccentric Tang dynasty calligrapher Huai Su's "crazy script"? Then their body will move faster and will sway more from left to right to make a good copy. There is a poetic interplay going on between the body and shape of the character and the human body. This has been conceptualized and thoroughly researched as a close relationship between the script-body (书体 *shuti*) and the human body (身体 *shenti*). The body-like character is created physically and mentally by the self-body, and in turn, that character demands precise movements, so that energy is passed from the human body into the script-body, infusing it with spirit.[35] Calligraphy theory is permeated with such bodily imagery of movement, force and body parts that serve as allegories to describe the calligraphic line, the energy of the brush, and the balanced shape of the character. Madame Wei, the teacher of Wang Xizhi, allegedly provided the first somatified images of calligraphy:

> In the writing of those who are skillful in giving strength of stroke, the characters are "bony"; in the writing of those who are not skillful in giving strength of strokes, the characters are "fleshy." Writing that has a great deal of bone and very little meat is called "sinewy writing," and writing that is full of flesh and weak bones is called "piggy writing." A writing that is powerful and sinewy is divine; a writing that has neither power nor sinews is like an invalid.[36]

This 4th-century portrayal is still used in day-to-day conversations on calligraphy. Characters are referred to as fat, bony, but also as having blood, which is linked to energy, and sinew, which allows for envisioning movement in the shape. A whole body is construed through the making, the description and the final form of the character. As Madame Wei also noted, writing can even appear sick, or invalid, which accentuates the intimate ties between body and calligraphy, as well as calligraphy as a practice for health. In the written character, ideas of both physical health and moral health come together.

Yen has described how the four main calligraphic bodily elements—bone, sinew, flesh and blood—are essential for the construction not only of a good calligraphic character, but also of a good person. The idea that a person's rectitude can be deducted from their calligraphy, as I developed in Chapter 1, hinges on the same metaphoric bodily imagery. The bone in particular, according to Yen, has special symbolic force. People who are weak are said to have "soft bones" (软骨头 *ruan gutou*), and strong-willed people are referred to as having "tough bones" (硬骨头 *ying gutou*).[37] The quality of a piece of calligraphy is defined by using the same metaphors: the calligraphy of people with upright moral character is referred to as very bony, or full of forceful bone (骨力 *guli*). The intricate and elusive conflation of metaphor, ancient belief and practical application connects practices of the body, calligraphy and the moral self. According to John Hay,[38] the ways in which calligraphy is anthropomorphized are closely related to and derive from traditional Chinese medicine. The combination of these calligraphic myths combined with the more quotidian *yangsheng* movement provide the foundational framework on which water calligraphy is built. Water calligrapher Xue borrows from both *yangsheng* and traditional Chinese calligraphy discourse when she tells me that "it is 'essence, qi, and spirit' (精气神 *jing, qi, shen*)" that imbues her calligraphy with life. These three elusive concepts are mobilized through movements of the body—the bone, sinew, blood and the flesh, and through the daily cultivation of these movements. The practices of these water calligraphers are somatically anchored and form an important creative interpretation of this bodily aspect of traditional calligraphy. The choreographed movements of the hand are magnified, as both brush and surface are scaled up and as such demand the involvement of, simply put, *more* body parts: arms, back, feet, legs and head. Yet, these movements remain intrinsically disciplined by external discourses of traditional calligraphy, because the shapes remain similar to those taught in the classroom and created in the artist's studio. This leads to the next consideration: how do these water calligraphers know how to write? And what to write?

Ephemeral Writing

> I have not graduated from high school, but now I am able to write and perform the *Orchid's Pavilion*. I go whenever I get the chance. Here, they taught me how to write, and now we are all learning from each other. When passersby compliment me on my writing, I feel such pride.
>
> —Conversation with Miss Zhang

Miss Zhang composes a Tang dynasty poem in regular script when I meet her in Ditan Park. Next to her writes a retired military veteran, who smiles when he adds: "We are all equal here. Among us are people from the countryside, some used to be professors. We act as each other's classmate and teacher here." There is no clear homogeneous profile to be drawn from the groups practicing in the parks. I have met water calligraphers with former occupations ranging from jade carving, the military, farming, nursing to civil servant work and professional dancing. Their common denominator today is their age group, hobby and their choice of public park where they form loose groups. Most of the water calligraphers I spoke to, unlike Miss Zhang quoted above, have learned calligraphy as a child. However, as their primary education happened to coincide with one of China's most tumultuous periods, many of them did not have the opportunity to cultivate their skill after primary school. A few water calligraphers conveyed, however, how they were involved in writing big-character posters during the Hundred Flowers Movement and the Cultural Revolution. Although a wholly different practice, this has made them confident in writing large characters, and confident in writing in public.

They use simple tools: park tiles, which are light-gray and are, as it turns out, conveniently laid out in grids quite similar to calligraphy practice sheets, water collected in a bucket from the public toilets and a brush. The brush is often an object of pride. It is homemade from leftover materials: a piece of yellowish foam is gathered from an old sofa or pillow found at a garbage dump and cut into a pointed brush-like shape; a broken mop, the shaft of a selfie-stick or umbrella is used as the handle; and a plastic water bottle cut in half attaches the foam tip to the handle (see Figure 2.3). In both parks, a few men were known to be good brush makers, and they would sell brushes or give brushes away. These foam brushes are now also industrially produced and for sale on online shopping platforms such as Taobao or at the kiosks in the park for tourists, but water calligraphers prefer their own homemade brushes. Most of my interviewees explained why their brush in particular works so well: the tip is well cut, the attached water bottle allows for a steady flow of water, or because the length of the handle is exactly right.

In both parks, I have observed a range of traditional calligraphic styles being written. Seal script, clerical script, running script and grass script are all used, but not often interchangeably: one calligrapher often sticks to one style. Most practitioners write from memory, and only rarely did I observe someone bringing along a copybook, although water calligraphers have mentioned they have used them when they started out going to the park. Some water calligraphers claim to also practice at home, with ink and paper, while others say they never do, and prefer the open and "cheap" style of practicing outside, as one water calligrapher mentions: "You can just buy a calligraphy copybook of Wang Xizhi to copy from for 20 yuan, it is all you need. As long as you practice and

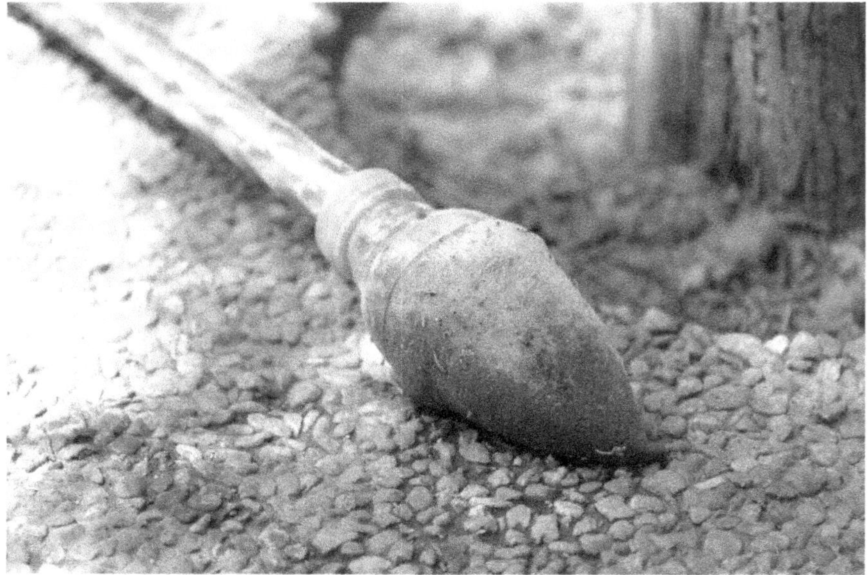

Figure 2.3: A homemade water calligraphy brush made from foam, a stick and a plastic bottle. © Laura Vermeeren.

persist, everybody can do it!" On several occasions, these water calligraphers would bring their paper and ink calligraphy to the park, to ignite a lively discussion on calligraphy on the spot.

In the ensuing paragraphs, I offer a visual analysis of three written pieces, seen from their inception until their disappearance, to shed light on both the content and the shape of the calligraphic characters. Figure 2.4 shows a piece by a retiree writing in Ditan Park. These are the first lines of a work composed by Liu Yuxi (772–842): "The Scholar's Humble Dwelling" (陋室銘 *Loushi Ming*).[39] The writer in the park remarked on his choice that it is not really important *what* you write, but that it is good to write something that you know by heart, so the piece can be written in a steady flow and the characters come out nicely. The frequently heard argument in calligraphy discourse that form precedes content persists in the parks. He learned calligraphy as a child, and now practices every day, in the park, but also at home. From Figure 2.4, it can be seen how, indeed, the poem was written in a steady flow: 14 characters are written in two almost perfectly aligned vertical columns of seven characters each, its anchoring aided by the grid lines of the tiles. The first character has

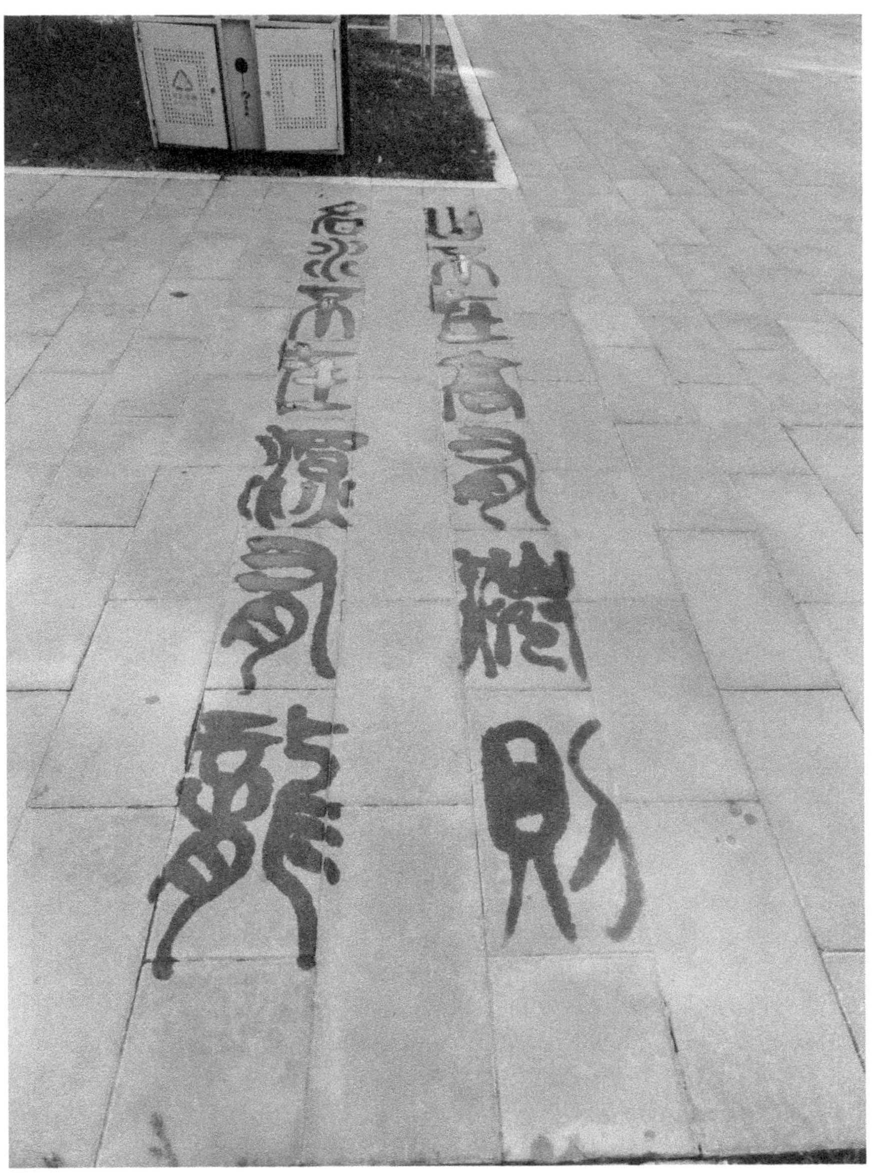

Figure 2.4: The first lines of a work composed by Liu Yuxi (772–842) entitled "The Scholar's Humble Dwelling" (陋室銘 *Loushi Ming*). © Laura Vermeeren.

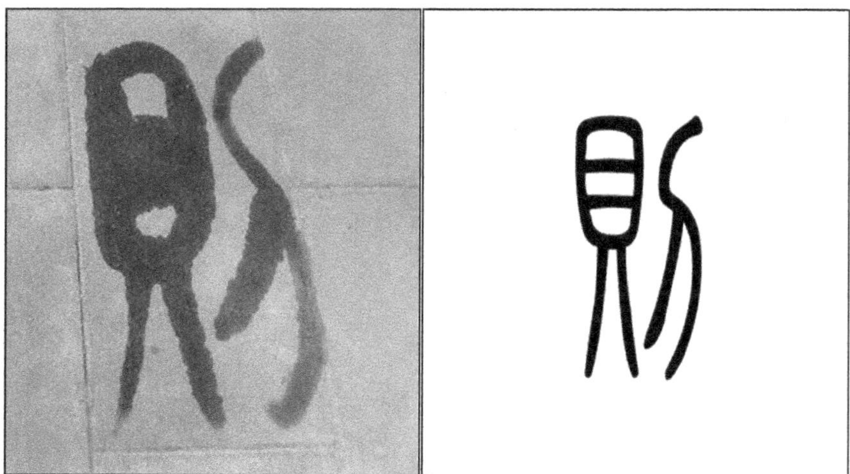

Figure 2.5: Close-up of the character 则 *(ze)*. Left: written in water. Right: in a digital font of seal script. © Laura Vermeeren.

not yet evaporated, and is as legible as the last one, implying that the 14 characters have been written in the span of less than five minutes.

Zooming in on the individual characters, we see how the thickness of the strokes is evenly divided, which is characteristic of seal script. It reveals a calligrapher's steady hand, as even pressure throughout the writing process of a whole character has to be maintained—not an easy undertaking. The empty spaces in the interior of most of the characters are evenly divided, but it is here that the specificities of the water medium become most apparent: the water bleeds out of its original penned shape, and fills up the interior of the character quickly. This is most evident in the last character of the right column 则 *(ze)*, shown in detail in Figure 2.5. The two interior strokes are linked together, but, as seen from the digital font on the right in Figure 2.5 for comparison, because the exterior shape remains intact the character is still recognizable. Altogether, the piece is a well-executed piece of seal script calligraphy, skillfully written according to the conventional rules of the art.

In several instances, this bleeding of the water allows for extra three-dimensionality in the piece—in Figure 2.6, the reflections of the surrounding trees can be seen. This calligraphy was made in Ditan Park and is a rendering of the well-known poem "Immortal at the Magpie Bridge" (鹊桥仙 *Que Qiao Xian*) by Song dynasty poet Qin Guan (1049–1100).[40] This flowing grass script reveals exceptionally supple wrist movement. The water has been evenly

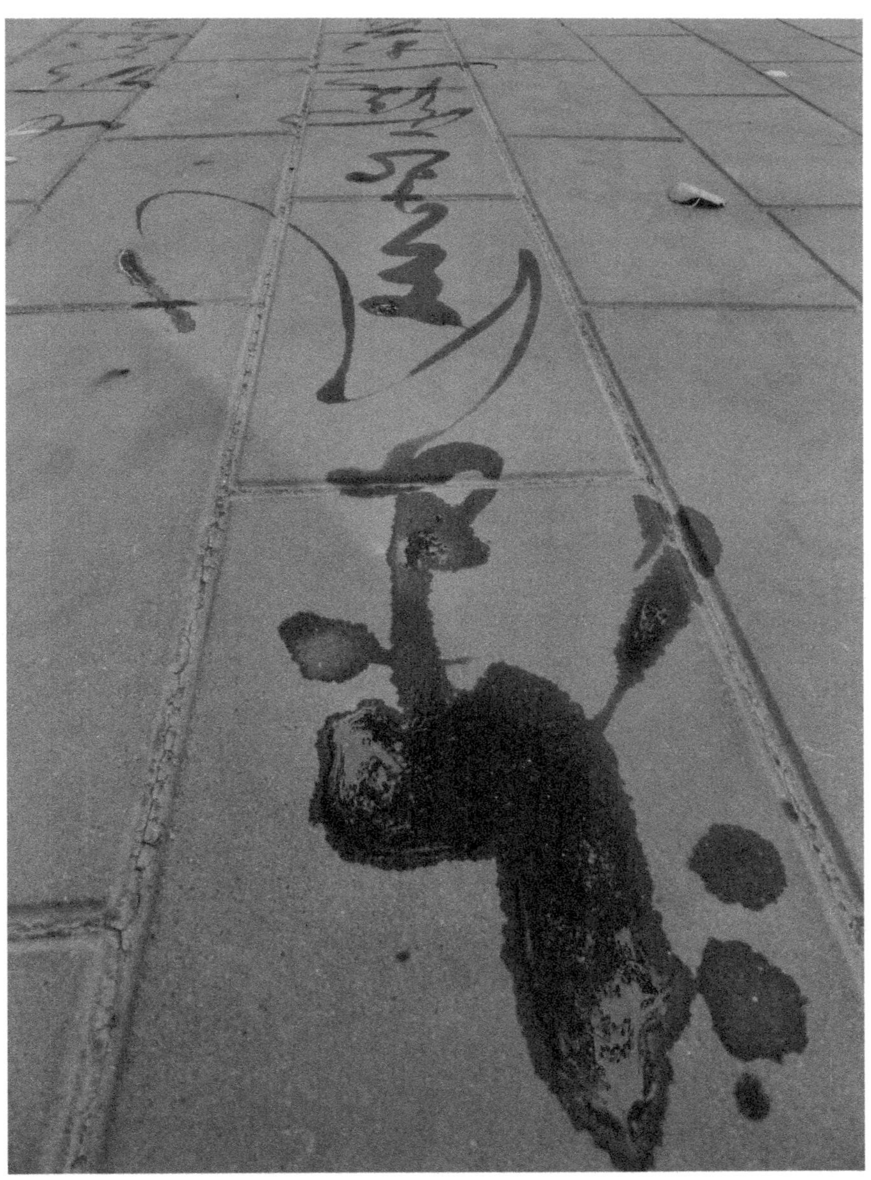

Figure 2.6: The poem "Immortal at the Magpie Bridge" (鹊桥仙 *Que Qiao Xian*) in grass script. © Laura Vermeeren.

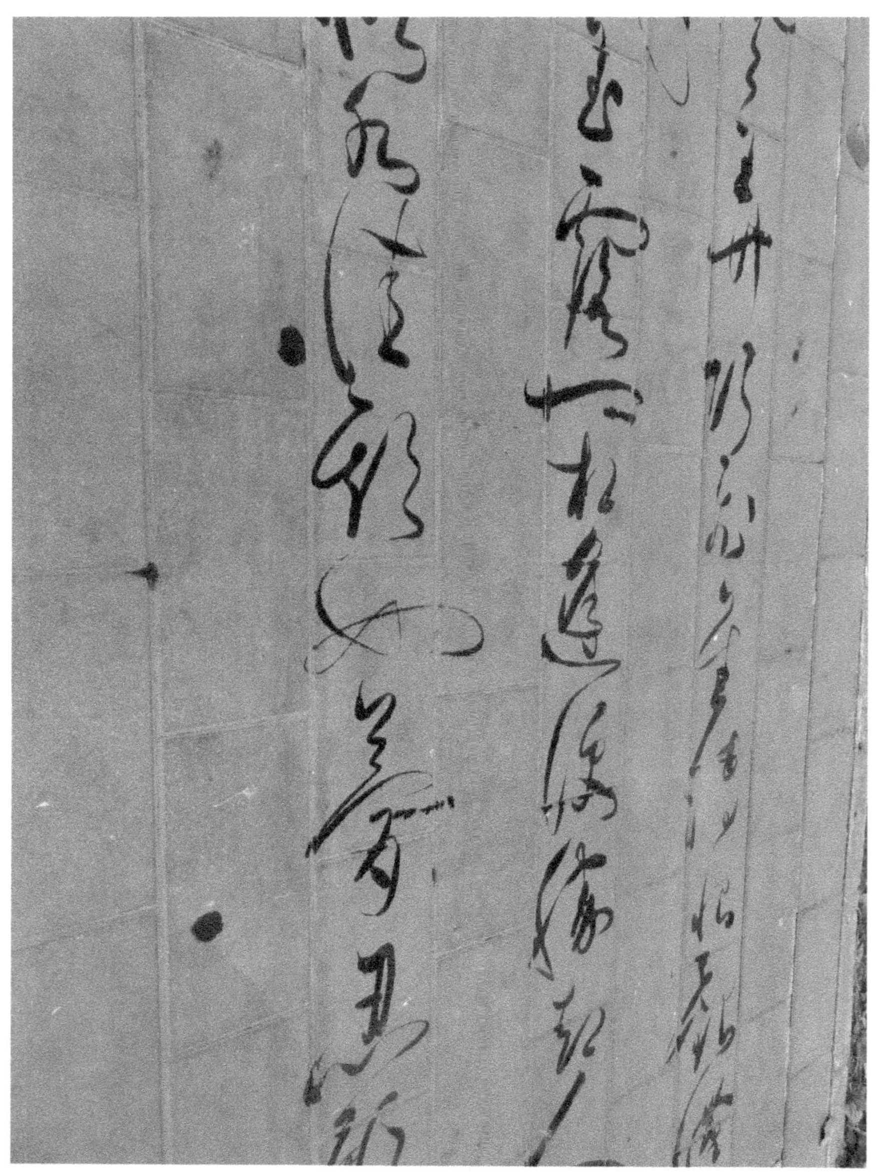

Figure 2.7: A close-up of the poem "Immortal at the Magpie Bridge" (鹊桥仙 *Que Qiao Xian*) in grass script. © Laura Vermeeren.

distributed with great control over the brush. It shows clearly how the calligrapher has hardly lifted the brush from the tiles throughout the composition of the work. The minuscule connecting lines are thin as hairs and bring liveliness to the piece. The large piece of calligraphy is legible from beginning to end, showing that the work has been made with speed. The subtle changes in width and thickness throughout and within each character, and the combined calligraphic methods of "hiding the tip" (藏锋 *cangfeng*) and "exposing the tip" (露锋 *lufeng*) reveal that this water calligrapher is highly skilled. He, too, practices ink calligraphy at home, and often comes to the park with a bundle of ink-written calligraphy in a linen bag that he sometimes takes out during the course of the morning to discuss with his calligraphy friends (书友 *shuyou*).

Although ink is exchanged for water, expensive brushes for brushes made of trash and *xuan* paper for gray tiles, the stylistic rules of Chinese calligraphy are rarely deviated from. Characters are vertically aligned and are written in traditional form (繁体字 *fantizi*)—although I have seen instances when simplified (简体字 *jiantizi*) forms were used. Most of the writers stick to writing in one style and model their writing after the style they have internalized, which allows them to write in a steady flow. Observation shows that a wide selection of well-known Tang dynasty poetry, idioms (成语 *chengyu*), Maoist slogans and poetry, Wang Xizhi's *Orchid Pavilion* and the popular the *Heart Sutra* (心经 *xinjing*) are among the most popular subjects of writing.[41] This makes good sense: verses like these have been taught since primary school and many retirees still know how to write them by heart. It is seen as a good brain exercise. Miss Zhang said with a wry smile: "My content is mostly positive, about long life, harmonious life, really 'typical old people's words' and poetry."

Then there is also spur-of-the-moment writing that responds to what is going on in the park. One calligrapher, who does not practice calligraphy at home, enjoys writing large characters with a brush of which he cut off the pointy tip to make writing easier. Every morning when we meet, he writes the word "friend" (朋友 *pengyou*) to say hello. On numerous occasions, the water calligraphers would write single characters or separate brushstrokes to teach others, or themselves. While the shapes of the characters remain in line with calligraphic stylistic conventions, *in what way* the characters are written down is more often subject to creative interpretation. One writer in Ditan Park has created his own "mirror script": he writes, da Vinci-style, the reverse of the natural way of writing; both left- and right-handed but still in a clear regular script style. The earlier mentioned calligrapher, Xue Fengli, is proud of the "double script" she created by herself: she holds two brushes in two hands and simultaneously pens down the same characters in regular script, intersected

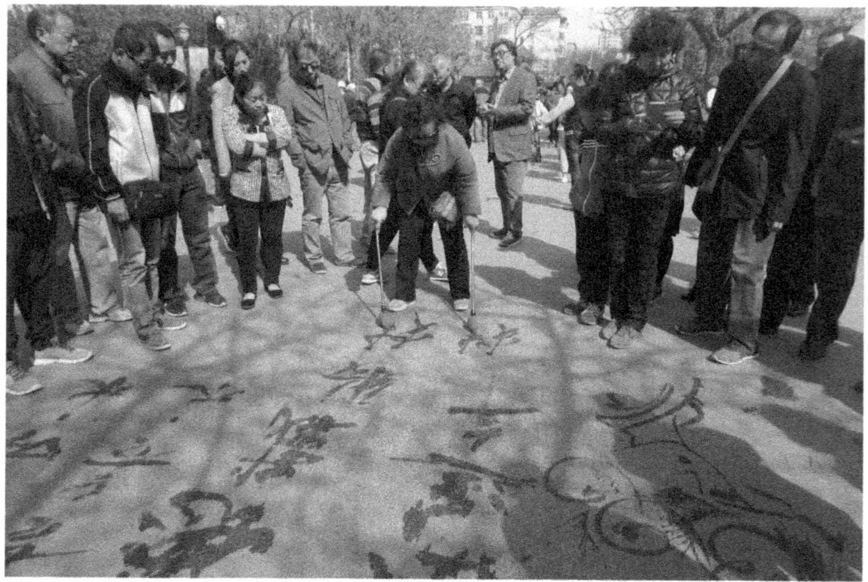

Figure 2.8: Xue Fengli creating a spectacle with her "double script." © Laura Vermeeren.

with drawings of animals of the Chinese zodiac or water sketches of the people in the crowd around her (see Figure 2.8).

Figure 2.9 shows Xue's double rendering of the idiom "A fragrant plum blossom comes from the bitter winter cold" (梅花香自苦寒来 *meihua xiang zi kuhan lai*), meaning that for good things to happen, one often needs to go through hardship. Her calligraphy is a fast-written and flaring regular script, pivoting on bold vertical strokes. Zooming in on the fifth character in both columns, 苦 *ku* (bitter), we see a good example of this frank and playful style. Both vertical *shu* strokes start with a splotch of water and remain thin. The vertical *heng* strokes are equally slim and have underdeveloped endings. The characters are better developed on the left side than on the right. What happens in the space around the characters is also noteworthy: far from an empty canvas, this water calligrapher plays around with images, and creates circles that seem to wear collars of water drops around the idiom. She uses the space differently than most calligraphers: she creates a social scene around her, drawing images of the passersby who enjoy her evaporating water spectacle.

Now of course, one of the more striking aspects of this practice is that the written characters do not last: depending on the weather, they remain visible

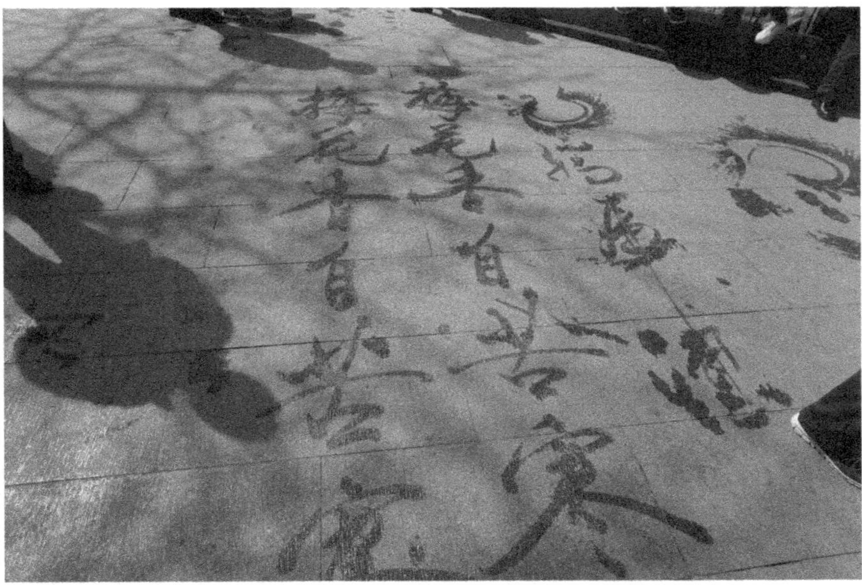

Figure 2.9: A rendering of the idiom "A fragrant plum blossom comes from the bitter winter cold" (梅花香自苦寒来 *meihua xiang zi kuhan lai*) written in "double script." © Laura Vermeeren.

only for three to ten minutes (see Figure 2.10) Two main principles emerged in conversations with water calligraphers, offering insights into the significance of this ephemeral quality. Water calligraphers talk about their hobby in terms of "just having fun" (只是玩儿 *zhi shi wanr*) and to "practice characters" (练字 *lianzi*). Both ideas imply a state of buoyancy, flexibility and deferral. To "just practice characters" (就练字 *jiu lianzi*) suggests that their writings should not be seen as serious calligraphic attempts and should not be taken too seriously. It is really just done "for fun" (只是玩儿 *zhi shi wanr*). They view their work as a cheerful exercise of skill—the disappearance does not hinder the training, nor the "fun" aspect of their hobby. The output, however beautiful, remains secondary to the reiterated movements that are necessary to acquire the skill, and the enjoyment. This is, of course, the nature of any practice: to try, and try once again, until we achieve the desired result. In this case, however, a result is not deferred, but will never take on a permanent shape. It is forever intangible and transient.

In further thinking through the idea of the ephemeral, a term that suggests a state of uncertainty, but also transformation, leading to its inevitable

Figure 2.10: A piece of water calligraphy evaporating. © Laura Vermeeren.

disappearance, I follow Anna Dezeuze.[42] There is, she argues, in ephemeral artworks a moment between appearance and disappearance. It is in that moment that the object exists as an independent entity. It becomes at that moment, as she mobilizes Herrigel's discussion on Zen Buddhism, an "art without art"—it only exists at the moment in which the spectator and maker engage with it.[43] Part of the appeal of the ephemeral, then, is the being there in that moment. If we are to grasp that fleeting moment of something ephemeral fully, we need a heightened form of attention as we move through our everyday lives.

At this point, Michel de Certeau's ideas on everyday life intersect. De Certeau developed a range of perspectives on how everyday life—a concept as fleeting and fragmented as ephemerality—can be approached as a field of possibility and opportunity for a life lived differently. Arguing that our modernity is made up out of a range of different temporalities, de Certeau singles out everyday life as an imaginative and inventive place, a place "scattered with marvels,"[44] where a critique on the dominance of an economic commodity order and the "rationale governing the present" can take place through creative deviation.[45] This critique should not be thought of as oppositional to the governing system, but rather as holding potential, as future generations can draw their cultivated culture from this inventiveness. Consumers, users and practitioners show a creative deviation by their ways of operating within a system that is constructed by someone else and, as such, de Certeau formulates a critique on modernity.

This elevated form of attention, which makes possible an imaginative and creative way of living, applies to both the spectators and the practitioners of water calligraphy. I observe creative deviations in the water calligrapher's creative *make-do* of trash and their insistence on cheap materials and self-learning, instead of following expensive lessons and buying the proper tools, as something highly valued within calligraphic tradition. We find creative deviation also in their voluntary collective mobilization that is now convivial, yet still resembles the compulsory Maoist mass mobilization sessions these water calligraphers have all experienced. Reading this as creative deviation from their shared former experiences, and not just a simple continuation, allows us to appreciate their practice as an emancipated and creative choice rather than instilled routine. They are intrinsically different, precisely because this instilled routine of mobilization has now become creative, voluntary and is created from the bottom up.

Water calligraphy practice further deviates from traditional calligraphy in several ways. It moves away from the bodily discipline normally demanded from the calligrapher, while yet, hidden in the sensuous movements of water calligraphers, we still find an ingrained master narrative of traditional calligraphy that centers explicitly on the disciplined body. Importantly, I have located creative deviations in the calligraphic sign: deliberate aberrations such as double script, mirror script or calligraphy intersected with drawings, as well as inadvertent deviations as a result of either writing tools or environment: the bleeding together of strokes; characters altered because of water drops; sparkling characters due to frost or sun; and half-evaporated characters. But none of those renditions have attempted to deviate from either legibility or conventional content. This raises the question—because the writing will inevitably evaporate within minutes—as to why these people do not write something completely different, be it rebellious, clandestine, mischievous or creative, either in style or content? This question was unanimously and unequivocally dismissed by calligraphers in the park. Calligraphy is perfect in its current form and it is not up to them to change anything, was the reply heard most often. As water calligrapher Li remarks, not looking up from his writing on the ground: "Why would I change something that has evolved over so many thousands of years? We should study the way of the masters."

Chastanet mentions that the presence of official guards remains a reality, albeit discreet, in the public parks. He argues that there is a tacit assumption shared by water calligraphers and these authorities: as long as the content remains neutral, you can write whatever you want.[46] How tempting to see in their choice of "safe" content a kind of self-censorship, as choosing approved texts surely ensures a minimum of government interference. Not only are all activities in China placed under conditions of forms of surveillance, but more to the point, I would argue that their choice of content is better explained within the frameworks of a traditional calligraphy discourse. As we know, acquiring calligraphic expertise involves a slow process of copying the works of ancient masters. A need to voice public opinion through lettering, something that might indeed meet with disapproval from authorities, is absent. What happens in the parks is no different from what people practice at home or in calligraphy class, and is subsequently no more and no less censured or altered. It should thus be approached as a type of calligraphy that is not deliberately opposing traditional calligraphy discourse, but rather borrows from it, expands it and celebrates it.

Expanding Spaces

The adherence to legibility and conventional content is an important observation that adds to our understanding of the specific ways in which calligraphy functions in contemporary contexts. It allows us, moreover, to complicate ideas of the vernacular and the everyday as positioned completely outside the institutions or symbolic boundaries of "real" or "official" art, a point made most authoritatively by Jean Burgess.[47] The practice exists in tandem with discourses of "official" calligraphy—operating outside, but necessarily in relation to it. It shows how we cannot simply separate what happens in "the everyday" from other means and spaces of cultural production. Michael Gardiner argues that "everyday life is vulnerable to the effects of commodification and bureaucratic structuring, and exhibits tendencies towards passive consumerism and an inward-looking, unreflective and routinized form."[48] This is indeed the case with water calligraphy. While water calligraphy started out as a loosely organized and spontaneous exercise, groups of water calligraphers are increasingly incorporated into neighborhood communities (社区街道 *shequjiedao*), Party-led committees that were set up after the gradual breakdown of the work unit were preserved as a way to maintain public order. In 2002, an interviewee disclosed, their activity in Taoranting Park was noticed by the neighborhood community and subsequently incorporated in

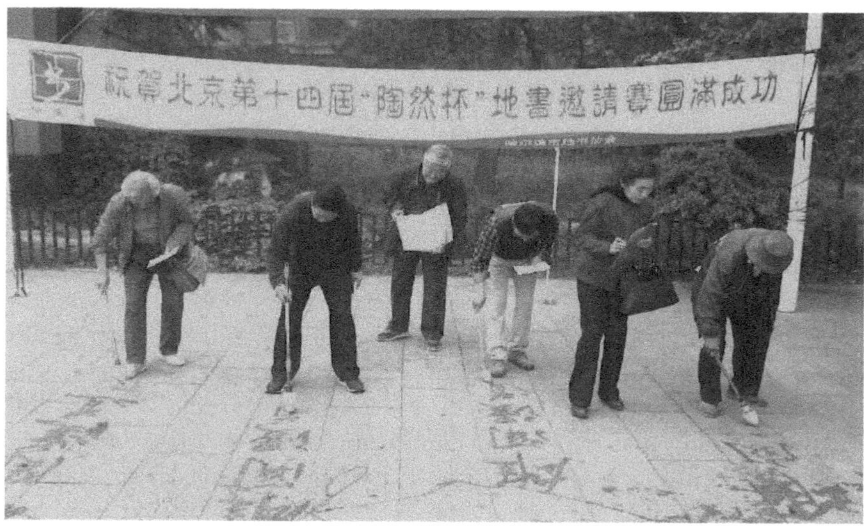

Figure 2.11: The 14th "Taoranting Cup" water calligraphy contest of 2016. © Jian Lin.

it, under the category of "culture, sports and health." With their help, water calligraphers now distribute their own newspaper and have their own logo, and sell caps and linen bags. An annual water calligraphy contest has been set up as well, which is now widely visited by other water calligraphy associations throughout the whole country. During the 40-year anniversary of the Reform and Opening Up Policy in 2018, this annual contest in Taoranting Park metamorphosed into a huge "Taoran Water Calligraphy Culture Festival" (陶然地书文化节 *Taoran dishu wenhuajie*) with the aim to "bring water calligraphy to the next level," and simultaneously promote a creative city (see Figure 2.11).[49]

The festival—with the hardly festive theme "Struggling for the new era: writing new Taoran" (奋斗新时代书写新陶然 *Fendou xin shidai shuxie xin Taoran*)—now also includes performances from famous calligraphers; visitors can try their hand at water calligraphy; and, importantly, a calligraphy contest for children is among the activities. "From an originally spontaneous personal leisure performance to an organized and disciplined team effort," the online newspaper 人民网 *Renminwang* reported,[50] reiterating the vulnerability of everyday activities, and how easy it seems for these to be incorporated into governmental agendas. The ways in which these groups organize and sustain themselves through contests reveal a degree of professionalism that ostensibly contrasts with the spirited, bottom-up nature of water calligraphy. Yet, it is important to keep in mind that the vast majority of water calligraphers do not travel to contests, and maintain their own daily routines of writing, within or outside an association.

In the Chinese media, water calligraphy is by and large praised as an innocent folk practice, a low-carbon one at that.[51] It is also increasingly employed by local and national authorities to promote awareness of calligraphy and, by extension, Chinese culture, while enhancing the city's image. Water calligraphy groups were invited to perform at events during the 2008 Olympic Games; a water calligrapher's design was chosen for the athletes' uniforms in the 2012 Olympic Games; and water calligraphy delegates are invited to kindergartens and schools to practice with children. In her article, "Writing in Water," on filmmaking and water calligraphy, Zito mentions that in Tuanjiehu Park in Beijing, where she observed and practiced water calligraphy from 2006 to 2009, passersby would often whisper in her ear that this is "not art," and one should not be confused thinking this might be a serious art form.[52] More than a decade later, I have had no such experience. During my interactions with traditional calligraphers, educators, artists, contemporary calligraphers, students and calligraphic font designers, I always asked their views on the practice of water calligraphy. No one disregarded the writings of the water calligraphers. While many might consider this merely a health exercise, there is a broadly shared view that the practice positively highlights the art of calligraphy as a whole. The "amateurs" are praised more than anything else for writing so skillfully. I hold that this change in attitude is a direct result of the attempts to pull water calligraphy from obscurity into public awareness, creating a dialogue with discourses of traditionally practiced calligraphy—water calligraphy is still operating outside of the discourse of more traditional calligraphy to maintain its charm, but it is necessarily existing in relation to it.

Practices reminiscent of—or identical to—water calligraphy have appeared in established artistic circles as well, which furthers highlights the way in which water calligraphy is becoming part of a general calligraphy and art discourse. Noted contemporary artist Song Dong (b. 1966) works with video and photography, and his works often focus on impermanence and the living conditions in contemporary urban China. In 1996, he created a transient performance piece by writing daily diary entries in water on a stone slab and documenting the process through photographs. A photo collage of this work is now for sale, transforming the transient nature of the original piece into something monetizable by relinquishing its ephemeral allure.[53] Even in western popular media, water calligraphy pops up—the second season of American

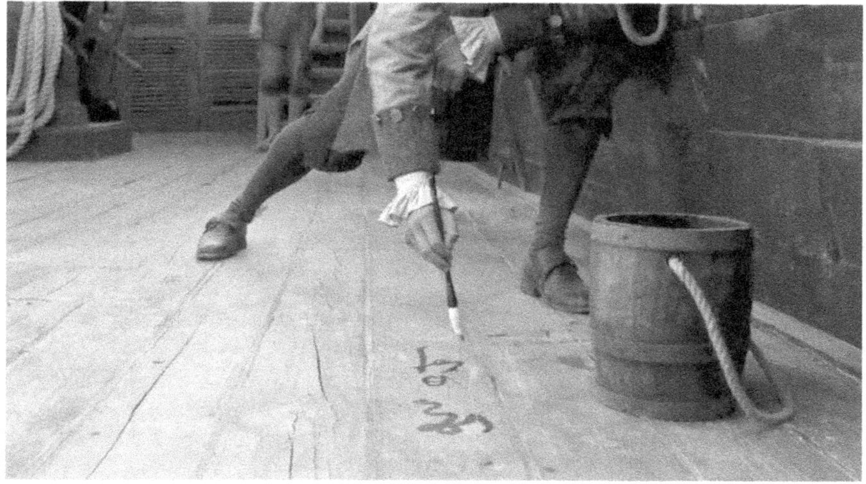

Figure 2.12: A snapshot of the series *Outlander*, Series 3 Episode 9: "The Doldrums" 2017. © Sony Television.

fantasy series *Outlander* features a Qing dynasty Chinese scholar-official (re)named Willoughby, who, in one episode, writes water calligraphy on the deck of a ship. Poetically, he muses that in order to tell his story, he needs to let it vanish (Figure 2.12). No larger contrast is possible between the character of Mr Willoughby, an educated poet who, accompanied by the vague orientalist tunes of a bamboo flute and the romantic background of the sea, writes in water to tell his own story, and the writers in the park in Beijing today who write familiar poetry and slogans with brushes made from plastic bottles and selfie sticks in a carnivalesque park heavy with the sounds of transistor radios and choir singing. But this is, of course, not the point. An image is imprinted on the viewer of a poetic orientalist figure, writing in mystic ephemerality.

Contemporary calligrapher Wang Dongling, whose work will be analyzed in more depth in the next chapter, also created a performance piece of water calligraphy in 2016, making an ephemeral rendering of the *Heart Sutra* in front of the Forbidden City using water and a hairy brush (Figure 2.13). He told me:

> In Hangzhou I also saw some people writing water calligraphy, and in Beijing there were people writing water calligraphy at the Temple of Heaven. Actually, the people and their written characters were really quite good. But it was done for health exercise. I think this is a very good thing. But then, because I am an artist, I was doing an exhibition in Beijing, a piece of

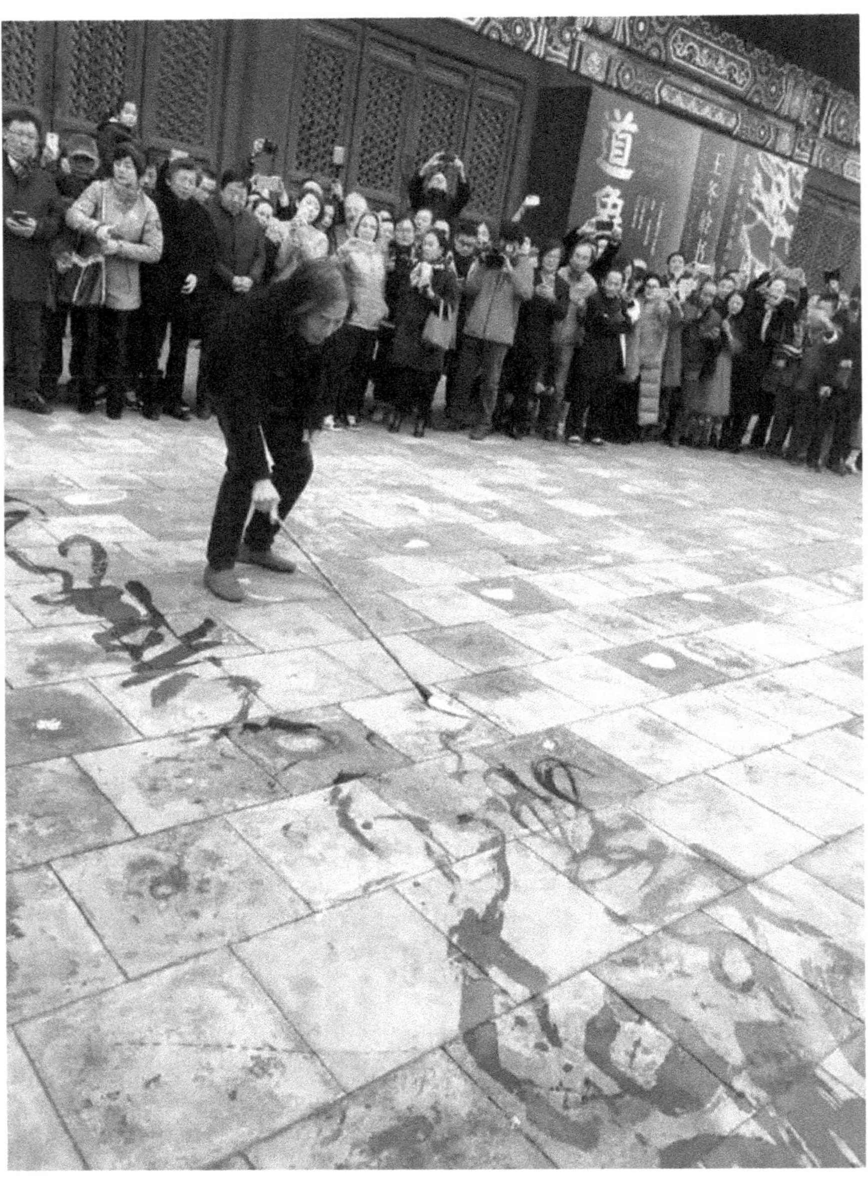

Figure 2.13: Wang Dongling and his rendition of the *Heart Sutra* in 2016. Courtesy of Wang Dongling.

> 3 by 27-meter, white paint on stainless steel. That was the main work, and then I wrote the *Heart Sutra* on the ground. That was also a piece. It was conceptual. On the surface it may look the same as water calligraphy, but in reality, it is not the same.
>
> —Interview with Wang Dongling

The conceptual boundaries drawn by Wang Dongling are important for understanding the discourse of calligraphy, and recap the whispers of Zito's passersby; that water calligraphy is not art and, at best, it reminds us of art, and allows for a reappreciation of the "real."

Water calligraphy, until now, remains to be valued as calligraphy's charming and innocent other, and is defined by contradictions: ephemerality as opposed to permanence; indifference to economic advantage as opposed to making valuable pieces; floor, park and water versus paper, study room and ink. But instead of focusing on contradictions, it might be worthwhile to approach these differences as creative deviations, to circle back to Michel de Certeau's terminology. I have attempted to sketch water calligraphy as a spontaneous ephemeral creative act in the context of the urban public park. The park is an active agent that helps produce these creative expressions by transforming into a temporary creative cluster in its own right; invented and maintained by retirees. By shifting the focus of creativity from clusters in designated creative industry spaces to the seemingly mundane setting of the public park, we can also begin to outline a new typology of creativity, one shaped by the ephemeral nature of everyday life.

I return to Wang Dongling, quoted earlier, as a point of departure for the questions of the next chapter. He argued that his ephemeral work in front of the Forbidden City, although very similar if not identical to the calligraphy made by water calligraphers, was actually very different. It was, as he maintained, a "conceptual" work, meaning in this case that it was created with different intent. But what are conceptual calligraphic artworks, and how might we begin to explore what they do? Throughout this chapter, I have argued that water calligraphy should be seen as an extension of traditional calligraphy—not existing outside of it, but rather borrowing from it, expanding it, and celebrating it. This practice is made possible within the graspable, ephemeral moments of everyday life. It is other, yet it does not resist, nor is it conceptual. But Wang Dongling belongs to a group of reformers that have deliberately tried to create *yet another other* to traditional calligraphy in content, in shape, in form and in purpose. The next chapter will engage with the scene of contemporary calligraphy, and probe the predicaments or openings it offers to the calligraphy discourse.

CHAPTER 3

Contemporary Calligraphy: Leaving Characters?

> Xu Bing's work is not calligraphy. . . . We have a consensus: you can play, but the bottom line is that you cannot leave Chinese characters. Once you go beyond that line, you play, but this is not calligraphy. Some people go over that line, but they still claim it is calligraphy. That is their business.
>
> —Interview with Zhang Rongqing

Xu Bing (b. 1955), whose works have by now become the go-to example for those who want to highlight the audacity, the creativity and the inventiveness of contemporary Chinese art, once was—and still is—a skilled calligrapher. Growing up between books, characters and prints, with his mother working as a librarian and his father serving as the lead of the Department of History at Peking University, Xu Bing's fascination with script started early on. "I love using the written word to create works of art," Xu Bing declared in an essay.[1]

The subtle juxtaposition posed here by Xu Bing serves as a good point of entry to the questions this chapter investigates. Instead of saying that the calligraphic written word *is* art, Xu Bing uses the written word as a tool that can be employed to create what today might be considered "art." He speaks out more clearly here:

> It might be said that I had such a skill, yet in my mind I have never truly created calligraphy, because my earliest experience with the brush—the tracing of red characters and the copying of classical steles—was not calligraphy: it was simply writing characters. To be precise: it was a method of cultural conditioning and a rite of cultural passage. I never thought of it as art.[2]

Xu Bing's thoughts here are at the heart of many debates on the intersections, overlaps and contradictions vis-à-vis craft, art, writing and calligraphy. These are not contemporary debates by any means: they were around as early as the Han dynasty. The difficult position of calligraphy in the present day follows, along with other factors, its synchronicity with a relatively new phenomenon called "contemporary art." Both calligraphy and contemporary Chinese art today struggle with a complicated position: the status of calligraphy as an independent art form—in the sense that it is both researched as an academic subject and evaluated and exhibited in designated (calligraphy) art expositions—is less than 40 years old, and continues to be ill-defined and open-ended. At the same time, the conceptual frameworks to demarcate the spaces inhabited by Chinese contemporary art are also still subject to debate.[3] When the two met in an artistic juncture around the 1980s, scholarship on Chinese contemporary art attempted to define this moment with imprecise terms such as: "calligraphic expression as a new artistic language"[4] and "combining calligraphic imagery and techniques with the modern forms of conceptual and performance art."[5] Minglu Gao, one of the most prominent art critics in mainland China, refers to this moment as "an investigation of language as part of the idea art (观念艺术 *guannian yishu*),"[6] and Xu Jiang concludes that these developments "use writing as shock tactics . . . intent only on extreme conceptualism, decoration, even at times treating calligraphy as a minor of video art."[7]

A good example of a work that is located at that juncture is *Book of the Sky* (天书 *Tianshu*), the famous woodblock art installation made by Xu Bing. During the advent of the avant-garde art scene in China around the mid-1980s, coined by Minglu Gao as the "'85 New Wave Art Movement,"[8] this piece became the defining artwork of the movement—and not much later also the focal point of governmental critique. *Book of the Sky* is an impressive work for which the artist spent four years designing and carving out thousands of Song-type woodblock characters, and printing them on volumes of books, scrolls and one enormous hanging scroll. Together, these pieces make up a monumental art installation, initially named *Mirror to Analyze the World: The Century's Final Volume* (析世鉴-世纪末卷 *xi shijian shijimo juan*), but collectively known as *Book of the Sky*. The text appears to be perfectly legible, but instead of real characters, the graphs made by Xu Bing are all deliberately illegible—they do not exist in the lexicon of the Chinese language. The work upsets conventions of writing, and forces the viewer to reassess their relationship with language and script—a configuration in which language is made meaningless and fake that was, and is, to many offensive, disturbing and unsettling. When I visited his studio in Beijing in 2016 to interview Xu Bing, he spoke about new artistic and linguistic expressions that should always be made "in accordance with the needs of the time":

> Most people consider artists geniuses. But I realized that IQ is not the most important thing for artists. The most important thing is whether you can absorb the energy of society, and transfer it into new expressive ways of art and language. I feel that this ability is the most important. I must always keep myself alive and creative, and this motivation must come from the attention to my societal surroundings.
>
> —Interview with Xu Bing

This makes every artwork, he argues, a reflection or translation of its time, echoing Baudelaire's credo of the western modernist movement *Il faut être de son temps* ("you must be of your time"). And this is ultimately the main issue I probe in this chapter: how to be "of your time," when you create something that is supposed to resemble works made more than a thousand years ago.

The burgeoning art movement of the '85 New Wave provides a foundation for investigating artworks situated at the intriguing intersection of Chinese contemporary art and calligraphy. This exploration aims to examine both the visual creations and their creators: what falls within the realm of "contemporary calligraphy," and what lies outside of it? And who decides where the boundaries of that realm lie? Can we go as far as to read the aesthetic alterations in these works as a critique on traditional calligraphy, or is contemporary calligraphy art actually not the locus of criticality that it is often made out to be? Birgit Hopfener observes that in the discourse of contemporary art, "there seems to be a dominant view that a commitment of art to criticality is obligatory."[9] This is especially the case for non-western artistic production. In the case of China, the freedom to create art was demanded by the Stars group, demonstrating in the streets of Beijing in 1979. This foundational avant-garde movement adopted western-style modern art to claim new liberties, a style that allowed artists to distance themselves from the style of Socialist Realism, mandatory until then. Hsingyuan Tsao argues that by then, "the term 'avant-garde' had become something of a comical concept in the west, leaving the Chinese contemporary art movement as the last real avant-garde."[10] Chinese contemporary art still seems to be burdened with an expectation of avant-gardism and, more precisely, an intention to dissent, because that might still be relevant "there."

Making changes to the written character almost instantly implies critique, geared not only at writing, but at the culture in which writing is embedded. "To strike at the written word, is to strike at the very essence of the culture," states Xu Bing.[11] Calligraphy, with its in-betweenness of word and image seems to function as a double-edged sword, and tampering with it—either transforming it into illegible or nearly illegible signs, blending it with other art forms or employing unusual tools to write it—seemingly renders it an ideal vehicle for critique. A prime example of this is the work *Copying the Preface of the Gathering at the Orchid Pavilion a Thousand Times* 重复书写兰亭序一千遍 *Chongfu shuxie lantingxu yiqian bian*, 1990–97[12] by Qiu Zhijie (see Figure 3.1). Qiu Zhijie chose to copy Wang Xizhi's *Orchid Pavilion* in the style of Wang Xizhi a thousand times, according to the traditional rules of calligraphy a thousand times, over the course of seven years. But instead of using a thousand separate sheets of rice paper, Qiu wrote on just one sheet of rice paper, writing the characters on top of each other. The result is a heavy and thick sheet of paper with monochromic black ink, on which all traces of legibility have vanished. When exhibiting, the artwork is made up of a multimedia installation combining video, photography and calligraphy: it comprises a 35-minute video with footage of the first 50 times that Qiu Zhijie copied the work, five digital photographic prints from different stages of the process, and the final original piece of rice paper and ink. Already after making 50 copies, the work was completely black, which means that for the remaining 950 times, Qiu wrote the *Orchid Pavilion* on a black surface with black ink, not being able to see the result of his labor. Of the multiple ways to probe this artwork, it is most easily read as a critical contemporary commentary on Chinese tradition and Chinese art at large, as it effectively renders the most well-known symbol of Chinese cultural tradition blacked out and illegible—it cannot speak and it cannot be read anymore. By not producing a thousand copies that are all legible, all shareable, and all separately affirming their place in the ongoing stream of contributions to the large body of calligraphic works, Qiu Zhijie deliberately places himself outside the historical narrative, and puts a considered halt to the traditional convention of production. Yet, he is not dramatically destroying them, by ripping them apart, burning them or not writing them in the first place. Instead, it is his own physical calligraphic labor that is doing away with the production. I therefore read this work as a personal destruction that carries implications for calligraphic practice as a whole. By emphasizing the artistic process over the finished product, Qiu Zhijie's intentionally futile copying frees the act of calligraphy from its traditional function, but also from the multi-interpretability of the calligraphic character, and as such returns to the act of writing itself. The work pulls calligraphy back to the core values of the tradition—copying, script, self-cultivation and discipline. Yet, the more frivolous parts, perhaps simply the joy, of writing the *Orchid Pavilion* have disappeared in the process: the original

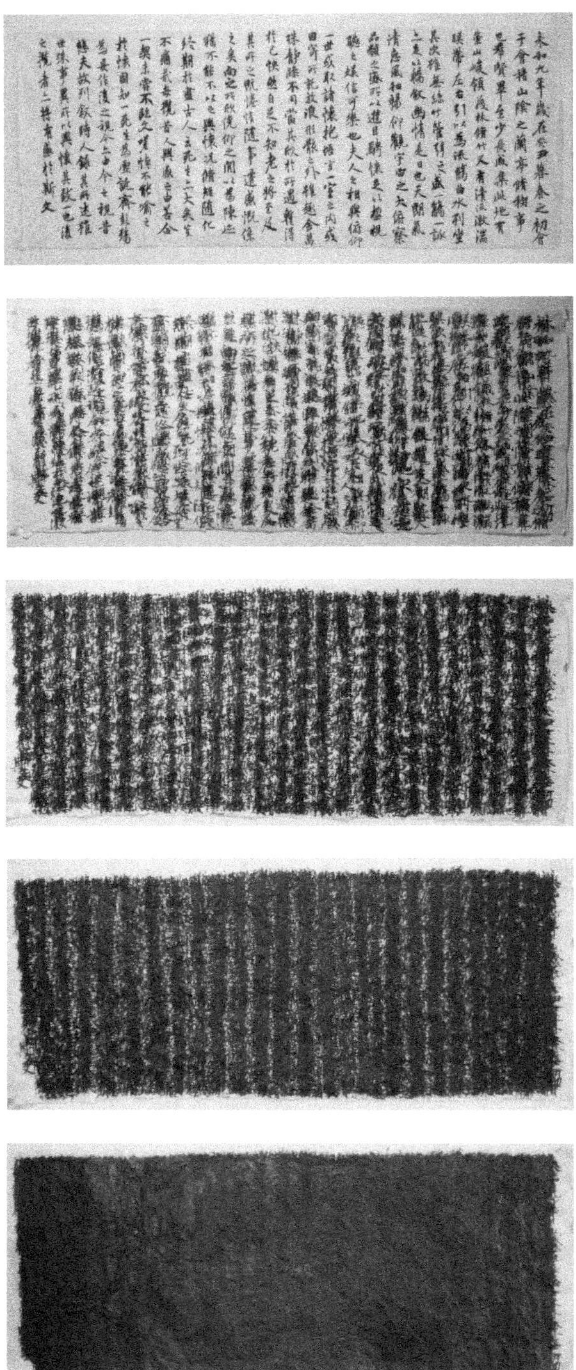

Figure 3.1: Qiu Zhijie, *Copying the Preface of the Gathering at the Orchid Pavilion a Thousand Times*, 1990–97. Single-channel digital video (color, silent) and chromogenic prints, overall (approx.): 276 × 105 × 1.3 cm; duration: 34 min. 48 sec. M+ Sigg Collection, Hong Kong. By donation. [2012.839]. © Qiu Zhijie. Image courtesy of M+, Hong Kong.

piece, written spontaneously and drunkenly, is turned into a laborious and pitch-black work, dull and devoid of its original legible meaning.

But as tempting as it is to link (contemporary) art directly to a form of criticality, I refrain from the familiar pitfall of seeing Chinese contemporary art objects as *inherently* critical: there is more to gain from a careful analysis of the artistic object. The blackness and visual negation of Qiu Zhijie's work can, for example, alternatively prompt the question whether Qiu possibly particularly dislikes the *Orchid Pavilion*. Or is the artwork perhaps a personal reflection on, or condensed visualization of, the time Qiu Zhijie has already spent mastering the skill, grieving the lost hours? Here we go into the muddy waters of authors' intent.

In analyzing how art critics (as Silbergeld[13] reminds us, for the artist, "those in power" include critics and art historians—aesthetic colonizers) interpret the artworks made by contemporary calligraphers and contemporary artists employing calligraphy, it is striking how often their reading is framed in negative prefixes—to underscore, it seems, that what is happening, *un-does* something very important. Yang Chengyin, for example, wrote that *Book of the Sky* is "anti-art, anti-traditional."[14] Wang Nanming referred to it as "anti-calligraphy,"[15] while Yuedi Liu labels the contemporary artworks that engage with calligraphy as "counter-calligraphy" and de Kloet proposes "strategic unmeaning."[16]

Considering that these artworks have generally been framed as being anti-, non-, or counter-, this chapter is interested in how these works coexist with the traditional calligraphy scene. By definition, their makers place their works outside of the traditional calligraphy paradigm, but how—both in theoretical conception and execution—are they indebted to traditional calligraphy, and how do they talk back to, interact with and view each other? What is to be gained from freeing the calligraphic form from the apparent burden of legibility: what subtle artistic interventions can be found in the broad spectrum from critique to reverence? My concerns on the inclusion and exclusion of different types of calligraphy, critique and politics can be better understood by turning to Jacques Rancière's notion of the "aesthetic regime."[17] For Rancière, human practices are ordered in a more or less structured way that is aimed at maintaining configurations of power. This is done by setting clear boundaries, delimiting what is made visible and invisible, made audible and inaudible, made possible and impossible. Rancière calls this the "police order": a symbolic constitution of the social.[18] Artistic practices, according to Rancière, "are 'ways of doing and making' that intervene in the general distribution of ways of doing and making as well as in the relationships they maintain to modes of being and forms of visibility."[19] In other words, art can make visible what had been invisible; audible what was not to be heard, and make possible what was impossible in an earlier configuration. It has the power to change patterns of behavior and is therefore political. Rancière's ideas are similar to the earlier defamiliarization paradigm that was put forward by Viktor Shklovsky in 1917. Shklovsky argued that art is a technique that carries the ability to make objects unfamiliar, as art removes objects from the automatism of perception.[20] Shklovsky maintains that an artistic object, therefore, has a potential to unsettle, and to shift a commonly held perception. What Rancière inserts in the debate here on the boundaries of calligraphic work is a specific emphasis on forms of sensory experience: the visible, the audible and the sensible. It allows for an analysis of the ways in which the works of contemporary calligraphy selected for this chapter unsettle modes of perception, and simultaneously construct and deconstruct patterns of what calligraphy should do or should be today. Rancière's focus on the sensible is pertinent in the discussion of new forms of calligraphy, as they introduce new visual, tactile, and in some occasions even gustatory and olfactory practices to an art form that for centuries has been imagined as made with black ink, rice paper and brush.

This chapter will scrutinize two contemporary artists whose works play with configurations of calligraphy. They each maintain a unique position in relation to calligraphy, allowing us to analyze the scene from two distinctive angles: Wang Dongling is seen as one of the founders of the contemporary calligraphy scene. His status has become almost sacrosanct, and he speaks from the position of an established innovator. Zeng Xiang, on the other hand, operates from the position of a traditional calligrapher who also experiments with bold new forms, and is heavily criticized for it. My motivation for selecting these artists is also based on experiences during on-site research: their works were debated and compared during interviews; talked about and sometimes fiercely discussed in WeChat groups and at educational institutes, rendering a study of their works important for understanding the current calligraphy scene at large today. Wang Dongling, who has become one of the most renowned living calligraphers in China today, stems from a long lineage of well-known traditional calligraphers. From that position, Wang set out to create a new paradigm for contemporary calligraphy, and has not only produced innovative works, but also has written extensively on the new directions that contemporary calligraphy should take, thus simultaneously creating and demarcating the field. The aesthetics of his works have unsettled, confused and in a Rancièrian way redistributed the senses in China's calligraphy scene, as well as abroad. But as I will show, he is not concerned with overthrowing or critiquing calligraphy, but aims to redirect its focus and purpose to secure its longevity. I will look specifically at his by now signature style of large-scale wild cursive calligraphy (巨幅大字书法 *jufu dazi shufa*) performed live in front of an audience, and his own invented style that he calls "chaos script" (乱书 *luanshu*).

Second, I look at four works made by contemporary calligrapher Zeng Xiang. He caused a sensation with his exhibition at Art District 798 in Beijing in April 2018, where he showcased his large and highly expressive works. Accompanied by a video of himself creating these artworks, he used a brush as large as a mop on a large sheet of paper laid out on the floor, moving his entire body fiercely while shouting and splashing ink around. Not well known in the west, in the calligraphy scenes in China Zeng Xiang is often mentioned as one of the frontrunners of a contemporary calligraphic category called "ugly calligraphy" (丑书 *choushu*), a category in which Wang Dongling is also occasionally classified. While some use the term derogatorily, others claim that these works, although maverick, are a necessity for calligraphy in the modern age and highlight its creative and innovative potential. The works of these artists should be seen as part of a longer lineage of artists who started to obfuscate the lines between calligraphy and contemporary art since the beginning of the 1980s. They in turn are indebted to their predecessors of the New Culture Movement, which took place around the mid-1910s and 1920s, and fundamentally influenced the intellectual and cultural discourses of society. In the following section, I offer a historical overview of reforms within the calligraphy paradigm to contextualize the evolution toward contemporary experiments.

"A Pleasure Ground for Script, a Paradise for Free Imagination"[21]

> Down with the tradition of copying!
> Down with the art of the aristocratic minority!
> Down with the antisocial art that is divorced from the masses!
> Up with the creative art that represents the times! Up with art that can be shared with all of the people!
> Up with the people's art that stands at the crossroads![22]

This manifesto, presented by painter and art educator Lin Fengmian (1900–91) at the first Beijing Art Meeting of 1927, serves as an apt illustration of the impassioned mindsets of young intellectuals around the first two decades of the 20th century, in what was at that time the Republic of China, ruled by a nationalist government. Lin belonged to a group of art reformers who tried to push the agenda for a reinterpretation of Chinese artistic traditions, as well as the adoption and blending of western art techniques with traditional artistic practice. Earlier in the century, in the face of the Japanese intrusion, young intellectuals began to demand reform, culminating in the politically inclined May Fourth Movement (五四运动 *wusi yundong*, 1917–21). This demand for change included a nationwide popular critique on traditional Confucian ideas and the archaic writing system—the reformers were convinced that the strengthening of society could only occur if it restructured itself through western models such as liberalism, pragmatism, nationalism and anarchism. All this was part of the New Culture Movement (新文化运动 *xin wenhua yundong*), and was primarily directed at the educated youth.

Alongside these cultural and political activities, new encounters with western art forms—associated with science and progress because of their realism—convinced the modernizers that cultural reform would break grounds for social progress at large.[23] Reformers argued that in order to improve Chinese art, a western spirit of realism had to be adopted. A schism emerged subsequently, and the field of painting became discursively separated into "Chinese painting" and "western painting" (国画 *guohua* and 西画 *xihua*).[24] This categorization was first and foremost a nationalistic project—a search for a national identity.[25] The arts and the rethinking of the purposes of art were invested in the project of constructing a history, as well as a future for a specifically *Chinese* art. It needed a way to be able to talk about art and aesthetics, and western concepts and language were considered most appropriate to do so.

Within this ideologically hectic context, calligraphy as a pastime, a means to climb the bureaucratic ladder and a tool for self-cultivation of the elite was understood to be no longer sufficient to fulfill the needs of a modern society. The introduction of western aesthetics had created a paradigm shift in the way Chinese intellectuals wrote about art, and western conceptions and categories of aesthetics based on Kantian ideas of beauty, such as "inspiration" and "aesthetic feeling" were employed, instigating reforms also of calligraphy criticism.[26]

For an accurate historical overview of reforms within the calligraphy paradigm specifically, however, we need to go further back than the New Culture Movement: to the late 17th century, when a new chapter in the books of calligraphic evolution in dynastic China commenced. The conquest of China by the foreign Manchus in 1644 who took over from the Chinese Ming dynasty led calligraphers who, facing these alien invaders, self-identified as ethnic Han, to seek out the ancient, inscribed Han dynasty steles for copying. These distinctively engraved texts were previously excluded from aesthetic discourse and dismissed as merely a technical—and anonymous—skill. Now, they became in vogue: the proponents of this new fashion grouped under "the Stele School"

(碑学派 *beixue pai*), maintained that ancient script types on these steles or bronze vessels were superior because they were original, and not deteriorated by endless copying, as had been the norm for centuries. The works produced by the followers of this new school were fresh, less refined, and recall the workings of a carving knife.[27]

This new turn impacted the renegotiation of the purposes and role of calligraphy, and informed the ideas about copying and creativity within calligraphy discourse that would take shape in later centuries, facilitated notably by Kang Youwei (1858–1927)—the famous political reformer, calligrapher and nationalist whose ideas inspired the reformation movement. Kang Youwei published his influential commentary on the arts, "Expanding on Two Oars of the Ship of Art" (广艺舟双楫 *Guang yizhou shuangji*), in 1891, which, according to Yuli Wang, stimulated discussions on "how to deal with the past in creating a viable 'modern' style in Chinese calligraphy."[28] Kang Youwei argued that painstakingly copying one calligraphic style, or following one master is impractical. Instead, he proposed a pragmatic and personal approach, when he argued: "Thus, I develop my own calligraphic style by drawing on those rubbings and my style has come about by itself. With skillfulness from practice and learning in other fields, one can become a calligrapher. Both gifted and ungifted people can succeed."[29]

By the 1930s, scholarship on the aesthetic nature of calligraphy really started to thrive when scholars, having studied overseas, took an interest in the topic. Their writings combined western aesthetic concepts with traditional calligraphy criticism. In 1931, critic and poet Zhang Yinlin (1905–42) wrote a persuasive treatise that would lay the foundation for the discipline of future calligraphy criticism. He began his treatise wondering whether or not calligraphy should be seen as an art form, a question still relevant today, and attempted to systematize the experience of beauty. Zhang arrived at the conclusion that *calligraphy indeed is art*, because its beauty induces positive feelings: "Works of Chinese calligraphy have structured perceptual forms, and in appreciating calligraphic works, we can always experience the positive feelings that are dominated by the internal laws of perceptual forms. Therefore, we can conclude that Chinese calligraphy is an art."[30] He further argued that calligraphy is thus equal to and should get as much attention as the other arts, and that there should be a systematic collection of the past achievements of calligraphy.

The intellectual dialectic between western and Chinese arts, tradition and modernity, and the explorations on how their forms and meanings combined could create new theories of calligraphy was, however, not resolved during that time. Brought to a halt by the invasion by Japan in 1937, the newly set-up educational art institutes closed down, and momentum was lost. In the years that followed, artists were mobilized to create propaganda and cartoons to serve the resistance against Japan, and many fled from the big cities or moved to the west. In 1942, after having established themselves in Yan'an after the Long March in 1935, the Communists proclaimed their political line on literature and arts at the speeches given by Mao at the Yan'an Forum on Literature and Art (延安文艺座谈会 *Yan'an wenyi zuotanhui*). Outlining their strategies under the slogan "revolutionary art for the masses," the principles demanded that all artistic activity from now on should serve the revolution: "What we demand is unity of politics and art, of content and form, and of the revolutionary political content and the highest possible degree of perfection in artistic form."[31]

The style that was deemed most suitable for this purpose was so-called Revolutionary Realism (革命现实主义 *geming xianshi zhuyi*), which combined Soviet-style Socialist Realism and (re-)invented folk traditions, and this would remain the dominant style of art for the decades to come. This narrow definition of the arts as a tool for the revolution reached its peak during the Cultural Revolution (1966–76), when the permitted arts were limited to a very small selection of paintings, movies, novels and music.[32] Throughout these changes, however, calligraphy was not prohibited. While other traditional pursuits were heavily criticized as unwanted remnants of the feudal society that the Communist Revolution attempted to eliminate, calligraphy proved difficult to give up. This was in part due to its dual function as both a traditional literati art and writing—for revolutionary propaganda to be successful, it had to be visually attractive, and calligraphy is the means to make Chinese characters appealing. At the same time, it was also thanks to Mao Zedong's personal fondness for calligraphy that this particular traditional practice did not disappear with the other traditional arts. As a fervent calligraphy enthusiast, Mao had practiced calligraphy all his life, and did not stop writing with the Communist takeover. To the contrary, his calligraphy practice intensified after 1949, as he sought distraction from his bureaucratic burdens by picking up the brush.[33] He wrote classical pieces as well as his own poetry in an eccentric and clearly recognizable cursive grass script and built up a traditional calligraphy collection from the revenue of his sales.[34] For ordinary Chinese at that time, it was more complicated to write as freely as the revolutionary elite did. Calligraphy was not banned at the resolution on culture in 1931[35]—it was after all the means to raise literacy, and so remained an essential part of the elementary school curriculum. But it had to stay a practical skill that could forward the revolution.

Characters, therefore, had to be written clearly and legibly, and grass script was to be avoided.[36] This changed in 1957 when Mao decided to employ the writings of ordinary Chinese to the advantage of the revolution. People were encouraged to write in the format of "big-character posters" (大字報 *dazibao*), large pieces of brush writing in a clear style, to vent their grievances about the political status quo. During this period, known as the Hundred Flowers Movement (百花齐放 *baihua qifang*), from 1956–57, people answered the call and everywhere in educational institutes, factories and public places, big-character posters appeared. Although this was not a new practice and had been used as an informal means to pass on information—from the mundane to the dissident—from the late 1930s during the Japanese war, this time, as Geremie Barmé argues, "new directions in mass propaganda created a format—and a calligraphic fluency—that could be utilized by people of all social strata for political expression, no matter how basic."[37] Mao maintained:

> Dazibao are something wonderful. In my opinion, they should become part of our heritage. . . . The more dazibao, the better . . . Like language, dazibao are "classless." . . . They can be used by either the proletariat or the bourgeoisie. Because most of them are on the side of the proletariat, dazibao are instruments favorable to the proletariat and not the bourgeoisie (1957).[38]

Mao ingeniously killed three birds with one stone with this directive: he urged China's citizens to use their own writings as propaganda while firmly maintaining power; he liberated calligraphy from its feudal taint; and offered a sense of autonomy and artistic freedom to the people at a time when there was very little of that otherwise. The triumphs of the Hundred Flowers Movement had shocked the Party rulers, and after a temporary moratorium on the use of big-character posters by the public, the practice then culminated during the Cultural Revolution. At this paradoxical time, many old scrolls and calligraphic works were destroyed by the Red Guards, brigades of militant students formed in 1966 and guided by Mao, while at the same time, an unprecedented frenzied production of new writings took place. Hua Sheng notes that within a week after the call of the Party in 1966 for more *dazibao*, in Beijing alone "more than thirty times the normal monthly consumption of paper was being sold each month, just to meet the demand for dazibao writing . . . and people began using old newspapers as paper shortages developed and mud as a substitute for glue."[39] People who were formerly enrolled in the art academies, or otherwise known for their capability of brush writing, were at this point recruited to mass-produce big-character posters, while later, factory workers, children and peasants were also included in the practice, collectively covering the entire nation in a sea of characters.[40]

The reason I am elaborating on the practice of *dazibao* is because the negotiations during the *dazibao* movement concerning the public and the private, propaganda and dissent, and art versus writing, were carried over to the new calligraphy movement in the 1980s. This influence can be seen both in the contents and style of their groundbreaking works, but also in the way in which writing calligraphy could now be imagined as a practice done by everybody, regardless of class and status. Moreover, many people who are given voice in this book—ranging from artists and educators to water calligraphers—learned how to write calligraphy through writing *dazibao*, as educational institutes were mostly closed at that time. Contemporary calligrapher Wang Dongling confided that the *dazibao* movement led him to feel a sense of artistic freedom within calligraphy for the first time,[41] and Xu Bing mentioned that the way the revolution was played out in public writing urged him to renegotiate meanings of language, writing and tradition.[42]

After the practice of *dazibao* was prohibited in 1979, and Deng Xiaoping's Reform and Opening Up policy (改革开放 *gaige kaifang*) in that same year caused an outburst of artistic and intellectual creativity, calligraphy organized itself in the first official Calligraphy Association in 1981, and new directions for the art form had, yet again, to be found. The questions asked by reformer and calligrapher Kang Youwei, quoted on p. 83, this volume, became relevant again: how do we deal with the past in creating a viable and "modern" style of Chinese calligraphy? This question could arise once more, because the Chinese script had survived attempts to abolish it altogether and replace it with alphabetic writing. Before 1945, cultural leaders on the left, such as writer Lu Xun; writer, archaeologist and Communist leader Guo Moruo; and educator and co-founder of the Communist Party Chen Duxiu, firmly believed that substituting the archaic and indeed elitist character script with alphabetic writing would speed up mass literacy and would be a step toward modernity. "It is, furthermore, the home of rotten and poisonous thought. I have no regret in abandoning it," said Chen Duxiu.[43]

Different experiments in romanization were undertaken in the 1920s,[44] and in 1950, Mao decided that characters first had to be simplified as an intermediate step to eventually phasing them out in exchange for alphabetic writing. The idea was, according to Shouhui Zhao, to maximize "the simplification of the graphic form until the components of Chinese characters became so simplified that the individual strokes themselves functioned as a phonetic alphabet, as has happened in Japanese."[45] This did not happen, but instead, in 1950, 1956, 1964 and again in 1977, lists of character reforms were published. These reforms were meant to reduce the number of strokes in one character, making it easier to write and to remember the characters. In 1958, the romanizing system *Hanyu Pinyin* (汉语拼音) was introduced, first as an intermediate step toward complete romanization but finally as a way to input characters in the computer, to write foreign names and as an aid for the teaching of Mandarin.

I started this section at a critical period for the Chinese arts, when the tradition of writing calligraphy had been in full swing for thousands of years. But of course, in the millennia leading up to these critical years, calligraphy was not a homogeneous art form, as I stressed in the Introduction to this book. To the contrary: vast watershed moments, far-reaching renegotiations and crises have taken place in the realm of calligraphy throughout the many dynastic cycles. The developments in the last hundred years, however, as described above, created three important paradigm shifts that I think should be seen as key points for a better understanding of calligraphy in the present. First, Zhang Yinlin and his reform-minded peers concluded that calligraphy induces positive feelings and *is therefore an art form*. Second, Kang Youwei attempted to redefine calligraphy as a practical art form that could be done by everyone—the skilled and unskilled alike, while elevating crude and idiosyncratic character forms. And finally, Mao Zedong's promotion of big-character posters and his own public writings made the calligraphic sign ubiquitous in the streetscape.

The second debate on modern calligraphy that took place in the mid-1980s coincided with larger governmental liberal reforms that brought a renewed interest in western philosophy, aesthetics and psychology, largely fueled by translations of these works that now became widely available. Gu Gan, a former traditional calligrapher and printmaker during the Cultural Revolution, became the frontrunner of the Modernist Movement (书法现代派 *shufa xiandaipai*) after organizing the First Exhibition of Chinese Modern Calligraphy (中国现代书法首展 *Zhongguo xiandai shufa shouzhan*) in 1985. The beginnings of that movement, as Gu Gan recalled in 1992, were anything but clearly defined:

> Our group from the first Modern Calligraphy Exhibition was really not clear-headed at all. It is just that we wanted to differentiate a bit from the same old grass, clerical and seal scripts that we could see everywhere. But I would have never thought that the exhibition would ignite such a strong reaction from the public. When that happened I, only still half awake, started to ask myself: "What is this all about?"[46]

His confusion then turned into excitement, prompting him to state that "Modern calligraphy is a pleasure ground for script, a paradise for free imagination."[47]

Gu Gan and his peers experienced this time as a period in which one was allowed to play around freely, with a cheerful difference of opinion on where to take these new shapes and forms, arguing that the different voices in modern calligraphy should never agree, or else it would mean the end of modern calligraphy as a whole. Gu reiterates the same statement in an opinion piece in 2016.[48] And indeed, in the time that has passed between Gu Gan's almost identical declarations in 1992 and 2016, exactly that has happened: a common agreement on what modern calligraphy defines has not been found, and also, the debate continues to be as heated as it is alive.

While bold experimentations unfolded one after another, not all output was considered calligraphy, but was often seen as a transitional concept, that, if anything, negates traditional calligraphy. Xu Jiang positions the different opinions on a spectrum, in which the traditionalists are at the one end, where they "adhere so loyally to the past that they fail to evolve either styles of their own or push forward new frontiers within their art." This conservatism, he argues, overlooks the "essential exploratory spirit of calligraphy as an ever-evolving art form that can be as boldly experimental and as innovative as any other." At the other end of the spectrum, he places those who abandon all tradition in favor of change for its own sake, and deconstruct Chinese characters without regard for their meaning.[49] The separation of literary content from calligraphic technique was most concerning of all. Authoritative calligrapher Qi Gong (1912–2005) concludes in 1991: "Recently, some people have suggested that calligraphic technique exists independently of literary content. After much thought, I have concluded this notion is unacceptable."[50]

The attempts that have been made—and are still being made—to classify and categorize all the different rhizomatic, unstable and ever-changing offshoots and imaginations of calligraphy since the first exhibition in 1985—by art critics who are, themselves, often also calligraphers[51]—are therefore not univocal. Zhu Qingsheng, for example, proposes dividing the artworks into 13 different schools,[52] while Gao Tianming differentiates five schools.[53] Zhang Aiguo suggests eight types of calligraphy and Liu Zhongcao proposes six types of style.[54] In western scholarship, a distinction made by Barrass into Classicism, Neoclassicism, Modernism and Avant-garde is most often maintained.[55] I should emphasize here that I am less interested in joining any kind of classification. Being aware of these classifications, however, does allow me to embed the analysis in the context of the modern calligraphy movement, and it helps us in appreciating how complicated it was, and is, to find a common agreement on the subject.

Theorists on these new calligraphic constructs focused their analysis first on the nature of the works, specifically on how the artworks experiment with the legibility of the written character. These experiments are done in various ways, either by a distortion of form and space, such as stretching it in size (for example, in the works of Gu Gan and Yang Jin Song), dissecting the characters as single brushstrokes (for example, in the work of Qiu Zhenzhong), using newly discovered archaic script types (for example, in the works of Zou Tao and Zhang Aiguo) and rediscovering the ancient structure and visual symbolism with regards to nature, and its pictorial backgrounds (for example, in the work of Wei Ligang, Xu Bing, Qiu Zhenzhong and Zeng Xiang). Another category of works sets out to create a complete erasure of lexicalized meaning through creating Chinese-looking characters that are not legible as they do not exist in the lexicon (for example, Xu Bing and Gu Wenda). From here, artists started to leave rice paper as their main surface of writing, and to venture toward creating calligraphies on a wide range of surfaces: on photographs, newspapers and bamboo (for example, Wang Dongling), with leftover foods (by the Yangjiang Group), written directly on human bodies (for example, Zhang Huan) or animals (Xu Bing), on rocks and stone (Lis Jung Lu, Song Dong and Qiu Zhijie) or on walls (for example, Lu Da Dong and the King of Kowloon). In yet another reincarnation, the artists leave the concept of writing surfaces altogether, and interpret calligraphy as dance (Guangdong Modern Dance Company) or as a videogame or installation (Feng Mengbo).

Two major artistic currents continue to be especially important sources of inspiration: Abstract Expressionism of the New York School and Japanese modern calligraphy. Abstract Expressionism, a movement that developed in New York around 1940, was committed to art as expressions of the self rather than its object. Their aim was to be non-political and non-ideological, and their commitment to total freedom of expression was the extent of their political position.[56] Many of the traits of these works we also find in works of contemporary Chinese calligraphy—the Abstract Expressionists valued immediacy, and their non-representational framework of expressive shapes and lines made the act of painting a dynamic means of expression. Its influence on the Chinese modern calligraphy movement should be seen as a three-way entangled exchange, as Abstract Expressionism, itself, was indebted to Japanese calligraphy, which in turn is entangled with traditional Chinese calligraphy. Antoni Tàpies, an influential artist of the movement, commented: "We, especially the artists grown up with the Abstract Expressionist school, owe so much to the Chinese calligraphers that we understand the emotional language of using the skills of the brush."[57]

Japanese calligraphy, or *sho*, had been relocated from the category of art to that of "crafts" during the modernization processes of the Meiji Restoration

(1868 CE), when a group of innovators called the *bokujinkai* (Group of People of Ink) artists set out to develop a new vision for Japanese calligraphy, in order to, as Eugenia Bogdanova-Kummer explains, "protect their territory on the international modern art map."[58] They created daring experiments with legibility to the extent of complete abstractionism. One of their major concerns was the quality of the brush line: is the line produced by the brush and hand a "painterly line" or a "calligraphic line"? And what are the theoretic delimitations of these distinctions? After the Reform and Opening Up of China, modern Chinese calligraphers raised similar questions and were now, too, making calligraphy that could be free of form and free of the burden of literary content, as a way to accentuate the emotion within the calligraphic line. The body as a tool plays a significant role in the execution of this modern calligraphy. While the imposing gestures and brushstrokes, the dripping paint and the large canvases of the western expressionists were inspired by their previous mural making in the Great Depression of the 1930s, the modern calligraphers' large scripts are redolent of their lived realities of *dazibao* writing during the Cultural Revolution. An example of that is the work of Wang Dongling.

Wang Dongling: Emotion in the Calligraphic Line

> Calligraphy really is an incredible art form. . . . First it was enough that some old men just wrote for themselves, but now, in the 20th and 21st centuries, calligraphy has entered the art academies and art education. Now that has happened, we need to dig deeper to find its artistic nature. Because the essence of art is creation (创作 *chuangzuo*), artists should express their views and emotions.
>
> —Interview with Wang Dongling

Wang Dongling speaks softly with a discernible southern accent when I visit him in his hometown Hangzhou. Having exhibited in the British Museum, the Art Academy of Rome and the Metropolitan Museum of Art in New York, to name a few, and as the only artist to have been granted three solo shows at the National Art Museum of China, Wang Dongling has made a name for himself as one of the most daring and important contemporary calligraphers of today, and is well known both inside and outside of China. Wang belonged to the very first group of five students to receive a calligraphy diploma from Zhejiang University in 1981. As the teacher of the first calligraphy class for foreign students, and as a result of an appointment as visiting Professor of Calligraphy in the United States from 1988 to 1992, Wang Dongling has been influenced and motivated by a number of western painters, including Henri Matisse, Pablo Picasso, Franz Kline, Willem de Kooning and Jackson Pollock, as well as his own calligraphy instructors, such as Lin Sanzhi.

Wang Dongling became convinced that calligraphy should be acknowledged as a fully independent art form, one that is also understandable for people who "cannot enter calligraphy, because of Chinese characters,"[59] and has set out to liberate the calligraphic stroke from only being the carrier of meaning; making calligraphy an art form that is approachable for everyone. He has created large works with single characters and polychrome calligraphy—writing on colored paper or using colorants instead of ink. He has written on bamboo-canes; on photography of female nudes; on glass plates; on pavements. Many of the works clearly take inspiration from the Abstract Expressionist movement. Yet, Wang Dongling's brush lines remain recognizably calligraphic, as I will show.

During my on-site research in Beijing and Hangzhou, it was quite perplexing how not one conversation with professionally engaged calligraphers or students of calligraphy left Wang Dongling and his work unmentioned: despite his experimentations, he was univocally considered a true calligrapher. Typically, remarks like Jiao's, a student of calligraphy I interviewed at the Renmin University in Beijing, would be made:

> What Wang Dongling tries to express is still calligraphy. His traditional lines, the feeling he gives people through brush and ink; that is important to him. It doesn't matter if he writes on bamboo, or with a mop on the floor, he still wants to express the essence of brush and ink. Brush, ink and the line, these things together, that is his way of working. And the feeling it generates; these are still matters of calligraphy.
>
> —Interview with Jiao Zihui

Wang seems to have set the standards and boundaries of what constitutes modern calligraphy, and the harsh polemics that a calligrapher such as Zeng Xiang receives, as we will see in the next section, are much less prevalent.[60] To the contrary, the rave reviews he receives often extend to admiration for his moral character, in the traditional way of judging one's characters by their writing. Mai Jia writes, for example: "He only follows his heart. And this to be sure, is one strong, independent heart."[61] Si Shunwei notes: "Through Wang's prolific works, I am very much impressed by Mr. Wang's glamour as a leading contemporary calligrapher!"[62] Such praise piques curiosity: why is Wang Dongling in particular so popular today? I propose two readings, the one dovetailing with the other. The first reading relates to his background as a former apprentice of Lin Sanzhi (1898–1989)—an eminent calligrapher who has been referred to as "the man with the iron line" and "the Sage of Cursive Calligraphy."[63] Guo Moruo, famous writer, calligrapher and Minister of Culture, praised Lin's work as the finest he had encountered in three centuries of calligraphy tradition. This high praise catapulted Lin to immediate fame. Lin, who wrote expressive and elegant cursive script, burned his hand in boiling water, fusing his three fingers together. After that, his calligraphy was no longer flowing and elegant, but his lines became thin and long, brushed on with raw and dryish ink. Barrass describes how these lines were interpreted as "taut with energy," because it reflected the inner strength and iron will of Lin, who despite his misfortunes persevered in his writing.[64] We recognize traces of characteristics of Lin's writing in this period also in the work of his pupil, Wang Dongling, which shows not only how notions of creativity and innovation are very much informed and shaped by the arbitrary occurrences in the everyday, but also how this can be transmitted through copying.

Lin Sanzhi's ideas on creativity have, according to Barrass, deeply influenced the inception of a new and modern calligraphy movement.[65] Lin is, in turn, the student of celebrated brush-and-ink artist Huang Binhong (1865–1955). This means that Wang is part of a solid lineage of established and revered calligraphers, which allows him a safe position, as well as the artistic baggage, from which to experiment. Lin Sanzhi's radical views on creativity, tradition and innovation were mostly informed by a dislike for insincere endeavors of the new, regarding them to be fake and pretentious.[66] Wang Dongling, in a similar vein, reiterates how innovation is necessary, but should always be grounded in a careful and sincere negotiation with traditional calligraphy:

> Since the creative conditions of the calligrapher have changed, the essence of calligraphy must transform accordingly. Traditional calligraphy emphasizes spiritual pastime and symbolizes the self, and contemporary calligraphy values self-directedness and the performance of art. . . . The inner force of the creativity of contemporary calligraphy is preserving the specific intrinsic spirit of calligraphy, and yet make it have an essential effect on the condition of today's mainstream culture.[67]

This leads to the second reading: scrutinizing his works, we notice how they are invested, similar to the famous and recognizable works of Lin Sanzhi, in preserving a cursive calligraphic line. His unusual execution of these lines, however, unsettles and redistributes, in a Rancièrian way, the senses, through different tactics: introducing live spectacle employing techniques of performance, change in reading direction and a different use of the body. This is, according to Wang, "what the 21st century needs."[68] I look at his large-scale calligraphy (巨幅大字书法 *jufu dazi shufa*), by now a signature style, performed live in front of an audience, and his "chaos script" (乱书 *luanshu*) style that developed from there, which is, according to Wang, the final culmination of his wild cursive script. Wang has been writing large-scale calligraphy since 1987, often performed live in front of an audience and displayed in various places. Perhaps the most eye-catching of all was his rendition of well-known poem "Drinking by the Lake: Clear Sky at First, then Rain" (*Yin hushang chu qing hou yu* 饮湖上初晴后雨) by Su Shi (1036–1101),[69] written on the giant flagship Apple store in Hangzhou in 2015. When I asked why he wanted to write on an Apple building, Wang unassumingly declares in our interview: "I just like Apple, I use their products too." The conflation of commercial purposes and art might seem unusual, but like Wang Dongling, who embraces every opportunity to widen the scale and scope of calligraphy, contemporary calligrapher Gu Gan was also aided by commodification to show calligraphy to the world—he was asked by the famous wine house Rothschild to design the wine label for the 1996 Château Mouton Rothschild. Wang Dongling wrote large cursive calligraphy, covering the entire front of the building. The video released by Apple shows the exterior of the Apple store: an immense modern building presented in awe-inspiring angle, standing out from the surrounding traditional roofs and covered in Wang's bold calligraphy. The video parallels the old, rich history of China symbolized by calligraphy with an exciting new future as the voice-over states: "The work he created celebrates the rich history of art and culture in Hangzhou and the exciting future the new Apple store will be part of." Wang's larger-than-life characters are supposed to symbolize traditional art as a thought-provoking antidote to the modernity symbolized by the Apple store, but in fact, little is traditional about his calligraphy.

The contemporaneity of his characters is evident in three distinctive ways. First, Wang employs his entire body and movement to create meandering lines with quick idiosyncratic hooks in the line, walking over the paper that is laid out on the floor, as can be seen in the video. In this way, he reinterprets calligraphy as a physical art form that demands the entire body to participate: the expressive power of the technique itself becomes evident through these bodily movements. As suggested, Wang's physical gesturing can be interpreted as inspired by the *dazibao* movement, in which he took part. Writing large characters publicly in cursive style, however, was strictly prohibited during the *dazibao* movement as it was deemed too expressive and bourgeois. Wang's embodied public writing in large cursive style today is therefore both liberating and emotionally charged.

Second, the exhibition space changes the work. Wang prefers people to be part of the spectacle by watching him while he writes (in the case of the work for Apple, the performance was videotaped). The audience resonates with the piece as it unfolds in front of them, which simultaneously emphasizes individual performance. Performative calligraphy is, of course, neither uncommon nor a new invention. Political figures are often asked to wield their brushes in front of a large audience to grace an event, and calligraphers asked to write the signage of shops or buildings often do so in public. Kraus infers that "when you are holding the brush, you are on stage."[70] Wang's contemporary intervention in this longstanding tradition is that he develops a deliberate performative setting: he is not asked to grace an event, but he creates his own performance event, in a designated art-space.

The third contemporary feature of Wang's large cursive style relates to this public visibility. Wang's work travels all over the world, performing in public spaces such as museums, schools, halls and, evidently, Apple buildings. This is part of Wang's larger strategy and often reiterated conviction that calligraphy should be displayed to the rest of the world, in order to keep it alive and relevant. Performance of calligraphic art, or a performative calligraphy, can transcend national boundaries. This gives the art form cross-cultural relevance. Within this international context, where *reading* the calligraphic works is quite simply impossible for an international audience, the distinct calligraphic line is now paramount. While the performative spectacle renders Wang's pieces attractive for a global audience—allowing those who cannot read the characters to still be moved by the works, the calligraphic lines ensure that the piece remains calligraphic.

Looking closely at the brush lines on the Apple building, we can infer that they are without any doubt informed by traditional calligraphic technique. They are made up of raw and dryish ink lines: white spaces remain within the black stroke because of this dryness. This is referred to as "flying white" (飞白 *feibai*) in calligraphic discourse. The characters are not linked together and are relatively similar in size, written vertically in columns. The brush moves from angular strokes—the "reverse-tip stroke" (逆风下笔 *nifeng xiabi*: when you begin a stroke with the tip of the brush in the opposite direction) to hair-thin connecting lines. The brush jumps up and down in unlikely sharp angular bends. The lines reveal that Wang used the technique of the "hidden brush tip" (藏锋 *cangfeng*) and the "exposed tip" (露锋 *lufeng*). The long meandering, almost hesitant lines that give this work liveliness and playfulness are referred to as "lingering" (留 *liu*) in calligraphy jargon and are often seen in Wang's work. These lingering, raw lines are clearly influenced by his master Lin Sanzhi, as Hertel convincingly demonstrated,[71] and Wang's calligraphy thus builds on earlier experiments with cursive script.

Wang Dongling pushes the idea of the charged, emotional calligraphic line to the extreme in his newly invented "chaos script" (乱书 *luanshu*), a type of calligraphy that plays with the notion of the legible: "This will shock the world with its groundbreaking features," Wang claims.[72] This chaos script, also often performed in front of an audience, indeed looks chaotic, and breaks with almost every convention of calligraphy. Figure 3.2 is an example: one can see, first, from the title of the work that this is a rendering of a canonical poem by Li Bai. In good traditional parlance, Wang copies a well-known classical Chinese poem. But then, all guidance ceases. On the large surface of paper, calligraphic lines, curves, dots and strokes are jotted together in an amorphous jumble. The writing and reading orders are subverted entirely, and there is no beginning and no end to the piece. While Wang claims to have reproduced a well-known poem, the chaotic discrepancy between reading and seeing confuses the senses. When trying to discern separate characters—in an attempt to make sense of the work as a legible calligraphic piece—the viewer is pulled into an almost musical rhythm, with a dancing alternation of black and white dots and lines. The work simultaneously carries the power to alienate the viewer who is used to looking at calligraphic works, and to absorb those accustomed to seeing works of abstract expressionist art.

But what remains in his chaos script is a discernible calligraphic line. These lines, in which we find remnants of those that Wang copied, studied and learned from, are the only feature that lift the work into the realm of calligraphy—Harrist's "graphic DNA" mentioned in the Introduction. Wang is resolute: "The lines I draw cannot be written without the skill I attained in thirty or even fifty years. I maintain my writing skill as a calligrapher."[73] This is an important observation toward understanding the field of contemporary calligraphy: deviation from the norm can be done in many different and creative ways. Yet, it is clear that this should be done with deference to the foundations of calligraphy. These foundations should be discernible—even if very subtly—through the contemporary work, in order to remain legitimate as a respectable innovator. We might, at this point, recall the students in Chapter 1 whose motivation to go to calligraphy class (partly) lies in the widespread idea that one's handwriting reflects their moral character, captured in the phrase 字如其人 (*zi ru qi ren*) [The writing reflects the man]. Is this ancient belief so easily abandoned by Wang

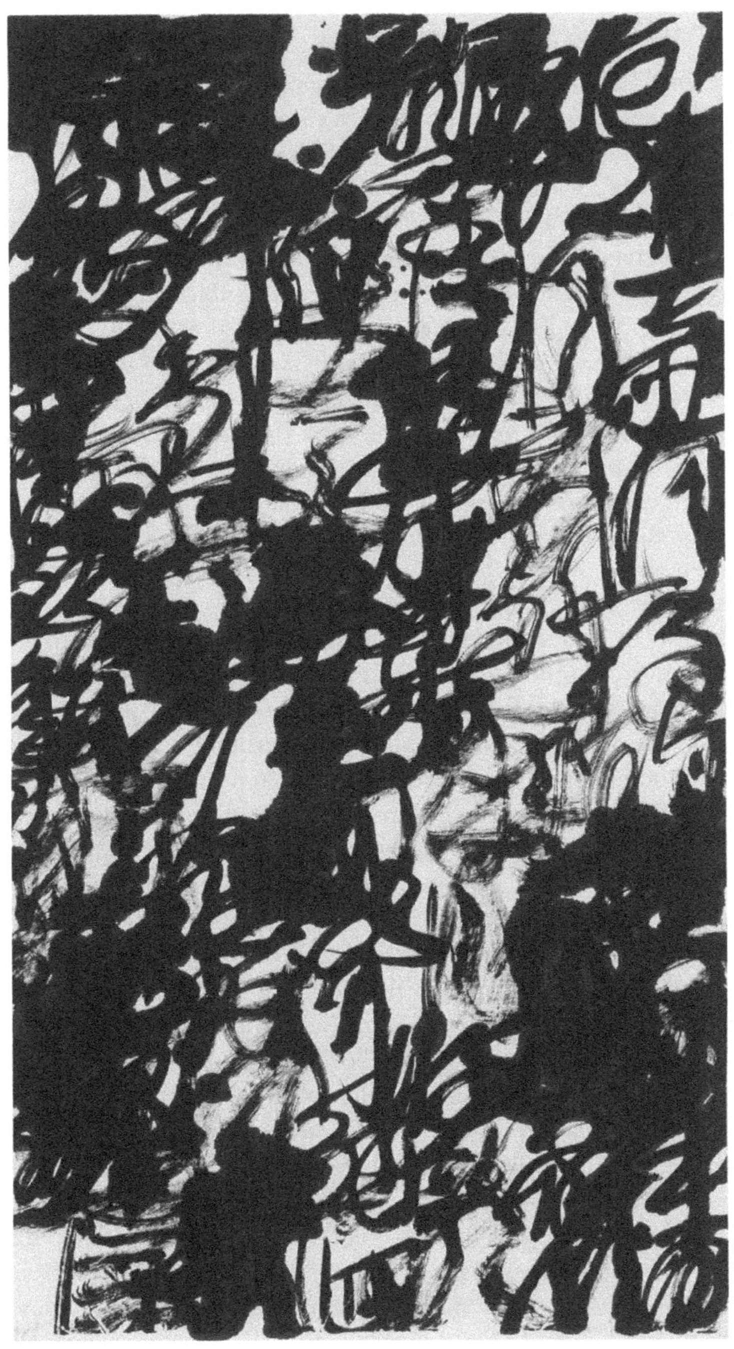

Figure 3.2: Wang Dongling, *Li Bai, "Drinking Alone in Moonlight: Verse One"* (2016). Ink on paper. 180 × 97 cm. Courtesy of Wang Dongling.

Dongling? It is not, he tells me in our interview: "Next time, you should see my studio, it is quite chaotic. It is the studio of an artist making chaotic script. . . . Calligraphy reflects personality at the deepest level."

In the next section, we encounter Zeng Xiang, whose work generates similar debates, but instead of being revered, he is critiqued for his innovations.

Zeng Xiang: (Not) Being Ugly

When I walk around in Art District 798 in Beijing on a particularly stuffy day in April 2018, looking for the gallery where the exhibition of Zeng Xiang is located, strange noises draw me closer to a gallery. I hear someone screaming at the top of his lungs, and, reluctantly, step inside. There, I see a tastefully set-up exhibition, featuring a large TV screen in the left corner of the room that shows Zeng Xiang while he is making the artworks on display to the left and right of the screen: he moves his entire body ferociously, while screaming and splashing around ink on paper laid out on the floor, sweat dripping from his brow and ink trickling from his brush. I suddenly got a hunch as to why this caused the stir that it did within the calligraphy scene of Beijing that early spring.[74]

Zeng Xiang is not well known in the west, but within China's calligraphy discourse he is often mentioned, together with Wang Hao and Wo Xinghua. They are seen as the major contributors to a contemporary calligraphy movement called "ugly calligraphy" (丑书 *choushu*), although he himself does not associate himself with that label. When I interview him at his exhibition, asking if he writes "ugly calligraphy," he bursts out in a cheerful laugh:

> Hahaha. No, this is not ugly calligraphy! That is just a secular view. Strictly speaking, people who have not received education in aesthetics would say that, they just don't understand. This is not ugly. They tell you: this is not calligraphy, it is insulting calligraphy, how can calligraphy be like this, how can you write calligraphy like this? For us, this is a development in calligraphy; it is a type of innovation. Wang Dongling writes chaos script, I think it is very good. And Xu Bing made *Book of the Sky*, who has not heard of that?
>
> —Interview with Zeng Xiang

"Ugly calligraphy" as a separate category also appeared in the 1980s, and has proved difficult to pigeonhole: although critiques and opinions proliferate, there is no common agreement of what constitutes this type of calligraphy.

Liu Zongchao argues that the "ugly" in ugly calligraphy should not be seen as an aesthetic category, but simply defines all those calligraphies that are disharmonious, asymmetric and inconsistent in appearance. Among them, some are "beautiful in their ugliness," while others are truly "ugly (non-art)."[75] Many consider 2002 the year in which "ugly calligraphy" acquired greater prominence as a distinctive category. That year, Wo Xinghua—an acclaimed calligrapher who himself writes what some have classified as ugly calligraphy—wrote the piece "Discussing Ugly Calligraphy" (论丑书 *Lun chou shu*).[76] In this article, like many ardent defenders of the field often do, Wo harks back to examples in calligraphic history in order to claim legitimacy for his contemporary practice. Pursuing the unbalanced, the ugly and the strange, proponents point out, is not unusual at all throughout the history of Chinese art. The "strange" or "marvelous" (奇 *qi*) rose to prominence as a concept in art theory in the late Ming, and the term carries a range of meanings: eccentric, bizarre, marvelous, shocking. With regards to the scope of this section, I do not pursue a critical investigation of the term, and translate 奇 *qi* as "strange." Liu Zongchao argues, moreover, that clumsy, ugly or childlike character writing has always existed, and traces the phenomenon back to as early as the Dunhuang manuscripts.[77] Galambos likewise shows how in Dunhuang manuscripts, mistakes were made, and instead of throwing the manuscript away, mistakes were corrected, which led to smudgy, scratched and uneven rows of calligraphy.[78]

Born in the culturally vibrant and politically chaotic last years of the Ming and early Qing dynasty, calligrapher Fu Shan (1607–84) in particular is often brought up in writings on ugly calligraphy. In the late Ming and early Qing dynasties, a new cohort of creative calligraphers such as Fu Shan and Wang Duo (1592–1652) actively pursued strangeness and ugliness in their works, Wang Duo believing that strangeness was hidden within the familiar structure of the characters, and Fu Shan taking the view that one should go beyond existing structures and outside notions of "beauty" in creating calligraphy. Calligraphers were producing writings that were, according to Bai Qianshen, "expressive and dramatic yet often playful, ingenious, puzzling, and entertaining"[79] and even parodied ancient masters. Fu Shan experimented with inventing bogus characters based on archaic scripts, wrote bizarre script types based on archaic seals, dripped blots of ink on his calligraphy, created long meandering lines, and blended script types together (see Figure 3.3). Dora C.Y. Ching says about Fu that "Concocting new character forms by experimenting with ancient scripts gave him an avenue to express his creativity"[80]—here, Xu Bing's creative character inventions 300 years later come to mind.

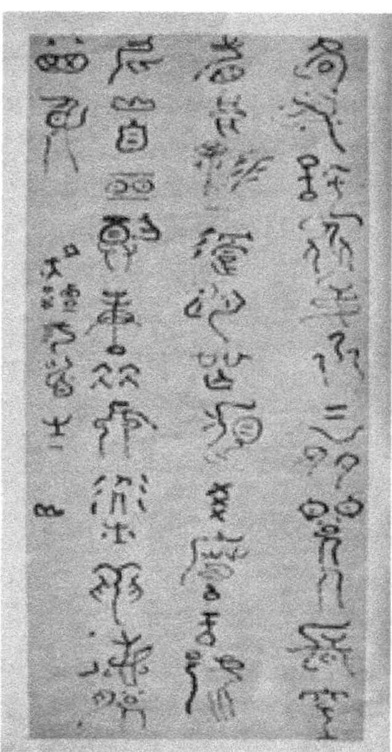

Figure 3.3: Fu Shan (1605–90), *Nocturnal Reading: One of Three Poems in Cursive Seal Script.* Ink on paper, 330 × 97 cm. Shanxi Provincial Museum, Taiyuan.[81] Every effort has been made to trace the copyright holders and obtain permission to reproduce this material. Please do get in touch with any enquiries or any information relating to this image or the rights holder.

But not only the urge to be creative, but also the deception upon discovering the questionable morals of his former models led Fu Shan to change his calligraphy style. Fu had always modeled his calligraphy after Zhao Mengfu, but after realizing that Zhao served the non-Chinese Yuan dynasty after the fall of the Song dynasty, Fu Shan regarded Zhao as a traitor and felt inclined to take on a new, more respectable, model: Yan Zhenqing, the morally upright calligrapher *pur sang* that we encountered in Chapter 1. He became "disgusted with the superficiality and vulgarity of his [Zhao Mengfu's] calligraphy, which has no backbone,"[82] and Fu Shan then chose to model his writing after something he considered less beautiful, but more sincere, writing the words that are so often quoted by proponents of the current ugly calligraphy scene: "I would rather [my calligraphy] be awkward, not skillful; ugly, not pleasing; deformed, not slick; spontaneous, not premeditated."[83] These were the beginnings of a calligraphy movement that purposely did not take the elegant and refined style of Wang Xizhi and his son as their models, but maintained that the calligraphy on ancient stone steles and bronze—the previously mentioned Stele School (碑学派 *beixue pai*), were superior, because they were original and not deteriorated by endless copying, as had been the norm for centuries. Fu Shan's writings are often used as a historic example by contemporary calligraphers to legitimize their choice for making daring works, but his work is employed in other ways as well. The exhibition on modern Chinese calligraphy, "Secret signs," in Hamburg in 2015, for example, displayed contemporary calligrapher Shan Fan's work, *Calligraphy of Slowness* (2015). This work is a copy of Fu Shan's work. Shan Fan copied this piece, slowly filling in the broad strokes—they were originally painted in one single brushstroke—with tiny strokes of his own small brush. The whole work took him 210 hours to complete. The duration of this work makes it a very different activity from the original calligraphy that would have been written with speed. This double layering of unusual methods and alienation is another tactic employed in the broad spectrum of contemporary calligraphy.

I am elaborating on the context surrounding calligrapher Fu Shan, not only because he is so often used as a leading legitimizing example when it comes to pursuing the strange or ugly in contemporary discourses of calligraphy, but also because his motivations to deviate from the norms were driven by a conflating mix of motivations and emotions that, I suggest, inform the current new wave of ugly calligraphies. It was first of all politically and morally motivated: Fu Shan was led by "disgust" with the vulgarity of his previous ideal model. Intertwined with political motives, there were aesthetic incentives as well: beauty, according to Fu Shan, should be found in the "ugly-yet-sincere"—it is a childlike kind of incorruptibility the movement was after. His attempt, in short, was to unsettle through aesthetic means, by breaking down "the symbolic constitution of the social."[84]

It is remarkable how more than 300 years after Fu Shan and his innovative peers, the power of ugly calligraphy to unsettle and upset has not waned. The opinions that circulate about ugly calligraphy today range from the absolutely offensive, like Wei Wei when he argues that it is "a plague," "spreading like germs" and is "polluting the younger generations"; those doing it are in "an abnormal state of mind, have a distorted soul, coupled with ignorance and shallowness"[85] to the more mellow:

> We welcome innovation. Innovation is the only way forward for the arts. To be able to innovate better, we must boldly and confidently fight against "ugly calligraphy." If we cannot distinguish the five beauties, cannot discern

> fragrance from stench and if our reasoning is unclear, then we are not able to have meaningful innovation. It is like poet Ai Qing said: "Art must have originality, but is it definitely not the case that all innovation is art. The madman is the most innovative, but he is definitely not an artist."[86]

I scrutinize the aesthetic construction of five of Zeng Xiang's works that were displayed in his solo exhibition of April 2018: "Spring and Autumn Calligraphy: The Lion Roars" (春秋笔 法狮子吼 *Chunqiu bifa shizi hou*). The centerpiece of the show is a series comprising four large works that all feature the single, and hardly discernable, character, 空 *kong*, meaning empty or space (see Figure 3.4).

The character "empty," in a twist of irony, fills up the surface of rice paper. The works are written with a hefty bespoke brush and it is immediately evident that they have been made with speed. The edges of the brushstrokes are rough, splashes of ink around the bends point at rapid movements of the brush, and the expressive lashes of ink connecting the separate strokes are

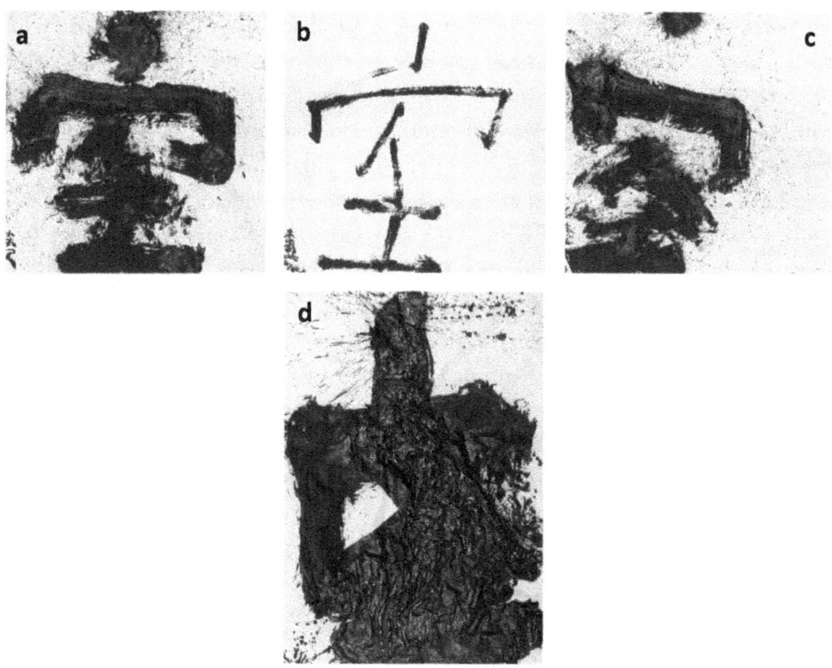

Figure 3.4: Zeng Xiang, *The Empty Series* (2018). Ink on paper. (a–c) 300 × 300 cm; (d) 205 × 145 cm. © Zeng Xiang.

unrefined and hastily made. Except for (b), which is made with lighter and narrower brushstrokes, the other three works in the series are heavily loaded with a deep blueish-black ink, dried up on the paper, giving the piece an almost three-dimensional quality. It is not clear from the work itself whether the ink is applied in layers or brushed on at once with a very wet brush. The immediacy of the aesthetics, however, suggests the latter. All the characters are square-shaped, and as such, the single characters are reminiscent of the square-shaped characters seen in calligraphies belonging to the Stele School. It is important to point out here that the character 空 *kong* is still legible. It shows that Zeng is not deviating from script, nor does he take away the literary content of the characters—as we know, staying within the boundaries of legibility is a common marker to designate whether something should still be considered calligraphy. The series is further reminiscent of the work of modern Japanese calligrapher Yuichi Inoue (1916–85), who created highly expressionist single-character works that he would often perform live. Also Huai Su and Zhang Xu (eighth century) come to mind, the two most renowned cursive calligraphers of the Tang dynasty who are generally referred to as "the crazy Zhang and the drunk Su," and known for their eccentric and explosive performances of live calligraphy, written while drunk, sometimes using their long hair instead of a brush. Zeng Xiang, sweating, screaming and panting heavily while he writes, argues, however, that the term "performance" (表演 *biaoyan*) does not do justice to what he attempts, as performance implies a staged insincerity. As an artist, he conveys in our interview, being in the moment of creation is not merely a performance, but should be understood as "a state of being" (状态 *zhuangtai*): "Many people in China too think that this is a performance. But in fact, it is not. It is the understanding of everything the artist has learned and practiced (修炼 *xiulian*) being mirrored on rice paper at the most effective moment" (interview with Zeng Xiang). The artist stresses that the inner feelings that come out at this well-timed moment are paramount. Although the outcome might be something anyone is able to produce, the artist, as an accumulator of artistic and traditional knowledge, is the only one who can create this particular deeply felt moment in time. Accompanying these works is a large television set-up that features prominently in the exhibition space. Entering the space, you hear loud screaming (hence, it is suggested, the name of the exhibition, "Lion's roar") coming from the video, featuring Zeng Xiang making the *Empty* 空 *kong* series. By showing the process of creation as well as the work itself, the work offers a logic of double immediacy. While the piece in itself is already highly suggestive of the full body movements of the artist, this is rendered acutely present with the added visual and audial demonstration of its creation. This immediacy, I contend, further suggests this sought-after quality of sincerity: with both process and result in full view, it is clear that no hidden methods, tactics or unnecessary embellishments have gone into the work.

The complexity of the notion of ugly and beautiful in Chinese calligraphy plays out in full here. In Chapter 1, I suggested that having good handwriting is typically associated with a corresponding good moral character—hence the insistence of proper learning and the careful selection of morally upright models such as Yan Zhenqing. Ugly calligraphy breaks with this paradigm: beauty, as Fu Shan noted as well, is in this sense seen as too affected, vain, insincere and self-aware. From this perspective, crude and ugly writings do not reveal a person's bad character, but quite the opposite: they show a brave searching for true emotion, and an earnest exploration of the boundaries and definitions of aesthetics. Deviation from beauty, however, still comes with a price. Calligraphers still carry a responsibility for culture, which, as it turns out, cannot be represented in the ugly without impunity. This is evident in the critiques that call Zeng's works "a national crime" and "poison."[87]

Lin Daojun, in commenting on Zeng Xiang, argues that his works are far from a national crime, but he is, instead, doing the nation a favor. "Calligraphy is already dead," he states: when in the west the invention of photography led to somber reflections on a loss of aura and the death of painting, in the digital age, the functionality of calligraphy likewise is gone.[88] Lin argues that instead of disappearing, western painting did reinvent itself: influenced by the light and everydayness of photography, creative currents such as Impressionism, Dadaism and Fauvism appeared. Like the works of the ugly calligraphers, these currents were initially ridiculed and mocked. Lin, therefore, argues that Zeng Xiang does the only thing possible with the "dead art" of calligraphy: he reinterprets it and makes it an artistic spectacle that unsettles. As such, Zeng allows the art form to survive in contemporary digital times where calligraphy has lost its practical application.[89] The second large piece of the exhibition is called *Origin* 起源 *qiyuan* and makes clear reference to the bronze and oracle bone scripts—as the title suggests, the origins of Chinese writing (Figure 3.5). The artist has composed a bricolage of ancient writings, pictographic characters, actual drawings, hieroglyphs, lines, dots and hints of animal traces in a seemingly arbitrary order. None of the symbols are actually oracle bone characters or other ancient script types: they are all creative interpretations. The ink is crudely brushed on, interspersed with *flying white* (飞白 *feibai*), thick black strokes and arranged in chaotic columns. The spectator is invited to stand in front of the work and to separate pictograph from character from image, and the legible from the illegible, thus drawing them in with its many possibilities.

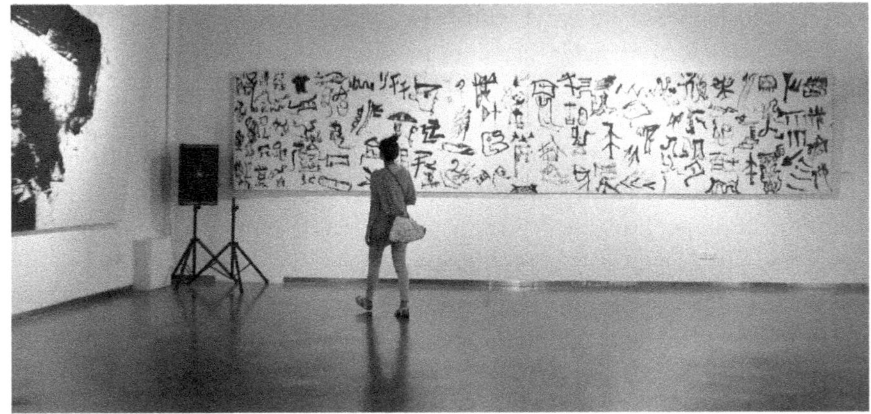

Figure 3.5: Zeng Xiang, *Origin*. Canvas 144×734 cm. © Zeng Xiang.

None of the symbols are part of the Chinese script, yet it is a convincing mix: the signs appear to be a part of the Chinese script system.

On ancient script types, Bachner considers how "a master narrative of cultural coherence and scriptural stability incessantly scripts them as recognizably Chinese."[90] Here, something similar occurs: the work looks convincingly primordial, yet with a creative twist—playful, distorted, messy. Placed in an exhibition together with Zeng's ink-drenched calligraphic works, this work contradicts and functions as antidote—while still very expressive, this is a work that hints not at an uncertain future, but at a common origin. In this work too, Zeng Xiang plays with the legible and the real. It is familiar, recognizable as some sort of oracle bone script, but not quite, and lingers between meaning and non-scriptural expression, image and script, this time leaving it to the viewer to extract meaning and decide what in the artwork is (still) image, and what is, or was in the process of becoming, ancient script.

As shown in the analysis of both works, both the *Empty* 空 *kong* series and *Origin* 起源 *qiyuan* allow for a reconfiguration of the sensible. The works visualize a new future for calligraphy as an expressive art form, and reshape perceptions of archaic script. They intervene on different levels. First, the *Empty* 空 *kong* series reinterprets calligraphy as emotional, ugly and spectacular, and introduces additional sensory perceptions by showing a video of the work's inception. Second, the piece *Origin* 起源 *qiyuan* deconstructs the idea of cultural coherence and scriptural stability through creative play with scriptural elements—and although this has been attempted before by innovators such as Fu Shan, this case shows aptly how the power of these tactics continues to unsettle. Rancière's contention that art is inherently political becomes acutely clear when looking at the responses the works evoke: they are seen as a national crime, as polluting the younger generation, even polluting China's cherished cultural heritage. Zeng Xiang himself, however, feels quite the opposite: his works are steeped in tradition, and he presents himself as a "dreamer": someone who takes traditional scripts and viewpoints and molds them for the needs of the modern world, where exhibition and play are important to its survival.[91]

The works of Wang Dongling and Zeng Xiang are considerate and deliberate aberrations from traditional calligraphic practice. They are part of the discourse of contemporary calligraphy in which, to reiterate Gu Gan's conviction, script can be imagined as a pleasure ground and a paradise for free imagination. This new position has led to deviations ranging from the absurd to the sublime. Much is possible, as we have seen: from screaming and splashing ink, writing chaos, and writing fake characters. But finding pleasure in creativity does not mean there is nothing at stake: this pleasure ground is also an inky minefield, where every line, thought and irregularity stems from a careful positioning vis-à-vis traditional calligraphy and remains under strict scrutiny. In this discursive minefield, Zeng Xiang's work can be denounced as a national crime, and Wang Dongling, with his continuous loyalty to the traditional calligraphic line, can be elevated as a national hero.

I asked at the start of this chapter if there is a case to make in approaching the aesthetic alterations in contemporary calligraphic works as a (political) critique. Rancière has argued that aesthetics and politics are inherently intertwined; a tie that is made through a "making visible." It is at that junction that these three artists should be positioned with regard to their criticality: their works contest the plausible and the standard, and are invested in making visible what was invisible in earlier patterns and, as such, they deconstruct the dominant image of what calligraphy should look like. But we have also seen how maverick calligraphers existed in the past, and these contemporary calligraphies take clear inspiration from them. How "invisible" then, should we consider these calligraphies? The crux, I suggest, lies in providing alternative representations of calligraphy that remain visually close enough to still be considered part of a calligraphy scene, and yet, still, do something quite different. Wang Dongling has redistributed the existing sensible by introducing body movements and expressive calligraphic performances. He does so in a conscious endeavor to make calligraphy available for a global audience that cannot read Chinese. Instead of focusing on content, Wang borrows tactics from contemporary art to get across an emotion—what he believes is the essence of calligraphy and lies within the calligraphic line. In his final experiment of chaos script, almost nothing from traditional calligraphy remains, except for the discernible calligraphic line. That line, in which we find remnants of the calligraphy styles of those Wang copied all the way down, allows his experiments to remain safely within the realm of calligraphy. Zeng Xiang maintains a conscious antithetical position: instead of validating the beautiful, the symmetric and the consistent, Zeng renders visible the ugly and the visceral, as such separating the conventional from the beautiful. Yet, the aesthetics of his work make clear reference to the calligraphic past. Zeng weaves historical fragments of preceding idiosyncratic calligraphies, showing that a construction of contemporary calligraphy is necessarily related to its past.

At the beginning of this chapter, I wondered how it is possible to be of your time, when you make something that is supposed to be similar to works made more than a thousand years ago. The works of the two artists manifest a noticeable preoccupation with time. What does this time need from us, the calligraphers of today? How can we keep calligraphy relevant? How do we rescue calligraphy from obsolescence in the digital age? What strategies and tactics must it adopt to maintain its relevance, as it is increasingly being surrounded by emerging western artistic influences and a thriving art market? The answers can be found within their works: modern times need spectacle—we create spectacle. Modern times are chaotic—we make chaotic calligraphy. In modern times, people spend afternoons going to museums and galleries—we create large works that can be exhibited. This self-awareness, the realizing that modern times are critical times for calligraphy, becomes a speculation on how to best *serve modernity*. The attitude of concern on what is needed, and how a calligrapher might attend to that need, still hints at a gentleman-scholar's attitude—the traditional calligrapher as the scribe who labors for the nation—and, in this reading, the question of critique fades to the background. This continual backward glance, while inevitably moving forward, creates a teleological perspective on calligraphy versus modern art—the notion that, over time, calligraphy must evolve into or increasingly resemble contemporary art to ensure its survival. Zeng Xiang articulated this view most clearly:

> I belong to the traditionalists, those who study the calligraphic line. They [Xu Bing and Wang Dongling] do too, but they became contemporary artists earlier on. It is like the rabbit and tortoise race; do you know that story? We are slow, but Xu Bing and Wang Dongling are fast like rabbits. I am the tortoise!
>
> —Interview with Zeng Xiang

Zeng thus juxtaposes calligraphy and contemporary art. He argues, however, that calligraphy is in a stage of becoming, guided by those who can think the quickest of new and creative ways: the "rabbits." The overarching concern regarding how and what to reform to preserve the art of calligraphy, how to enact those reforms, and what the future implications will be, remains pivotal. This issue is also central in the next chapter, where I delve into reinterpretations of the calligraphic sign within the specific domain that many believe threatens the survival of calligraphy: the digital realm.

CHAPTER 4

Calligraphy and the Digital: Remediated Calligraphic Community

> With the rise of the information age and the increased popularity of computers and mobile phones, people begin to get accustomed to the keyboard, thereby alienating themselves from ink and paper. This results in people spending less time writing Chinese characters. Currently the problem is not how to write a character beautifully, but to pick up the brush and simply remember how to write the character (提筆忘字 *tibiwangzi*).[1]

Navigating the calligraphic circles in Beijing is as much an analog as a digital undertaking. Connecting with calligraphy friends (书友 *shuyou*) to discuss recent developments, exhibitions and news on governmental directives on calligraphy now takes place on digital platforms such as WeChat. A multitude of apps and social media platforms such as *Douyin*, *Bilibili* or *Kuaishou* allow calligraphy enthusiasts to livestream, upload, compare and buy or auction calligraphy. In the calligraphy classes I audited, apps are more frequently used than paper copybooks to find models for copying. Digital calligraphic fonts are increasingly employed, and scanned original calligraphy is integrated into online copybooks, dictionaries and virtual museum galleries. Jing Tsu[2] summarizes: "As more characters enter digital circulation, the Chinese language is being ever more widely used, learned, propagated, studied, and accurately transformed into electronic data. It is about as immortal as a living script can hope to get." Increasingly, and more and more convincingly, "digitally native" calligraphy is now a possibility: a computer that is able to generate a "real-looking" calligraphic sign from learned examples. All these digital tools render the consumption of calligraphy increasingly accessible and mobile, and mediated experiences of calligraphy seem to be as much a part of the wider calligraphy scene as those experienced and consumed through sensory unmediated perception. We might even argue that such unmediated life does not exist at all anymore—Couldry and Hepp add here that it would be bizarre to separate a "pure experience" from a "mediated experience" as we have known mediation since the time that humans started writing.[3]

Meng Lei, a professor of calligraphy in Hangzhou, tells me how apps are convenient tools in calligraphy education, but that they should be used with care, as it makes his students lazy:

> We used to have a reference book, like a dictionary, to look up the characters written by the ancients, and then we would write those down. The apps we use now have their pros and cons. The pros lie in their convenience; for example, I now think of an ancient poem, and I want to write four characters, all I need to do is look it up, and all the different calligraphy styles pop up. This is the convenience that the mobile phone gives us, but the downside of this fast pace is the effect on the memory; people will become lazy. You don't have to go to the source text anymore, and you will miss this research experience, it becomes more a practical feeling. So, when we are using this, I advise my students that they can do it if they need to be quick, but it cannot be a long-term solution.
>
> —Interview with Meng Lei

Young calligrapher Chen Cong explains how digital apps help him with his business of selling calligraphy. He is a calligrapher and a calligraphy salesman working at a small shop at Liulichang (琉璃廠) in Beijing, the traditional street for selling art, antiques, calligraphy and paraphernalia dating back to the Ming dynasty. But the physical shop is not doing well, which has led Chen increasingly to sell works through *Taobao* and *Weipaitang*, a social C2C art and print auction platform released in 2017 backed by Tencent, surpassing 74 million users in 2021:

> Here, we have some tourists, or people who have calligraphy as a hobby. You often have these groups here, they buy one or two pieces, that type. And then there is, do you know *Weipaitang* (微拍堂), the one under WeChat? We sell our works there now too, but the prices are not very high, just a couple of hundred *kuai*. . . . The prices are not as high as in our physical shop, because such a shop is more expensive to maintain.
>
> —Interview with Chen Cong

These developments and opportunities for calligraphy exposure and sales in the digital realm coexist with a growing fear for the demise of calligraphy *because* of that very realm, carrying wider consequences with regard to culture, identity and nationality. While nearly every interviewee is at least in one way digitally aided in their everyday calligraphy activity, at the same time, almost all conversations on calligraphy referred to the pressing and anxiety-inducing problem of *tibiwangzi* (提筆忘字), which translates as "picking up the pen, and forgetting the character"; often—somewhat clumsily—rephrased in English as "character amnesia," or the more appropriate "dysgraphia." The problem is as pressing as it is simple: because of the global shift toward digital communication, the method through which we write Chinese characters has irreversibly and fundamentally changed. We swipe with our fingers, drag characters to our screen, draw one or two strokes and let the computer figure out the rest of the character, and in mainland China we choose characters from a list of the official romanization system for Standard Mandarin Chinese, Pinyin (汉语拼音 *Hanyu Pinyin*).

We use voice recognition to get our characters on the screen, and increasingly just skip text entirely and simply use voice messages. The extensive use of GIFs and memes in, for example, WeChat further facilitates communication without having to resort to writing characters. It all reduces the time actually spent writing characters on paper. Jing Tsu remarks: "One scarcely has to learn Chinese characters the hard way—by memory or by hand—anymore, it seems."[4]

The *tibiwangzi* (提筆忘字) problem originates there. Writing characters, as Victor Mair notes, is a highly complicated neuromuscular task because of the complexity and multiplicity of the characters, and it takes hundreds and hundreds of hours before character writing is mastered.[5] This time is simply no longer there to spend. Already in 2001, Jennifer Lee noted how character writing is deteriorating due to word processing and as technology is increasingly permeating our everyday lives, this problem has only been exacerbated since.[6] Calligraphy practice at home or school is the best way to combat character amnesia, according to the MOE. As we saw in Chapter 1, efforts to facilitate better and more frequent calligraphy classes for children nationwide have been ongoing since 2013. National and regional calligraphy contests, and more lectures and exhibitions by well-known calligraphers are also seen as part of a solution, or at least as part of the remedy. We might find it slightly ironic that these proposed resolutions are mainly activities that take place offline, while the problem—most people agree—can be traced back immediately to the effects of modern online communication technology and the fact that we spend so much time on our screens. It highlights how we remain attached to the notion of a dichotomous relationship between the online and offline worlds. But this dichotomy is rapidly dissolving. The question whether communication technology should be judged as either a "good" or "bad" phenomenon at all seems by now an outdated and redundant notion. Our lives are inevitably permeated by online technology, and living with the internet comes intuitively to most of us, especially to the post-1980 (八零后 *balinghou*), the post-1990 (九零后 *jiulinghou*) and post-2000 (零零后 *linglinghou*) generations in China. This permeation has only increased over the last years when communication technologies occupied, and continue to occupy, a central position during the COVID-19 pandemic. Not only has the use of social media increased significantly as a result of severe social lockdowns, the internet provides online mental health education, online shopping has sky rocketed and social media platforms are used as a propaganda tool and promote public policies under the control of the government. That the digital realm is now rarely seen as a separate space anymore, but as a part of the social totality of the everyday seems evident. David Berry argues that since digital media are not a separate space, digital objects therefore also do not come out of nowhere to disrupt our analog lives: "It is not that we should be thinking solely in terms of 'digital object' but rather that we must be able to dialectically think in relation with a number of moments within instantiations of the digital."[7]

Creating, sharing, or appreciating calligraphy online exemplifies such an everyday interaction with the digital world. This is perhaps challenging to imagine, as calligraphy is so deeply intertwined with its bodily engagement and analog tools of brush, ink, inkstone and paper. Moreover, these analog tools are all supposed to be properly mastered through education before we can even speak of "calligraphy"—how might we even start with bringing all of that online? And even if we can envisage such a calligraphy, the continuing conundrum of technology replacing or even obliterating analog writing is not immediately solved by its perceived permeability or "part of everydayness." The moral panic over the loss of writing due to the digital lies much deeper, and relates closely to a fear of losing an essential part of culture, or even culture itself. The forceful argument made by Benedict Anderson,[8] who asserted that the written language of a nation is instrumental in the idea of a national identity, is specifically apt in the Chinese (digital) context. He maintains that the written language of a nation, and the dissemination of that language through the capitalist endeavor of printing, is instrumental in the idea of a national identity, as it creates an illusion of a national community. China is linguistically extremely diverse, with 302 officially recognized living languages and many more regional dialects. Such linguistic diversity has historically posed communicative and administrative challenges, and continues to impact this idea of a national consciousness. Since the end of the Han dynasty, all the diverse spoken forms of Chinese continued to deviate from each other, and also from the only written form of Chinese, classical Chinese (文言 *wenyan*), which remained unchanged until the early 20th century. But for most people, it was nearly impossible to become part of the small elite that could read and write the highly complex classical Chinese. This meant, in practice, that while the writing of Chinese was carried out in all regions in an almost uniform way, making use of an almost unvarying character script and thus linguistically unified large areas, this sense of unity remained largely an abstract notion for most people living in those areas. The idea of belonging to a larger state, unified geographically and by a shared written language, then existed mainly in the collective consciousness of the elite.[9]

The emergence of China as a nation occurred in the late 19th century. When at the beginning of the 20th century nationalist reformers sought to stimulate a broader sense of a national consciousness, they estimated that facilitating ways to communicate effectively throughout the country would be instrumental. Efforts to achieve mass literacy and the establishment of a unified national written and spoken language accessible for all were two successfully implemented strategies. Around the 1920s, propaganda by the nationalist Guomindang helped to stimulate a wider perception of belonging to a nation among all the people, which was then further pursued by the Communist Party. Now, there is only one official state language, Standard Mandarin, or 普通话 *Putonghua*, which serves as the lingua franca in the PRC with around 80 percent of the people within mainland China speaking and understanding the language today. The written word is fundamental to Chinese national identity and, for many, the thought of a new generation of Chinese youth losing this hard-earned skill, especially now that China has nearly achieved a 100 percent literacy rate, is deeply troubling. Today, nationalism and China are hand in glove. Moreover, as Florian Schneider observes, nationalism today "interacts in complicated ways with advanced information and communication systems, political discourse and decision-making, at times powerfully shaping the state's policy efforts."[10] That means that state-led nationalism is "disseminated, adapted, negotiated, contested and redeployed by a dizzying array of actors who interact in China's digital communication and media networks."[11] The question of this chapter, then, is what calligraphy is doing in this constellation of an imagined national Chinese unity, fear, community and consumption. I am interested in how the technical affordances of digital platforms permit particular forms of affective engagement with calligraphy. The written language is not the only thing that helps in building a sense of national community—it is endlessly more complex and much more banal at the same time. Symbols of nationhood, argues Michael Billig, "hardly register in the flow of daily attention, as citizens rush past on their daily business."[12] While Billig refers to very specific symbols, such as flags, national colors or newspapers, I want to explore whether online everyday calligraphy practice might achieve a similar effect of transforming "background space into homeland space."[13] In the final chapter of this book I will lay out how the aesthetics in type font design mobilize, revisit or appropriate calligraphic qualities. In this chapter, I explore the digital calligraphic sign as it is created and used in online and app-based communities that connect together through calligraphy learning, motivational friendships, exhibitions and online auctions. First, I explore the ways in which calligraphy becomes hyperreal, brought to us through our screens by way of scanning and encoding. Then, I move on to analyzing how communities can be formed around these simulations by looking at two digital calligraphic communities: (1) the WeChat group *Handwriting Temperature* (手写温度 *shouxie wendu*), which is a spin-off of the arts and craft sharing app *Little Interests* (轻趣 *qingqu*) and (2) the calligraphy app *Ink Pool* (墨池 *mochi*). I examine both communities by combining ethnographic data with the "walkthrough method" as proposed by Ben Light et al.[14] A walkthrough of an app is "a way of engaging directly with an app's interface to examine its technological mechanisms and embedded cultural references to understand how it guides users and shapes their experiences."[15] User interface arrangement, textual content, tone and "a semiotic approach to examining the look and feel of the app and its likely connotations and cultural associations with respect to the imagined user and ideal scenarios of use"[16] are all part of the walkthrough method, and will tell us something about how users engage with the app, and how it shapes their experiences. With this method, the researcher mimics everyday use of the app, and by slowing down these everyday actions and documenting the technical, visual and symbolic aspects, they become available for critical analysis.[17] By examining the digital infrastructure, we can better grasp the app's intended purpose and ideal user base. Through these case studies, I analyze the role of two online platforms in fostering calligraphy consumption, promoting connoisseurship and building appreciative communities. How should we approach digital calligraphic signs, and how might they be important actors in these case studies? Are they mere skeuomorphs, reminiscent of an earlier real sign that is somehow more authentic, or are they perhaps a "digitally assisted genetic mutation of Chinese" as proposed by Bachner?[18] I think that in the case of digital calligraphy, it might be useful to borrow David Bolter and Richard Grusin's term of "remediations."[19] Bolter and Grusin argue that when examining new media, we should consider how these media have evolved from or "remediated" earlier practices. "No medium today," they maintain, "seems to do its cultural work in isolation from other media, any more than it works in isolation from other social and economic forces."[20] New media, in an attempt to confirm their existence as a new form, need to visibly build on an earlier form to be legitimate successors. Both new and traditional media, Bolter and Grusin further emphasize, work along a double logic of remediation: immediacy and hypermediacy. Immediacy attempts to erase the medium as much as possible in order to facilitate an immediate relationship with the content of the medium. We should forget that we are in the presence of a medium, but rather believe that we are in the presence of the represented object.[21] A digitally created calligraphic character, then, should as much as technologically possible look like brushstrokes made on paper, so that the link with its preceding form is unmistakable and we believe that we are consuming calligraphy. This experience without mediation is then countered by hypermediacy which makes the user constantly aware of the media they are using: it requires us to recognize our experience as a mediated one that we ultimately will come to desire.

Digital Calligraphies

That we encounter calligraphy on our screens has been enabled by computer experts through one of two methods, the first facilitating the scientific development of the latter: scanning or character encoding, which is assigning code to written characters, allowing them to be transformed, stored and transmitted by a digital computer. The two mechanisms work very differently. Scanning is a method of conversion: an image on paper is converted into a digital image, where it remains a static image. You can look at it, store it or classify it in specific databases, but it cannot be manipulated. These works serve multiple purposes. Professor Meng, who I quoted in the beginning of this chapter, for example, needs them to teach his students the first principles of calligraphic strokes. Connoisseurship and research are among the main goals of bringing the vast volumes of scanned calligraphic images online, which has been happening over the last ten years. Museums and libraries have taken impressive strides toward digitizing their objects and records through scanning, as it can lead to improved visitor experiences, but mostly opens up access to collections and enhances and increases research opportunities. Additionally, when a piece cannot be directly handled due to its fragility or high value, a digitized image can serve as a substitute.

CADAL (China Academic Digital Associative Library) is one of those digitized databases. CADAL is a collaborative project launched by the Chinese MOE and the US National Science Foundation. In 2002, it started to build a digital academic library through the scanning of paper books, providing digital access for learning, teaching and research-support purposes. There are now

2.5 million full-text books available, making CADAL the world's largest non-profit digital library. There is a large collection of books containing calligraphy available on a designated section on the CADAL web page. There, the internet user can do several things with this scanned calligraphy: they can browse ancient calligraphic works based on time-period and calligrapher or even search for separate characters within a single piece—they have been pried apart per character. A scanned character can be blown up by an interested researcher to study ink layering, or traces of the original calligrapher's wrist and hand position. Calligraphy can be easily compared, shared and classified when it is digital, to answer questions on authenticity and written content. Researchers working in different geographical areas can communicate and work together on a single piece because images are visible to many people at the same time. And finally, scientists can use the characters as models for deep learning of calligraphy structures,[22] which leads us to the second method of encoding.

Encoding or digitizing schemes allow for the graphic information of a scanned calligraphic character image to be edited and manipulated. Techniques such as Optical Character Recognition (OCR) and Handwritten Character Recognition (HCR) are typically used. The complex shapes and anatomy of a calligraphic character, however, pose major challenges to these systems. Brushstrokes within a character can be highly complex and intricate as they are often unpredictable in shape, and the differentiation in calligraphic styles and shapes make input difficult. To add to that complexity, calligraphy scanned from stone steles are often filled with excessive "noise" such as stone degradation due to the natural weathering of the tablets. To be able to extract the general properties of a character so it can be utilized as a statistical model, excess noise needs to be filtered and removed.[23] Xu et al. maintain that calligraphy is "type fonts on the loose."[24]

Another hurdle for automatic recognition is the large character set of the Chinese script. It is only possible to recognize calligraphic characters through OCR or HCR if a digital counterpart has been encoded. So far, over 80,000 Chinese characters have been encoded in Unicode. In 2006, the government, in cooperation with universities, research institutes and enterprises, launched a large-scale digitization project named "China character library project" (中华字库项目 *Zhonghua ziku dingmu*) with the aim to further digitize another 500,000 Chinese characters that are currently not available in digital form. This project is listed as one of the larger projects in the Outline of the Eleventh Five-Year Plan for National Culture Development in 2006 and was included in China's Plan on Reinvigoration of the Cultural Industry in 2009 according to developer Founder International.

These 500,000 characters should be made up out of 100,000 ancient Chinese script characters, 300,000 regular script forms and another 100,000 characters in minority scripts. The idea is to place all of these, together with already encoded oracle bone script, bronze characters, grass script characters and old characters found on manuscripts or unusual characters used in names, on one large platform.[25] There is, however, some skepticism about this grand number of half a million. Matt Anderson wonders, "How could there be 400,000 more unencoded graphs, even including every script ever used by every people who ever lived within the borders of China, however defined?"[26] Elsewhere, Anderson concludes that while one of the largest dictionaries of single characters (the *Ocean of Chinese Characters* 中华字海 *Zhonghua zihai*), contains 85,568 graphs, the great majority of those characters are erroneous and alternate forms, characters which have almost never been used and with unknown meaning. "The question of how many sinographs . . . there are is fundamentally unanswerable, as different approaches result in wildly different estimates" he concludes.[27] As a reference, it is good to realize that only 6,600 characters make up 99.999 percent of all graphs in typical Modern Standard Mandarin texts.[28] Over the last two decades, computer scientists have been developing more methods to realize real-looking calligraphy simulations on the digital screen: attempts to recreate the movements of the calligraphy brush, and to mimic the layering of ink and the way ink reacts to rice paper thickness, velocity and so on, as accurately as possible. Su et al. maintain: "Though a computer cannot capture the creative spirit of an artist, it can simulate the brushstroke characteristics that are so important in its manifestation."[29] Studies show how calligraphic brushstrokes can be simulated through a model based on a "parametric curve";[30] the "skeletal strokes method"[31] or a virtual brush that is able to capture three-dimensional geometric parameters, brush hair properties and ink variations by Wong and Ip.[32] The invention of Parametric Hairy Brush[33] (see Figure 4.1), especially designed to realistically duplicate the affordances of a Chinese brush (毛笔 *maobi*) was followed up by Yu and Peng,[34] who presented a framework to synthesize realistic grass script calligraphy through texture mapping, based on brush texture patches collected from handwritten calligraphy. They claim to be able to reproduce typical grass script strokes, brush variations, the wetness of the brush and even the visibility of the amount of ink. The results are indeed striking, as shown in Figure 4.2.

When developing a system to synthesize digitized calligraphic characters that most resemble the "real," the level of precision demanded from scientists again reveals a desire for immediacy.[35] All studies take as their point of departure that "real" calligraphy is written with a soft Chinese brush and ink on

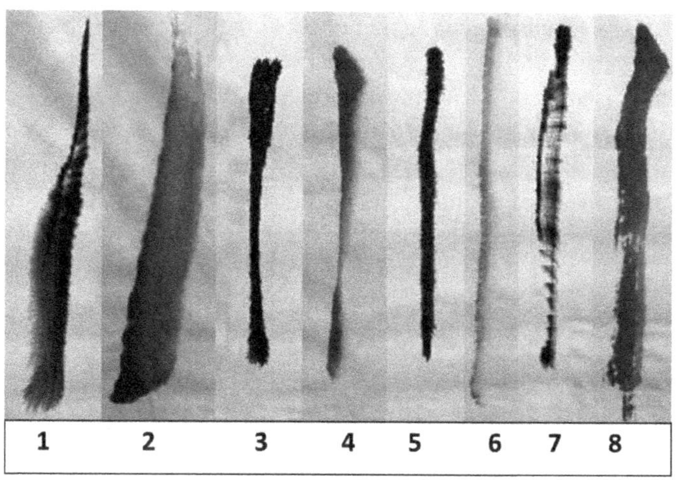

Figure 4.1: Real versus simulated strokes: (1), (3), (5) and (7) are digitally simulated. (2), (4), (6) and (8) are written by hand with ink. Retrieved from Girshick 2004: 30 with permission. © Girshick.

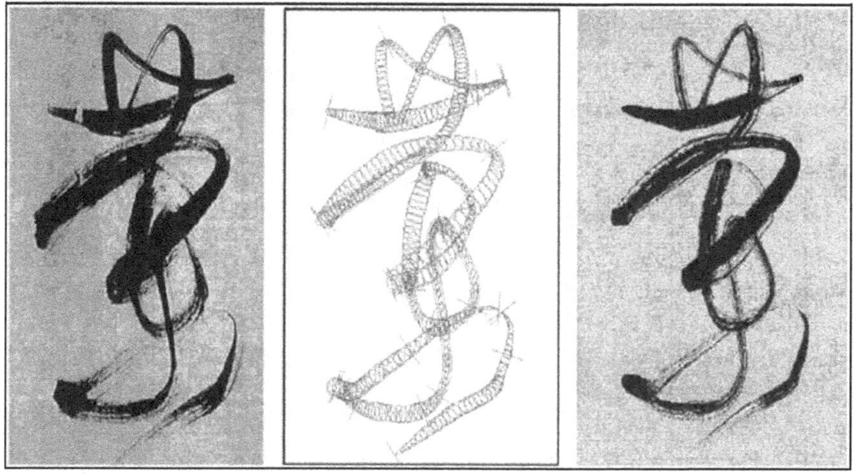

Figure 4.2: The left image shows the original work, the middle displays digitized strokes, and the right presents the synthesized version. Retrieved from Yu and Peng 2005: 150 with permission. © Elsevier.

paper. Yet, this does not mean that developers then assume the "real" is also the best possible version. Xu et al. developed an algorithmic framework that simulates the human process of learning calligraphy skills. It allows the computer to automatically produce new calligraphy based on these learned examples. "For the first time," boast Xu et al., "it is possible for the tool's performance to surpass the skill level of the user."[36] If, given the right parameters, a digital application can surpass the skill level of the user, who might we then identify as the calligrapher? A final illustration of research in digitally generated calligraphy is the study by Cao Shi et al.[37] They created a five-layer framework that can generate Chinese characters based on calligraphic prior knowledge. In an experiment, generated characters, based on the handwriting of Yan Zhenqing, were mixed with Yan Zhenqing's real, analog calligraphy, and shown to a test group of 14 people. When the group was asked to select the characters with the "worst visual acceptance," the results revealed how the computer-generated characters received "almost the same visual acceptance relative to Yan Zhenqing's calligraphy."[38]

These results point toward another tactic of remediation: the tradition of modeling after the master continues in the digital, but this time a machine serves as apprentice. When the artwork made by the computer no longer has a clear correlation with the skill level of the tool's user, we should ask ourselves again the earlier posed question with regard to immediacy, leading to an overarching question of reality. When immediacy is achieved, it has successfully closed the gap between signifier and signified, so that we feel we are not in the presence of a representation. But what if this signifier transcends, or at least claims to do so, what it aims to represent? Here we enter the stage of Jean Baudrillard's hyperreal,[39] where there is no clear distinction anymore between what is real and what is fiction. Hyperreality is not simply "unreal," it is something experienced as more real than real, because it has broken down the boundary between real and imaginary. Today, hyperreality has become a permanent feature of our everyday lives, as our multiple virtual presences are at least as real as our physical one.

But before we lament how calligraphy simulations have replaced or obfuscated the real, we must consider what "real" actually entails in calligraphy discourse. Very few people have ever seen the original copy of the *Orchid Pavilion* by Wang Xizhi—especially since the original piece has been lost since at least the Tang dynasty. But this has not diminished the significance of the piece, and the devotion so many feel toward it—in fact, it has done the opposite. Simulations of this real are now *the only real*: countless handwritten imitations and ink rubbings of engraved copies have circulated for millennia and acquired significance of their own. Of course, this is not exclusive to Wang Xizhi's calligraphy; it applies to all calligraphic works. Both the skill as well as the physical reproductions of calligraphy have survived by the grace of this widespread copying culture, done through painstaking techniques such as tracing lines, rubbing stone steles, and the exact and creative copying of the ancient calligraphy masters. And although the adaptation, integration and assimilation of new tools, writing surfaces, cultural shifts and societal changes have all played their part in the changing purposes and ways of appreciating calligraphy, Chinese calligraphy has remained strikingly homogeneous in both form and shape because of these meticulous copying techniques.

Now, we find ourselves in a moment in time where this culture of copying is executed in unprecedented ways. Calligraphy has become more ubiquitous, and perhaps more real than real, but we can no longer touch and smell the ink, hear the brush move or caress the dried-up characters on a sheet of rice paper. What then, are the potential affordances of digital calligraphy in today's context? I propose that digital calligraphy, among other things, affords a specific form of community making, and the following sections scrutinize digital communities in which online calligraphy is shared, enjoyed and consumed, brought online by scanning.

Online Calligraphy Platforms

Worldwide, we are currently in the middle of a "platformization" of society. José van Dijck, already in 2013, has described how internet users have increasingly moved their everyday activities to digital environments.[40] Social media platforms permeate more and more of our daily lives, not only by facilitating activities that would otherwise have been ephemeral and private, but also because, as van Dijck argues, "the construction of platforms and social practices is mutually constitutive."[41] A platform is, in its original meaning, a simple construction from which to freely speak or act. Tarleton Gillespie warns, however, how this metaphor hides how platforms are highly dynamic and increasingly intricate infrastructures: "Information moves in and around them, shaped both by the contours provided by the platform and by the accretions of users and their activity—all of which can change at the whim of the designers."[42]

When I argued at the beginning of this chapter that "doing calligraphy" seems as much an online as an offline undertaking, these platforms take up a large space in that assertion. Also in the Chinese online context, life is increasingly structured through a wide array of digital platforms, actively supported by the government's Internet Plus and China 2025 policies.[43] These platforms are user-friendly apps, those we use to organize our friend groups, order food, get our news, form our opinions and feed these opinions back online. While the early rhetoric on platformization (much like early theorizations on "the internet" a few decades ago) lauded its democratic potential, and the way in which they could provide marginalized communities opportunities to engage in cultural production, now the platform society is contested,[44] because interaction, socially and economically, is increasingly global and interconnected, and as such informing and altering the ways in which power is distributed.[45] Platforms, markets and cultural producers have become intricately connected, as Poell et al. maintain, which has large consequences for the "sustainability of cultural production, and the diversity and vitality of culture at large."[46]

On top of that, the content that is generated on Chinese online platforms has to align with the expectations of the authorities, who are increasingly demanding that all content providers "disseminate socialist core values and cultivate a positive and healthy online culture."[47] As the widely used online catchphrase "positive energy" (正能量 *zheng nengliang*) has been co-opted by authorities and platform companies to encourage social media users to share positive and uplifting messages instead of negative stories,[48] a new online discourse is emerging where positivity, encouragement and enjoyment take center stage. Increasingly, the Chinese party-state is committed to enforcing a singular and mainland-centered notion of Chineseness, aligning with Xi Jinpings vision, calling for everyone to " tell China's stories well."[49] Calligraphy can serve as a powerful discourse in such a framework, one that government institutions can mobilize to express patriotism, devotion to the motherland, and an embodied engagement in a strong and culturally self-assured China. The online platform, we can conclude, is not a neutral and open stage for free expression but rather, it functions as a state-supported mechanism that governs and restructures our social interactions and cultural preferences through its technological affordances. With these considerations in mind, we can now explore what I call "appreciative communities" on WeChat and the *Ink Pool* app. WeChat is the most popular and widely used Chinese social media platform, launched in 2011 by Tencent. It offers many services, from instant messaging, chatting to strangers, shopping, gaming, online banking and ordering taxis. The technological affordances of a platform shape the way in which the user can move and act: WeChat is specifically designed to facilitate intimate social interactions. A user can have a maximum of 5,000 friends, and WeChat groups cannot be larger than 500 people. WeChat groups are widely used to form small communities around interest groups. During the course of my research for this book, I have gained many valuable insights by being part of WeChat groups organized around a particular interest in calligraphy: groups sharing information on calligraphic font design, a group interested in contemporary calligraphy in Beijing, a group sharing information on teaching calligraphy, etc. One of those groups is WeChat group *Handwriting Temperature* (手写温度 *shouxie wendu*).[50] This is a self-sustained WeChat group organized by a group of people who found each other first on the arts and craft sharing app *Small Interests* (轻趣 *qingqu*). In this particular WeChat group, around 400 people—the number fluctuates as people come and go—have gathered with the aim to share a line of their handwritten characters with each other every day. They are inclined to do so, as they want to "keep the beauty of handwritten calligraphy alive." Every morning, a friendly message appears, with instructions for the project of the day: "Good morning friends! Let us persist in writing by hand and 'punching in' (打卡 *daka*) every day to experience the beauty of calligraphy and literature!" What then follows is an image containing a short classical poem, a slogan or aphorism in a digital font, accompanied by an image that is readily indexed as something "traditionally Chinese" such as a poet in traditional dress, a peony or an ink drawing of a court lady. As seen in Figure 4.3, this digital font is placed, traditionally, on the right side and runs vertically. The participants of the group then have the whole day to copy these characters on paper at home, take a photo of their work and send it to the group, by saying "punching in" (打卡 *daka*), as if they are evidencing their attendance at the beginning of a working day. The group motivates each member to practice every day and to improve themselves by sending each other appreciative emoticons, thumbs ups, hearts, flowers and encouraging words along the lines of: "I admire you for your well-written words and your hard work!" or "Well done today!"

The aim of the group is to encourage members to maintain the habit of writing, and the output that is posted in the group demonstrates a great variety: quickly scribbled ballpoint writings knows as "hard-pen calligraphy" (硬笔书法 *yingbi shufa*) alternate with skilled and less skilled traditional calligraphy in every type of calligraphic script. Often, heavily digitally edited written works are posted. Different apps are employed to alter these writings: converting the backgrounds, so that the works appear to be hanging in museums, bus stops or gallery halls, for example. Or writing surfaces are transformed digitally, so it appears the characters are written on traditional stone steles, or are framed in elegant frames, as seen in Figure 4.4. The handwritten calligraphy is

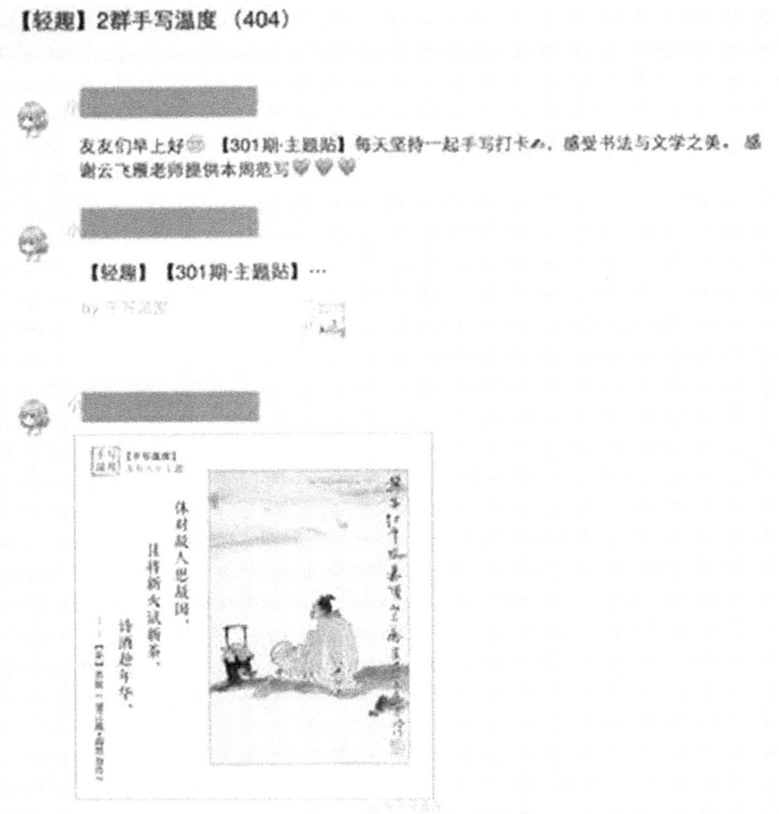

Figure 4.3: The daily message in the WeChat group.

transformed through these digital edits: color is added and shapes are made thicker, coarser or more flowing, and as such, it is nearly impossible to discern if this is an initially handwritten, uploaded and edited work, or that a pre-made calligraphic font is used and edited afterward. Such edits obfuscate even more the already imprecise differences between producers and consumers, but also between the skill of the digital designer and the calligrapher writing on paper and uploading their works on the screen.

The variety of handwriting and digital edits posted in the group—all receiving equal praise regardless of skill level—as well as the ease with which these works are digitally modified and remediated, suggest that concerns about realness are not on anyone's mind. The creativity of this exercise seems to lie as

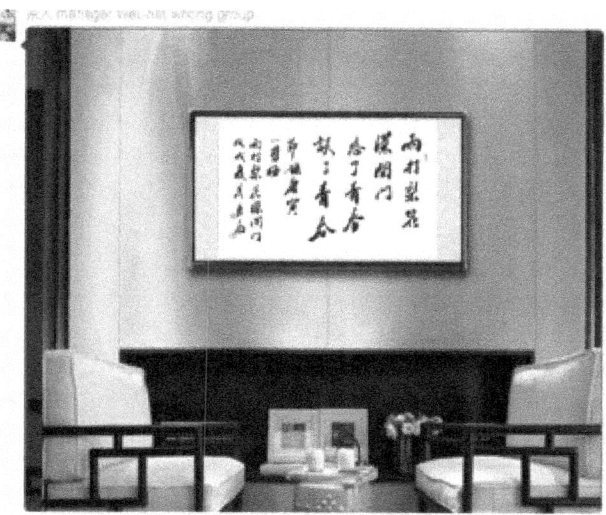

Figure 4.4: A digitally edited, handwritten piece of calligraphy. Screenshots taken on May 16, 2018.

much in the writing itself as in the employment of creative editing apps. This reveals the ultimate concern of this online calligraphy group: the practice of craft and the maintenance of skill through an online appreciative community. I read a responsibility toward the art of calligraphy here. This is further evidenced by the prevailing narrative in the WeChat group, which views their daily writing as cheerful labor—a routine task the community must persist in to improve, yet paradoxically, one they engage in before calligraphy becomes obsolete. Throughout this book, I have made the argument that the detachment of calligraphy from its practical use—ballpoints and computer screens have taken over as the dominant tools of writing—has rejuvenated calligraphy as predominantly an *artistic* skill. This skill needs to be preserved through daily practice, and the WeChat community encourage each other to do so. Most explicitly through the daily message of the group host to "persevere" (坚持 *jianchi*) in writing. A reminder is given to those who have not submitted a piece in a while, and people whose calligraphy might need some extra practice receive extra encouragement. The affordances of WeChat as a platform have allowed for this affective space of calligraphy practicing. It operates as a virtual collective space in which participants who do not know each other and who do not meet still are part of an imagined calligraphy community. Keeping calligraphy alive has become a small, daily team effort.

The app *Ink Pool* (墨池 *mochi*) is a spin-off of the popular calligraphy site shufawu.com and China's first calligraphy community platform, established in 2015 and currently boasting 600,000 registered users. The app's vision is to "use the power of technology to popularize traditional calligraphy." The app is designed to offer everything the calligraphy lover could wish for: associated with reputable consortia such as the Central Academy of Fine Arts and the Chinese Calligraphy Association, the platform features a mentor scheme allowing subscribed users to learn from more than 1,600 well-known professional calligraphers; a large community of calligraphy lovers to discuss calligraphy-related matters and exchange written works; online calligraphy courses; a vast library of high-definition scanned calligraphy and competitive exercises in copying calligraphic models together. When opening the app, a single vertical column appears, stating in traditional characters: "Do not let writing characters be a solitary devotion anymore" (让写字不再是孤单的修行 *Rang xie zi bu zai shi gudan de xiuxing*). Underneath the digital font, we see an image of a calligraphy brush resting on a wooden brush holder (see Figure 4.5). The double logic of remediation resurfaces here in these types of visual reminders of the analog; possibly designed in an attempt to alleviate a tension between the analog skill and its remediated online twin. The app remains in constant dialogue between the remediated and the authentic. The elements that are supposed to convey "real" calligraphy (images of a brush, calligraphic fonts, a yellowish background similar to the color of rice paper) are countered by a hypermediated interface: hyperlinks and animations make the user acutely aware of the medium.

The calligraphy enthusiast can navigate through the app with buttons in recognizable symbols: books, shopping cart, the familiar house-shaped home button, while the "special column" section shows more markers of traditional calligraphy: backgrounds of faded traditional calligraphy overlaid with calligraphic fonts. The large "plus" button allows users to upload their own works, and as such affords access to a community of calligraphy enthusiasts. Through algorithmic organization, user content is divided into "recommended," "newest," "videos," "calligrapher" and "single characters" and "topics." In this last section, user content is organized by calligraphy script: regular, cursive, grass script, and so on. When swiping through the home video section—the app affords a vertical video feed much like Douyin or Tiktok, we see a striking resemblance across the vast majority of uploaded videos. The videos last around 15 seconds and feature a single POV shot, showing only the hand holding a brush, and a single character or sometimes a whole column, flowing out of the

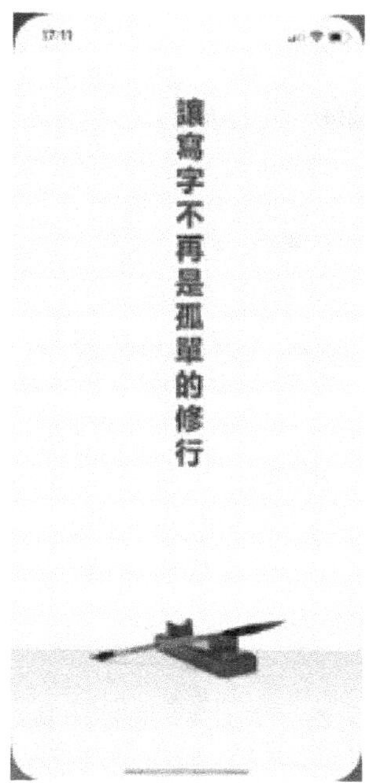

Figure 4.5: The first screen when opening the app *Ink Pool*: "Do not let writing characters be a solitary devotion anymore" (让写字不再是孤单的修行 *Rang xie zi bu zai shi gudan de xiuxing*).

brush. The videos are serious and often completely quiet, but narration also occurs when the calligrapher explains what they are doing or when background information about the written piece is given.

One major feature of the app is the "exhibition tool." The write-up of the app reads: "You want to give yourself a solo-exhibition that never ends? Distribute your works through Ink Pool and set up your own solo-exhibition with your own topic, for example #Xiaomings exhibition, and thousands of calligraphy lovers will see your work. You can enjoy the attention of a wide audience!"

By adding the hashtag: "#please criticize!" #请大家拍砖! *qing dajia paizhuan*, app users ask their online app community to help them improve their calligraphy skills. This feature caters to the needs of many calligraphy enthusiasts, as it provides a convenient and safe way to test ability and talent—no physical space is needed, nor is there a benchmark-level set-up; everyone is allowed to exhibit in this digital space (see Figure 4.6). The revenue model of *Ink Pool* relies on advertising and selling online courses. Arranged by calligraphic style, calligraphy

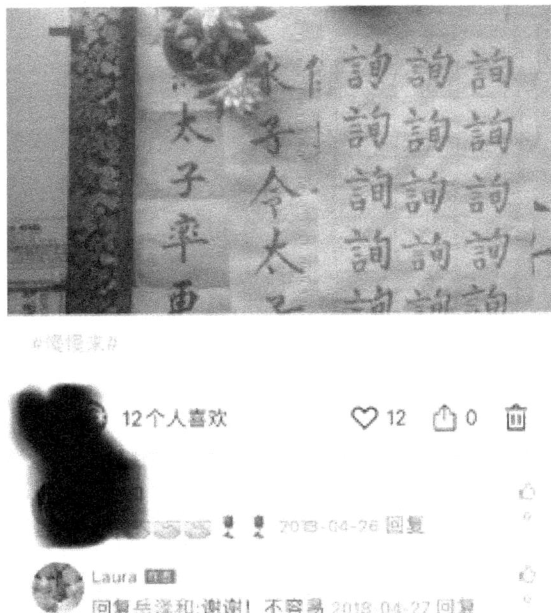

Figure 4.6: Anyone can join, as shown by my calligraphy on *Ink Pool.* © Laura Vermeeren.

teachers—the vast majority of them male—introduce themselves and have unlocked a few of their instruction videos for free. The app does not include a tool to design a type of digital calligraphy but instead, users upload photos of their brush-and-ink calligraphy created offline, to allow for a larger audience to see, comment, critique or praise, similar to what happens in the WeChat group. This "offline to online" move shows a fluid interaction between the natively analog and the digital, underscoring the earlier mentioned proposition that online practices are embedded in offline everyday practices. In this capacity, *Ink Pool* appeals to all users—hobbyists and professionals—and invites everyone to create and share in convivial spirit, all the while improving their offline, analog calligraphy.

Online platforms enable, but also limit forms of cultural production. The particular affordances of both WeChat and *Ink Pool* change the way in which calligraphy can be consumed. The vertical video feed of *Ink Pool*, for example, allows a user to flick through a dizzying array of written calligraphies with one thumb, organized by script type. These videos are visually rather stripped-down and austere, especially in comparison with calligraphy home videos found on, for example, *Kuaishou*, where we find much more variety in applying filters, background music, color and edited speed. Affordances that allow liking, sharing, commenting or critiquing help in constructing an imagined online community of calligraphers. While the specific affordances of both WeChat and *Ink Pool* have introduced new modes of calligraphy creation and consumption, they also influence our perception of what calligraphy entails. Do we, perhaps, increasingly envision calligraphy as a simple art, quickly done by a floating hand and neatly fitting into the square of the video screen? A body, so important in calligraphy discourse, seems to be missing, and omitted from view is the hand dipping a brush in ink, the quivering hesitation of the brush, and the many fails it takes before producing a piece of acceptable calligraphy. Why indeed would anyone upload a photo or video of a miserably failed piece of calligraphy, when you can just upload your successes to your imagined community? Unsuccessful executions will end up in a bin somewhere far out of view from the community, no matter how appreciative.

I started out by stating that there is some anxiety surrounding the idea that younger generations may forget how to write, and handwriting and calligraphy may subsequently lose their significance in the ongoing processes of digitization. But a clear-cut binary distinction between what is "real" calligraphy and what is "unreal" has quickly proven unsustainable, making the idea that we might lose the art of calligraphy to the digital much more complex. In our current reality, we have online calligraphy museums to visit, numerous ancient calligraphy reference books to browse, online calligraphy communities to meet, discuss and share work with, and calligraphy auctions and exhibitions to attend. Calligraphy enthusiasts copy directly from the screen, digitally embellish their handwritten works, and consume or write with calligraphy simulations that are rated just as well-executed as the characters once written by Yan Zhenqing. We are more and more surrounded by such instances of the hyperreal. I suggested that when we start to consider what that might mean for the art of calligraphy—a loss of aura, authority or expressiveness, but also texture, color and physical proximity in the process of digitization—we should take into account how important the role of authenticity or realness is for the discourse in which the artwork exists. The longstanding tradition of copying suggests that reproduction *an sich* might not necessarily be problematic. On the other hand, there is a vast field of research in calligraphy, Chinese painting and seals that concerns itself with questions of authenticity and connoisseurship. The subtlety and preciseness with which brush movements, layering of ink and calligraphic shapes are assessed would imply that every digital alteration would carry large consequences.

A final thought on community shaping. In recalling Billig's remark that banal quotidian practices may have the effect of turning "background space into homeland space,"[51] the potential of an imagined online community of calligraphers is very powerful. The members of these communities are connected through a love for calligraphy, which however remediated or hyperreal remains deeply ingrained in the collective memory as pointing at something unquestionably "Chinese," indexing a cultural China. These online communities then might also be inadvertently "telling China's story well," and their everyday practices are again an instantiation of "serving the nation"—here I recall the discourse employed by the contemporary calligraphers that we met in Chapter 3. Digital communities complicate calligraphy yet again, and simultaneously complicate ideas of Chineseness, which was already multifaceted, fragmented and contested.

CHAPTER 5

Creative Calligraphic Fonts: The Skin of Culture

Everyone is an expert in creativity[1]

When you are walking on Ghost Street (簋街 *guijie*)[2]—a bustling street in central Beijing renowned for its many seafood and hotpot restaurants—and look at the characters that light up in the evening when the street is at its busiest, the mind boggles. Digital calligraphic signs are literally on every spot the eye lands: beaming on restaurant doors, advertising billboards, movie posters, public toilets, the packaging of goods for sale in the shops, the beer bottles that people are drinking outside while waiting for their tables, and on the clothes people are wearing. They are plump, thin and spidery, edgy, rounded, square, brightly colored, neon-lit, black, white and everything in between. But there is nothing really specific about Ghost Street: such abundancy of characters can be found in every large street in every city in China and Chinatown abroad. Through my interviews with font designers and lectures on typography in Beijing, I learned that there is now a pastime called "typography strolling" (字体散步 *ziti sanbu*): walking around the city, enjoying and feeling creatively inspired by all the differently designed characters—a literate *flânerie*.

The Chinese character in the landscape of the everyday is plentiful, varied, multicolored, and serves many purposes. This is, of course, not a new development: cityscapes have been jam-packed with calligraphy for centuries. But the present manifestation of the calligraphic sign as a playful digital typeface that can be morphed into myriad shapes and colors is quite new, and is due to the rapid expansion of the creative industries within the last 35 years. This expansion has shaped and transformed many aspects of material life, and has allowed the works of creative professionals to proliferate. Young graphic designers have grasped these new creative openings to letter, or, more accurately, to *character* the landscape of the everyday. Among these graphic designers are "font bank designers," a direct translation from the Chinese term 字库 (*ziku*), who create complete sets of 6,763 characters required for digital character fonts. They meticulously craft new Chinese font banks character by character, adhering to traditional rules and methods, and the meticulous attitude of the calligrapher. Bachner asserts that the Chinese script is envisioned in contemporary typography "in many instances as a fragmented script that is vanishing stroke by stroke," thus "spelling out the death" of the script.[3] She argues that this is due to a cultural angst for the loss of Chinese culture under the pressures of globalization, which is expressed through the corruption of the written expression. And indeed, as I have established previously, the fear that people are losing the ability to write by hand resonates widely.

In this chapter, however, I propose to consider an alternative to Bachner's assumption that the demise of the handwritten sign is simultaneously due to and embodied in the typographic design. Instead, I have observed quite the opposite: a development toward a very deliberate revitalization of calligraphic features within contemporary font bank and typography design. This development is facilitated by techno-linguistic innovations and motivated by an increasingly thriving realm of the cultural industries that grows in tandem with a desire to strengthen Chinese national culture. The mobilization of calligraphic aesthetics in design is, as I will argue here, further proof of its longevity, and its versatility as a marker of cultural Chineseness. And it challenges the idea of linearity—in which writing methods move straightforwardly through new technologies, discarding the old by every new invention. Through this observation, I attempt here to complicate and add to current notions of Chineseness, by arguing that Chinese font designs embody a double logic between creativity and national interest. Chinese fonts, to put it plainly, are not just fonts: it matters, a lot, what the digital fonts on your screens look like. They are, as with calligraphy, loaded with cultural significance, personality, emotion and implications about Chinese culture at large.

So far we have seen how, in different iterations, calligraphy has been employed as an irreducible articulation of Chineseness. The notion of a 5,000-year-old cultural China takes up a large space within the concept of Chineseness, and has become a normalized conviction, one that has been ascribed with the status of truth. Calligraphy, and the continuous use of the Chinese sign throughout this long history, serves as a potent attestation of this idea. It is, as I have argued throughout, used in the context of moral education in service of the Chinese nation; as a means to discipline the (Chinese) self; to serve modern times; and as a nostalgic retreat. But the concept of Chineseness should not be that straightforwardly applied—the notion has been hitherto critiqued and deconstructed thoroughly for over three decades for its narrow politics of identity; the hegemony of mainland China in using the notion; and for the way it often ignores the "other Chinas."[4] Indeed, how can we use this term unreservedly after such rigorous deconstruction?

One specific tactic that I see as a unique articulation of Chineseness will be taken up in this last chapter: font designers locate creativity in the Chinese calligraphic past, and employ it to enrich the present in fonts and popular media productions. As such, creativity—the much sought-after quality heralded as a productive force in the present—is located in a very distinctive Chinese past. This is an important observation: the Chinese calligraphic past is not often framed as particularly creative—rather, "excellent," "profound" or "unique" are adjectives applied much more frequently. Firmly set in a standard of imitative reproduction upon which present-day practitioners can further build, this past is usually presented as a rock-solid foundation. As I have shown throughout this book, this rock-solid foundation can become the starting point of creative interpretation: inspired either by western contemporary art, Japanese calligraphy, stone steles, or by the innovative spirit that ignited post-Reform and Opening Up developments, new types of calligraphy are imagined and created. In the discourse of font design, however, the calligraphic past is heralded and mobilized as an exciting *creative* past.

The mobilizations of this creative past through contemporary font design renders national interest, creativity and Chineseness mutually constitutive. It also ties in with recent governmental directives: one of Xi Jinping's signature political strategies is the "doctrine of confidence" (自信论 *zixin lun*). This doctrine is aimed at building the confidence of the Party as well as the nation as a whole in the chosen path, the guiding theories and the political system of "Socialism with Chinese characteristics." These three pointers were initially referred to as the "three Doctrines" (三个自信 *sang ge zixin*), but in 2014, Xi Jinping decided to add a fourth confidence, which he regards to be the most important: a confidence in one's own culture (文化自信 *wenhua zixin*). According to Xi, this is "even more foundational, even more wide-ranging, and even more profound."[5] Xi further articulated this in his speech at the Symposium on Literature and Art Work in 2014, made public in June 2019:

> Both history and reality have proven that the Chinese nation has a great cultural creativity. Inheriting Chinese culture is not simply nostalgic (复古 *fugu*),

> or blind exclusion, but it is making the past serve the present; making foreign things serve China; investigative decision-making; innovation; abandoning negative factors; inheriting positive thoughts;[6] starting your own unique creations based on the creative rules of the ancients to achieve a creative transformation; and the innovative development of Chinese culture (Xi 2019,[7] my translation).

The speech is a typical display of Xi Jinping's management of cultural politics. He constructs a creative Chinese history, one that should guide creative individuals to grow in their cultural confidence, simultaneously disciplining the ways in which this individual should create: based on and inspired by ancient, creative and Chinese ways—here we are reminded of Foucauldian governmental tactics. Xi's speech forms a tool to manage the creative individual's relation to Chineseness efficiently: it leads and directs behavior to improve the condition of the population by increasing its self-confidence, and it enhances the nation as a whole, because creative individuals support the "innovative development of Chinese culture."

With this in mind, the question arises as to how the font (bank) designer should then, practically, create: how to adhere to calligraphic rules while being a prolific creative worker at the same time? The creative visions and ideas of the designer are deeply entangled and become, as I will argue, a complex balancing act. On the one hand, they are asked to depart from a culture of imitation, but they are also expected to draw on historical models to foster creativity. Simultaneously, they must create marketable fonts that meet rigorous calligraphic standards. This chapter is based on interviews with a selection of professional font bank designers working at the Type Design Research Center, also known as FounderType or 方正 *Fangzheng*, the largest font design company in China.[8] Their fonts are used by 90 percent of the newspapers, publishing houses and printing houses in China as well as major TV organizations and tech companies. FounderType is a state-owned cultural enterprise (SOCE), and, according to Jian Lin, as such is "required by the Chinese government to shoulder a double 'responsibility' to achieve both social and economic benefits."[9] I have also interviewed graphic designers who publish their calligraphic designs on ZCOOL .com.cn, an online community platform for designers to exchange designs, photos and information. Finally, I closely followed an active group of font designers, some of them working at FounderType, others aspiring to become designers.[10] Instead of claiming representativeness, I use these interviews and conversations as well as visual analysis to construct and contextualize the current field of font design. Through these tools of analysis, this chapter will provide insights into a complex and quite new discursive field. Complex, because creative font design is not only visual, it is also semantic, and involves city branding, advertising, entertainment and communication, all of which influences its contexts of viewing, production and consumption. It is therefore paramount to consider the historical—and in this case techno-linguistic—innovations that have occurred before the cultural moments of the current study, and have led to the ongoing usage of the Chinese sign in the contemporary. Here, I am inspired by Thomas Mullaney to refrain from using the word "continuation" of the Chinese sign, as he argues that continuity is not synonymous with conservatism: "To continue something—in this case, to continue character-based Chinese script—can be avant-garde, iconoclastic, radical, and even destructive. Phrased differently, while it is virtually a cliché to speak of the 'destruction' often entailed in acts of creativity, rarely do we pause to reflect upon the destruction central to acts of continuation."[11] In order for the calligraphic sign to be reimagined, and to remain, as a digital font, much had to be destroyed first. The next section will hence provide a brief investigation of the techno-linguistic turns in China, placing those in a wider context of technological and cultural changes that have facilitated the development of technical aids to handwriting and calligraphy. Understanding how these innovations have set the stage for calligraphy to be re-envisioned in our technologically advanced era helps answer the initial questions: what aspects have persisted, and which discontinuities have facilitated new representations of the calligraphic sign at the intersection of creative font design and traditional calligraphy?

Techno-Linguistic Innovations

Before the invention of paper, bamboo slips were commonly used as mediums for writing characters. These slips date back to the Shang dynasty (17th century BCE) and were in use at least until the Jin dynasty (300 CE). Tsien and Needham argue that stencils were made as early as the second century BCE, and during this time, animal skins or thin silk fabrics treated with varnish or tree sap were used.[12] Technical methods to duplicate characters on paper have existed in China since as early as the second century BCE, the sixth century, and the seventh or eighth century CE, respectively, coexisting with handwritten calligraphy for centuries. They are stenciling (模子 *muzi*), rubbing (碑帖 *beitie*), and woodblock printing (钻版 *zuanban*) or xylography.[13] These methods paved the way for the invention of movable type in the 11th century, and they all work according to the same simple principle. For the technical reproduction of characters on paper, you need three elements: a flat surface with an inscription cut in relief, the preparation of the mirror image and the transfer from the original on to the surface to be printed.

Stenciling is done by forming designs on a thick piece of paper, through perforation, after which the stencil is put on a hard surface, and ink is applied through the perforation.[14] Rubbing is the process of making a reproduction of a (calligraphic) inscription carved into a hard-surfaced material such as stone, metal or bone, or three-dimensional objects such as round or square bronze vessels. The paper is first prepared by moistening it with rice or lotus water, after which the paper is laid out on the engraved surface, is tamped into every depression with a hard brush and tapped with an ink pad, to then be peeled of the hard surface. This results in a negative image: a white text on a black surface. For the method of xylography, or woodblock printing, a craftsman carves in a woodblock with mirrored characters by placing a piece of handwritten calligraphy face down on the wooden block, which means that anything the calligrapher writes, is exactly transferred. When the ink is applied to the block, and the paper is pressed against it, the characters appear in black on white, appearing as if it was written.[15]

This final method evolved into the dominant printing technique, reaching its peak during the Song dynasty, a period often referred to as the "golden age of printing." It allowed for great changes in the production and dissemination of texts, which prompted major cultural and intellectual changes. First, as Cynthia Brokaw and Kai-Wing Chow note, although publishing centers, predominantly located in Zhejiang province, existed before, printing now became mobile, in the same way that handwritten calligraphy was a mobile way of producing text: a portable set of tools allowed block carvers to travel around and offer their services to literati or religious institutions, to print texts, sutras and religious texts, provided that the client had access to the right woods, paper and ink.[16] This coincided with—or more accurately, woodblock printing allowed for—the commissioning by the imperial government of large projects in this period, such as: the (re)printing of editions of the Confucian classics, new dynastic histories, compendia on medicine, literature and law, after which Taoists and Buddhists started to print their entire canons.[17]

Printing was here to stay, and continued to proliferate in the subsequent Mongol Yuan dynasty and especially the Ming dynasty, when commercial publishing houses started to churn out texts such as popular novels in the vernacular, fortune-telling handbooks and household manuals, making them even more appealing through the development of the woodcut with multicolor prints and illustrations. This meant that lower classes, craftsmen and peasants, could now enjoy more opportunities for upward mobility.[18] This also meant that many people were able to see a variety and a multitude of calligraphic characters on a daily basis, just like in China today. Brokaw and Chow note, moreover, that "woodblock-printed books in fact never broke away from the model of the handwritten text, as western books did; in China, the finest texts were often those that managed to reproduce, largely through elegant and striking calligraphy, the appearance of a manuscript."[19]

Hang Lin adds that printing in China coincided with one of the great periods of calligraphy. Although the great Tang masters (such as Ouyang Xun and Yan Zhenqing) did not make woodblocks themselves, the calligraphy master carvers used rubbings of the famous inscriptions that were executed by these masters and copied them to produce texts for blocks.[20] This indicates that calligraphy remained the dominant representation of the Chinese character, despite undergoing different layers of remediation: handwritten calligraphy was first written with ink by a master calligrapher, then carved into stone by a craftsman, then a rubbing was made of the carving, after which it was used to be carved into wood and to be pressed again on paper. Through all this, the aim was to remain as close to the calligraphic shape created by the master calligrapher as possible.

Around the 11th century, the use of movable type in wood, earthenware and enamel began, although, according to Tsien and Needham, this was never the preferred method as many types had to be cut and it was therefore labor-intensive, expensive and impractical.[21] With the invention of a bronze type, printing with bronze movable type began to be widely applied in the late 15th century. By the 18th and 19th centuries, new technological advances such as stenography, typewriting, Morse code and, indeed, digital typography, were all invented with the Latin alphabet as their foundation, after which they were tweaked to incorporate non-Latin alphabets. Western inventions were influential in the development of China's printing technology, but as Christopher Reed maintains, again the adaptation of these techniques was influenced by a deeply ingrained preference for calligraphic aesthetics:

> Contrary to received wisdom, nineteenth-century Chinese were making constructive choices when it came to identifying the Western technology closest to the literary and aesthetic culture that they venerated. Their choices were influenced by the range of literati values . . . particularly those concerned with calligraphy and relevant to extending the life of calligraphic and manuscript culture.[22]

By the mid-1920s, western-style printing, by then characterized by a blending of the calligraphic aesthetics of the Chinese literati with the technology of the Gutenberg revolution, would become an inseparable part of China's modern civilization.[23] It is important to recognize that, well into the 1930s, all these methods of reproducing Chinese characters—hand copying, stenciling, rubbing, woodblock, movable type—were employed at the same time, which effectively subverts the idea that technological progress moves in just one direction, leaving behind earlier practices with every new invention.

With the developments in printing based on western methods, attempts were made to break up the Chinese character in order to fit it, quite literally, into the mold of European typesetting, which resulted in the decision to break the character down in Chinese radicals.[24] This is not to say that radicals are a western invention. Radicals are graphical and semantic components that build up the Chinese character and are used to categorize or systematize lists of characters in dictionaries. The Chinese dictionary 说文解字 *Shuowen jiezi*, dating back to around 100 CE, was already structured through a system of 540 radicals. The divisible type went on to be used as the basis for a transmittable code when telegraphic messaging entered the stage around 1871.[25] After trial, error and many attempts to transform the Chinese character into a workable and sizable piece of code, the Chinese character was now a four-digit and Arabic number, based on a deconstructed sign, which also became the basis for computing later in the century. Unlike the movable type, the calligraphic hand copy or the woodblock, the input now no longer related directly to the output. In other words, whereas before the idea was to duplicate the original as accurately as possible, now the input—what you need to do to end up with Chinese characters on the other end—was based on a shared technological agreement. Historical overviews on Chinese mechanical writing from the invention of the telegraph until the age of computing have been scarce.[26] How and what kinds of technological advances were made in order for Chinese consumers to input their text into personal computers has also received less attention, but this has recently been remedied by Jing Tsu's *Kingdom of Characters*,[27] which gives a full account of China's language revolution. Between the telegraph era and the computing era, the Chinese typewriter saw widespread use during a brief period from the 1950s to the 1980s. Organized first by radicals, typists later found ways to organize the setting based on the frequency of usage, and inventing predictive text.[28] The first Chinese computer was produced in 1958, and Guo and Sun describe how the development of the computer industry can be divided into three periods. In the initial period (1956–71), "the computer industry advanced freely" with its main user base being military and research organizations. In the second period, the industrial development from 1972–79, a total number of only 2,000 computers was mostly installed at universities and other institutes. And from 1980 to date, the fields of application have changed exclusively from research and defense purposes to the entire society."[29]

When China moved on to develop personal computers (PCs) in the 1980s, the first Chinese PC85 could generate and display Chinese characters and process information in Chinese. The input system used was Cangjie (仓颉输入法 *Cangjie shuru fa*), invented in 1976 and based on the alphabetic keyboard, since the developers realized the QWERTY keyboard had become universal. With Cangjie, Chinese characters could be entered by selecting a radical that corresponds to an alphabetic key. Over the years, different systems were added, either based on phonetic readings such as Pinyin input, which has become most common today, or root shapes such as Wubi. Now, new techniques such as OCR, HCR and voice recognition have been added to the arsenal of input methods, further blurring the lines between the digital and the analog. There are, notes Tsu, currently 900 million internet users in China, all using Chinese input methods when posting on social media; buying, selling online and "making the Chinese internet smarter, faster, and ever more rich in data." "The country," she concludes, "is poised to create its own Han script sphere of influence, once again, in the current millennium."[30]

With the transformation of the Chinese character into a four-digit number, based on a deconstructed sign, the visual output—the character that appears on the screen—has become dependent on the skill of the font designer, who in turn is led by concerns of salability, convention, artistic negotiations and, as we shall see, national interest based on calligraphy. The next section will analyze designs and designers of font banks: high-quality and uniform sets of around 7,000 characters available for download and printing.

Font Bank Design: "Fonts Are the Skin of Culture"[31]

When I arrive at the open workshop of the National Museum in Beijing, organized by the Cultural Innovation Center in 2018, to learn about the basics of digital font bank design, the room is packed with young urbanites, men and women in equal number, of whom no one seems to be more than 30 years old. The event is organized as part of the larger project "Everyone is an expert in creativity" (人人都是创意家 *renren dou shi chuangyijia*) of the National Art Museum of China, which is aimed at urban cultural consumers, and encourages cultural innovation and promotes urban cultural consumption.[32] With such emphasis on innovation and urbaneness, it is slightly surprising, upon entering the room, to see the familiar copies of rubbings from model calligraphers Yan Zhenqing, Ouyang Xun and Mi Fu, as well as grid paper and freshly sharpened pencils prepared for all participants. At the back, an image of a giant oracle bone carrying ancient carvings is projected on the screen: it seems we will be guided through the well-known narrative of 5,000 years of glorious tradition and civilization.

And indeed, throughout the lecture, there will be a constant tracing back from design to calligraphy, emphasizing the impossibility of being a good designer without being able to recognize the different calligraphic styles and masters, the necessity of practicing calligraphy yourself, and the need to understand how woodblock printing gave way to font design in the digital realm. The lecture ends with all participants taking a copy of an ancient rubbing to first study the composition, style and center of gravity of the characters, how the lines are formed and how they link to each other. Then, inspired and informed by this calligraphy, they start drawing their own typeface on grid paper. The host ultimately selects a winner: the individual who has most successfully integrated calligraphic elements from traditional styles while also creating a clear and modern typeface. The winner is chuffed: she truly is an expert in creativity.

As a branch of the creative industries, font design is on the rise. According to Wang Wen, deputy director of FounderType, after years of experimentation, we are now in "the spring period of great development of Chinese fonts":

> We had the most extreme designs in the 1990s, when we had just entered the desktop era. That was the most radical; there were many designs that were overstepping all boundaries. . . . Why did we use those technologies and such dazzling use of skill in publishing or design? In fact, it was to show what we were capable of doing, all of which traditional printing could not do. This was the beginning of the digital age. Now, ten or 20 years have passed and we see less and less of this phenomenon. Before 2010, there was no particularly good development. It started after 2010, and we are now in the spring period of development, it is booming. This period will definitely produce vast amounts of fonts, but we must see if they will stand the test of time. In ten years' time, we can see which ones are still in use, and which ones have been knocked out of the competition.
>
> —Interview with Wang Wen

Wang further argues that the obligatory calligraphy classes in schools will aid the current development of digital fonts:

> We now have a national policy, right? Calligraphy has now entered elementary schools. So this period will not be so turbulent, and primary and secondary students will be able to write well. We [at FounderType] now have two fonts that were designed by ten-year-old primary school children, and they already write better than adults.
>
> —Interview with Wang Wen

Digital fonts, according to Wang, will be of higher quality when those creating and consuming them are skilled at calligraphy—Wang Wen welcomes the statutory calligraphy classes in elementary and high schools.

In creating a complete font bank, every single character needs to be written and designed individually by hand. This takes one employee about a year, and the whole process from the start of the design to a saleable font can take up to three years. Therefore, a company cannot afford to produce a font that is only mediocre and will not be sold, or a font that is very innovative, but not certain to stand the test of time. Senior font designer Liu Hanxu has created multiple well-selling fonts for FounderType. Creating fonts, he says in our interview, is slow and laborious work and starts with the SongTi typeface. The SongTi typeface—the name allows for an immediate association to the Song dynasty woodblock-style fonts, a style that confusingly was established in its recognizable form only in the Ming dynasty—is a clear and readable font and is used in the main body of text on most large Chinese web pages, together with Heiti.[33]

The digital SongTi typeface is a digitized remediation of the woodblock-printed characters: thick horizontal lines, with a small serif on the top right and thin, straight, horizontal strokes with serif on both sides. The distinct shape of the SongTi typeface stems from its direct connection to its woodblock predecessor. In woodblock printing, the grain of the wood ran horizontally, making it easier to carve thin horizontal strokes, whereas vertical strokes which ran against the grain, had to be thicker to prevent breakage. Because the ends of strokes were prone to wear over time, they were made thicker, eventually making what we now recognize as serifs. Woodblock printing adapted calligraphic forms to maintain textual legitimacy, and shaped how characters were standardized in print. This process of remediation continued with the development of the digital SongTi typeface, which preserves the influence of its woodblock predecessor. By maintaining its recognizable structure and visual authority, SongTi has managed to remain the dominant and most widely accepted typeface, even in the digital era.

> When you feel inspired (灵感 *linggan*), you start by taking SongTi as a model and write about a dozen characters, before showing it to your manager. You need to have a strong theoretical ability. If the manager agrees, you can continue, and write another 50 characters. They all need to be uniform, and all need to be representative of the style you are aiming for. Generally, each new font should contain around 7,000 characters, but at least 6,763.
>
> —Interview with Liu Hanxu

The font designer, in Liu Hanxu's account, needs to have acquired both manual writing skills and digital savvy to commence such a project. Although in alphabetic type design "variable type"—a technology that enables a single font file to be tweaked into multiple fonts without having to create more data manually—is increasingly used, this is, according to Wang Wen and Liu Hanxu, still not satisfactorily viable for character-based fonts, as they are too intricate in composition. There is still, according to my informants, only a handful of people in China today who are designing these high-quality complete font banks. However, this is changing fast. Big tech companies such as Alibaba, Tencent and Xiaomi as well as Adobe are eager to use their own distinctive font in order to convey a specific and recognizable brand identity and ensure brand consistency. In the last three years they have each developed their own distinctive and open-source font banks, with Vivo and Oppo following at pace.

At the design company FounderType, a font designer's job security depends on the success of their fonts. If a designer creates a well-selling font, they can continue their work, but if not, their position is at risk. Creative work in this branch is precarious, and the incentive to create a good, saleable font is high. Does this, I wondered, result perhaps in safer, or less creative designs? Liu rejects this idea:

> I think every character design is based on creativity (在创意的基础上 *zai chuangyi de jichu shang*) even if they are based on regular script, or if they are very legible and clear fonts. This creativity entails many things: the style, the shape, the outer silhouette, and although western fonts also have a shape, Chinese characters also have 中宫 *zhonggong*[34] which determines whether people will feel relaxed or uncomfortable looking at the character.
>
> —Interview with Liu Hanxu

For Liu, creativity within contemporary font design means transferring calligraphic concepts properly to the digital screen—style, shape, outer shape and 中宫 *zhonggong*—resulting in a font that is "comfortable to look at." Young font designer Tao Di, winner of the FounderType typography competition and now working as a junior font designer, expresses a similar view. He too believes that innovation and creativity in new designs should be based on traditional calligraphy—making something new without considering the past is impossible, he says. Font designers should instead "dig out" the creative treasures of the Chinese past:

> I personally think that Chinese traditional culture is very deep, right? So, countless classic calligraphy works have been handed down to us from

> history; this is an endless flow of creative inspiration for us (源源不断的创造力 *yuanyuanbuduan de chuangzaoli*). What we modern people can do, I think, is dig that out, and try to express that again, in accordance with the aesthetics of modern people. The roots are still here, so we should not just make things up without any foundation. What we are doing as font designers is extract its characteristics, extract its strongest features, and then use appropriate design techniques to express it, and then unify it into a font.
>
> —Interview with Tao Di

Successful font design, thus, relies on an intricate balancing act between handed-down calligraphic traditions and the aesthetics of modern people. Here, we find the same attitude so often expressed in the scene of contemporary calligraphy: what does this time need from us, and which elements of the national calligraphic past are useful for people today? How to extract from tradition what suits the tastes of people today and encapsulate that in a font is an ongoing concern for the designer.

A fascinating case is the rags to riches evolution of a calligraphic style developed by Cui Xianren (or as he is known online: "Brother chalk" (粉笔哥 *fenbi ge*)) who is neither a calligrapher nor a font designer—he has in fact only received three years of primary education. In 2011, online movies of Cui writing a very distinctive calligraphic style on the streets with colored chalk began circulating widely on Weibo. Cui suffered from an explosion accident, which left him with severe burns on his body. He started writing chalk characters, and asking for money or food on the streets of Yantai. Given that his fingers became deformed and fused together after the accident, his ability to write such a distinctive, uniform style astounded passersby and caused quite the stir among netizens. FounderType, after recognizing how trending his characters had become online and seeing potential in his script, asked their online community if they could help in locating and identifying Cui. They found him in Qingdao, and offered to turn his script into an official FounderType Font. Cui wrote the first 1,000 characters, after which the company further developed a complete font bank named after him: Xian Ren Simplified (方正显仁简体 *Fangzheng Xianren jianti*; see Figure 5.1).

It was the very first font developed by a grassroots writer. During the COVID pandemic in 2020, Cui Xianren's font resurfaced publicly: FounderType selected a range of fonts that could help in "fighting the pandemic" (Figure 5.2). They are believed to be specifically fitting to be used for propaganda, pandemic prevention and to pay tribute to the "front-line heroes" of Wuhan and cheer China on during the crisis. Xian Ren Simplified is one of those fonts: "Cui Xianren's mental strength complements the brave and firm qualities of the front

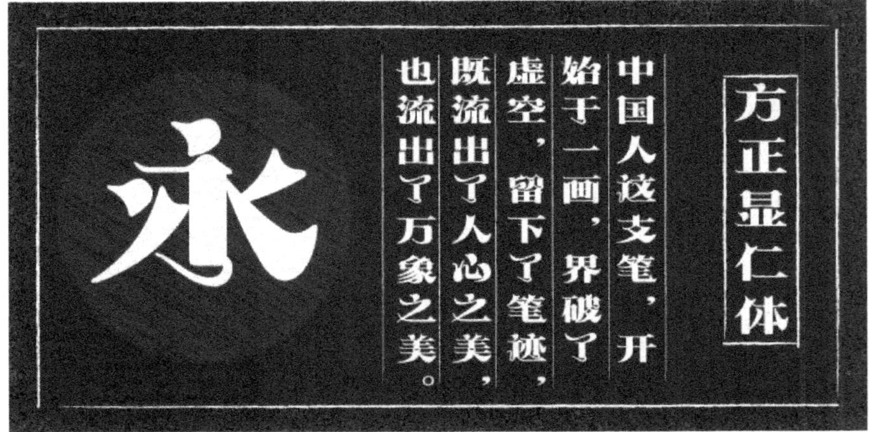

Figure 5.1: The font developed by Cui Xianren for FounderType. © FounderType.

line workers," is the rationale.[35] Here we are reminded again of the trope "the writing is like the man" (字如其人 *zi ru qi ren*). This is, of course, a rather rare case. After all, it is rare for a chalked character to evolve into a profitable font and ultimately become a propaganda tool in service of the nation during a global pandemic. But it highlights how fonts connote so much (more) in the Chinese context. The idea that fonts are significant players in the realm of everyday life is acutely clear here. Their applications are informed by the ingrained convictions that are still stacked upon the calligraphic character: we see the moral character of the writer shining through the written sign. Cui's mental strength and strong character make for a suitable font to apply in situations where the people need moral support.

Another way to find out this "trend of the time," according to interviewee Tao Di, is to find inspiration in the designs made for movies and games, and he observes a trend in the post-90s' generation for design "with a bit more personality and unconventionality." FounderType Deputy Director Wang Wen shares Tao Di's view, identifying this search for "personality" as a nostalgic and even psychological need to go back to ancient calligraphy:

> So, although we have actually entered the digital age, the computer, and the mobile internet era, in fact, there is now a trend towards handwritten and personalized fonts. Handwritten fonts (手写字体 *shouxie ziti*) are very popular in our society today. We don't write much ourselves anymore, but when we see a handwritten font, everybody loves it. This (third) trend is a

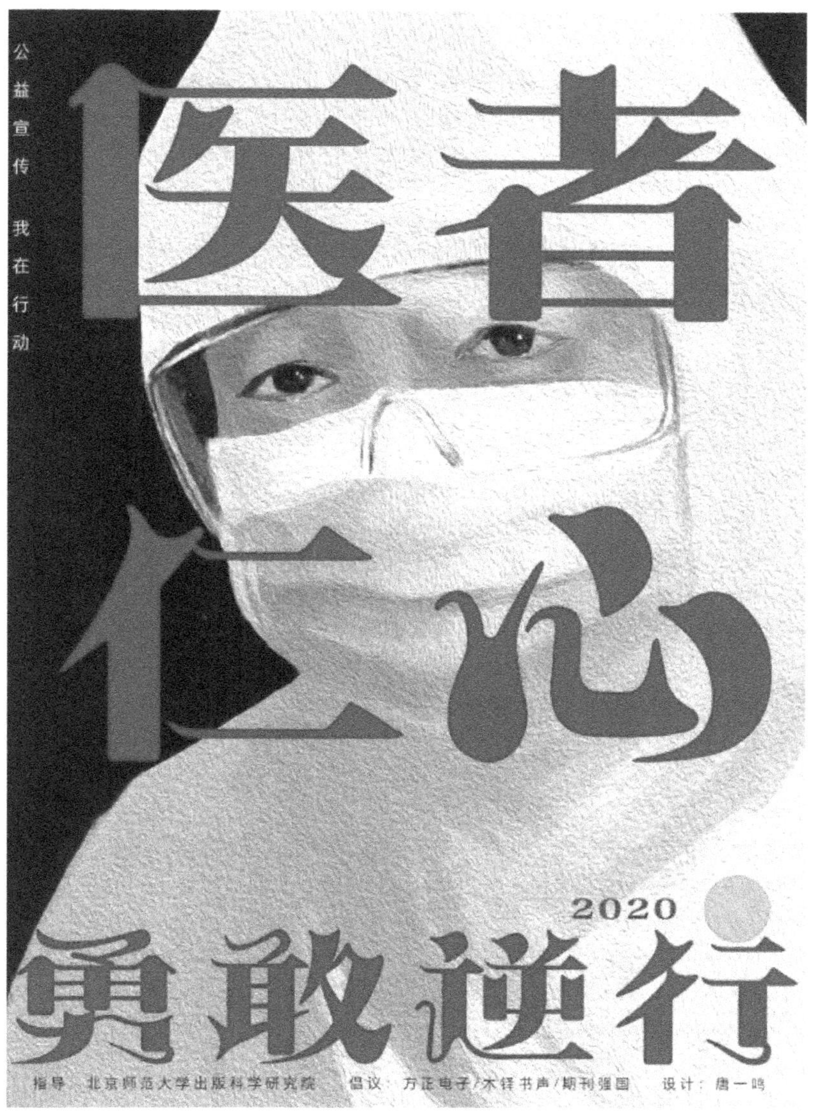

Figure 5.2: The font is promoted by FounderType as specifically applicable for anti-epidemic propaganda. © FounderType. Retrieved from www.sohu.com/a/375443101_671708

> collision of the modern aesthetic and the classical aesthetic. . . . On the one hand, we crave innovation, while on the other hand, all Chinese people still want to go back to our old culture, and we still hold the things of ancient people in high regard. We believe that the things made by ancient people are elegant, and we believe the classics are full of elegance. Based on this situation, we should produce our new fonts.[36]

Let us pause here to interrogate Wang's remark further: "all Chinese people still want to go back to our old culture." In a significant self-orientalizing move, it expresses a desire to set Chinese preferences apart from western equivalents. Moreover, it reduces "all Chinese" to one homogeneous group harboring the same aesthetic preferences, and the same longing for their shared past. Wang's comment, therefore, resonates with Chinese Communist Party (CCP) policies that use nationalism as their unifying ideology. Handwritten fonts become even more significantly Chinese—and more specifically locatable—when the hand originally writing them belongs to a well-known Chinese hero. This encompasses not only the handwriting of renowned calligraphers but also extends to prominent Chinese figures more broadly. For instance, the handwriting of actress Xu Jinglei, writer Lu Xun and calligrapher Qi Gong has been transformed into downloadable fonts (see Figures 5.3–5.5). In an interview with *China Daily*, Qiu Yin, Director of FounderType, describes the process behind creating Lu Xun's font: "We gathered his manuscripts from museums and then

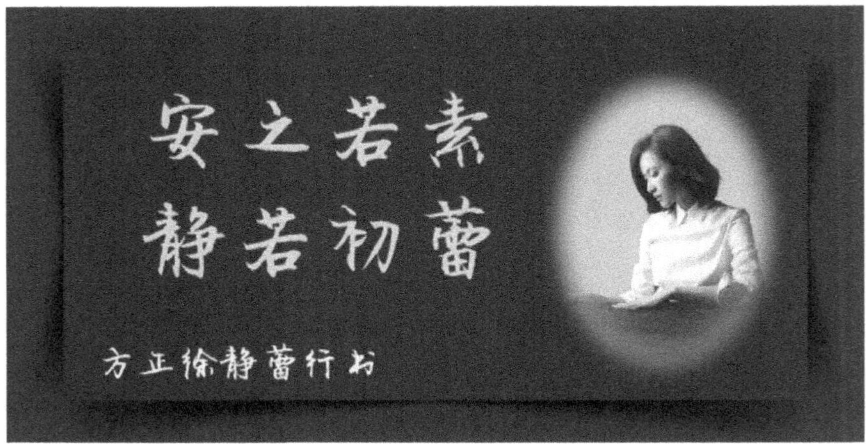

Figure 5.3: A font based on the hard-pen calligraphy of actress and director Xu Jinglei, developed by FounderType. © FounderType.

Figure 5.4: A font based on the calligraphy of Lu Xun, developed by FounderType. © FounderType.

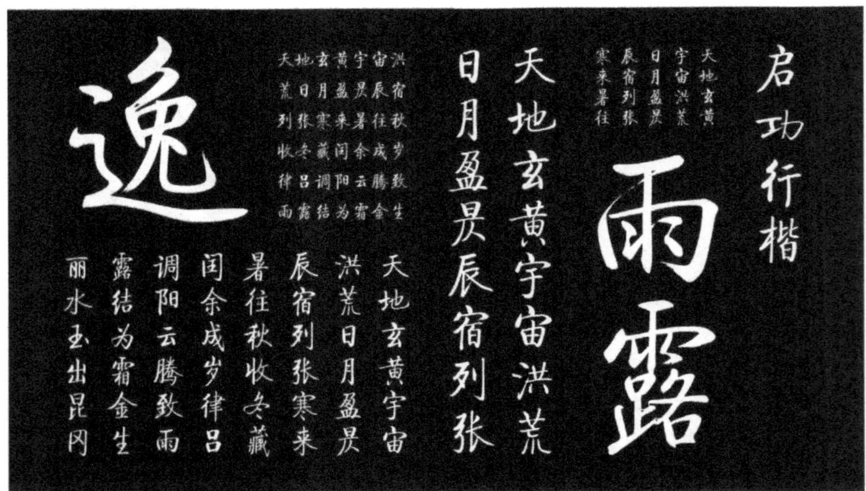

Figure 5.5: A font based on the calligraphy of Qi Gong, developed by FounderType. © FounderType.

chose about 2,600 characters, studied his style, and created the characters that could not be found or were illegible in his manuscripts." The project took a team of four designers 18 months to complete. Qiu emphasizes the cultural significance of such work, stating, "Seeing their handwriting, people can draw inspiration and connect with them in a digital way that transcends time and space."[37]

Based on the popularity of these personalized calligraphic fonts, a hypothesis can be put forward that a lack of physical handwriting in daily life might be *made up for* by contemporary font design, underlining Xi Jinping's earlier mentioned directive to "make the past serve the present." Font designers, then, do two things. First, they mobilize the past as a source of creative inspiration, rather literally by taking rubbings and copies of historical calligraphy. This past is construed as a continuous Chinese cultural history that affords an affective production—a cultural product with the ability to bring modern people, detached from their heritage, closer to a common national origin. In his research on Han clothing, Kevin Carrico argues that a "perpetually impassable gap exists between an ever-expanding nationalist imaginary and an inherently limited national experience."[38] There seems to be a discrepancy, he argues, between the national imagery of the Chinese nation as five millennia of tradition and the underwhelming modern lived reality. In the case of font design something similar occurs. The revival of calligraphic aesthetics in handwritten font design can be viewed as a strategy to bridge this perceived gap and reconnect with the analog past, a past inhabited by illustrious Chinese figures such as Lu Xun and Qi Gong. Seeing their writing and having the embodied agency of typing with their characters brings not only their handwriting close, but the person as well—might their lofty character traits perhaps rub off on the typeface user? Writing, again, reflects the man.

These types of designs are attempts to imitate handwritten calligraphy as accurately as possible, thus essentially relying on a mode of copying. At the same time, creative calligraphic font design that is less recognizably linked to calligraphy—yet, importantly, still claims descendance—is increasingly on the market.[39] What follows is a sample of two winners in the professional font designers' category of the annual FounderType Design Competition of 2018. The competition, celebrating its 20th anniversary in 2021 with a brief halt during the COVID pandemic, is aimed at promoting font design innovation and discovering font design talents. What is striking about the submissions in all categories are the outspoken references made to calligraphy and woodblock carving in their creative concepts. But looking closely, we see that their designs do not necessarily clearly (have to) correlate to any specific typographic predecessor. Lan Zezhen created "Rubber Stamp Square Characters" (橡皮章方块字体 *Xiangpi zhuang fangkuai ziti*), see Figure 5.6. The characters are thick and black, and are squeezed to fit into a square, leaving little white space in between the strokes. While the composition of the character remains intact to make the character still recognizable and legible, calligraphic references are difficult to isolate: there is no distinguishable stroke order, there are no discernible calligraphic lines and all rounded elements of the character have been made into a square. Evocations of woodblocks or rubbings are also not immediately obvious. Font designer Tao Di suggested that "perhaps the excess of blackness hints at ancient rubbings, and movable type was made through squares, like this square shape. But I think it is very far-fetched." Altogether, the font affords a modern, fun and almost graffiti-like impression. In the short explanation of the designer, however, Lan Zezhen explains that he has been motivated by historical calligraphic models, drawing inspiration from three historical writing methods: he has interpreted the single unit of a character as in movable type and the mechanical typewriter, while at the same time noting that "from an innocent childlike perspective, it looks like the rubbings of an ancient engraved stone tablet."[40] A clear discrepancy is noticeable here: with a font so unlike those seen on rubbings, and so unlike traditionally carved or written characters, the designer still insists on inspiration from earlier writing methods. This insistence

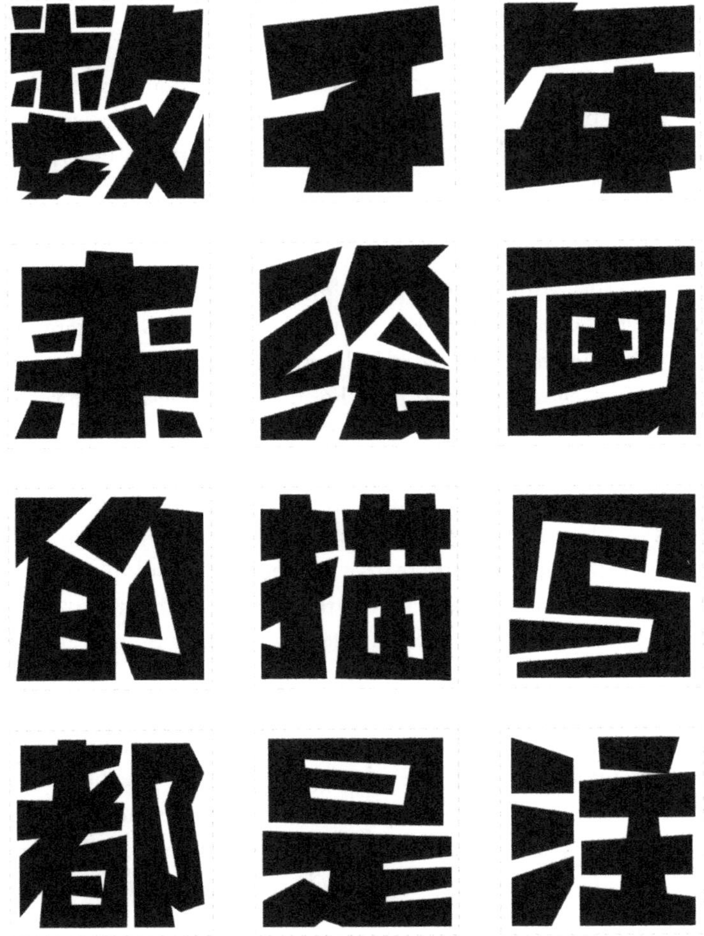

Figure 5.6: Font design "Rubber Stamp Square characters" (*Xiangpi zhuang fangkuai ziti* 橡皮 章方 块字体) made by third prize winner Lan Zezhen for the 9th FounderType design competition. © Foundertype, reproduced with permission. https://ztds.foundertype.com/?c=HuoJiang

is significant. Instead of claiming to have been innovative, the legitimacy of designers' creativity is still, or *has to be*, fixed in an interpretation of the traditional.

I began wondering whether the space of the digital would allow for more imagination and creativity than the handwritten calligraphic character is able to offer. The kind of diplomatic juggling that we see in this design allows for a nuanced answer. By creatively interpreting—and thus remaining faithful to—the aesthetics of a typographic predecessor, the design is allowed to be modern, creative and innovative, and carries national, as well as commercial, value. The contender finishing second, Zhu Rineng, has created a font called "Jin Nong Ink Clerical" (金农墨隶 *Jin Nong moli*; see Figure 5.7). The font appears to resemble a handwritten type, but does not follow traditional calligraphic directions: the characters are squared, and the horizontal strokes are very thick compared to the thin, sharp strokes downward. It looks as if they were written with a reed pen instead of a calligraphy brush, resembling Tibetan script rather than Chinese. The variation of heavy strokes with vertical slenderness within the characters further gives the font a dynamic impression. For this design, Zhu Rineng took as his model the hallmarks of Jin Nong (1687–1763), a calligrapher living during the Qing dynasty who is known as one of the "eight eccentrics of Yangzhou"—a group of radical calligraphers known for deviating from the official calligraphic rules to explore their own individual interpretations. The font design is based on a special variation of clerical script called "lacquer style" (漆书 *qishu*) invented by Jin Nong (see Figure 5.8).

Figures 5.7 and 5.8 reveal how Zhu took the hallmark of Jin Nong as an inspiration for his font design (and of course, while the font may be inspired by Jin Nong's style, it is not an exact copy due to the simple fact that Jin Nong has not written all the 6,763 characters needed to create a font bank). This design reveals another approach to negotiating the demands for creativity, national interest and calligraphic prowess. By taking an eccentric, but well-respected and prominent calligrapher as his model, the calligraphy in itself is the innovative and creative factor in this design. The negotiation in this case lies not in translating calligraphy to modernity, but rather in digging into that calligraphic history, and finding that there was maverick and surprising creativity there.

Not only SOCE companies such as FounderType, but contemporary artists have started creating their own fonts as well, turning their artworks into commodities. Two examples can be found in the fonts of Xu Bing (2015) and digital artist Feng Mengbo (2017). Xu Bing has refashioned his renowned artwork *English Square Word Calligraphy* (1994–96) into a downloadable font, see Figure 5.9. Characters in this font are built up from different layers of appropriation and assemblage: visually, the shape is inspired by woodblock, but more specifically, by the very recognizable woodblock characters that Xu Bing created in his earlier canonical piece *Book of the Sky*. In the original *English Square*

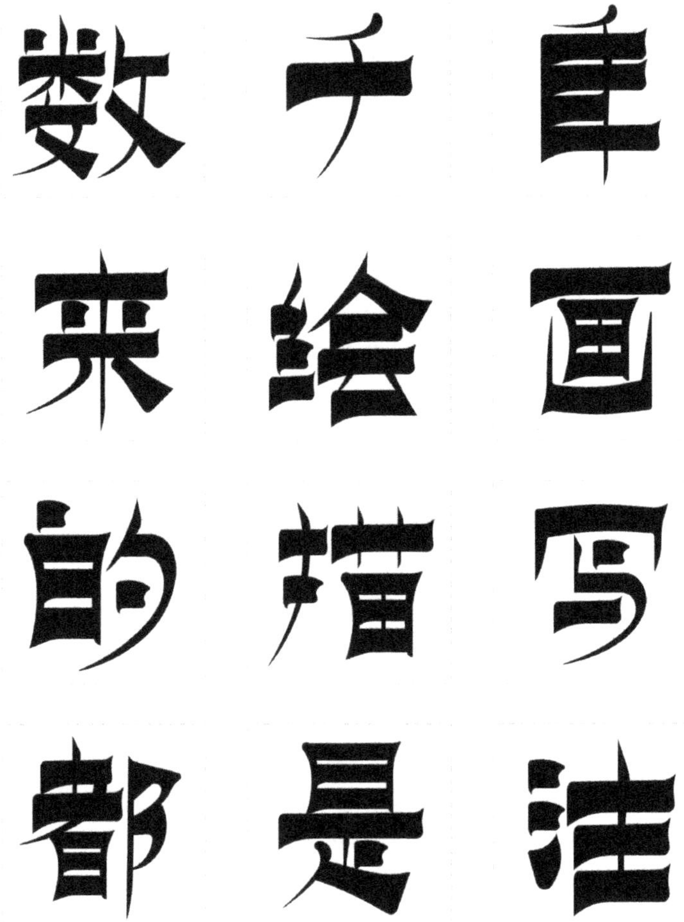

Figure 5.7: The font design by Zhu Rineng. https://ztds.foundertype.com/?c=HuoJiang

Word Calligraphy, Xu Bing developed a system for writing English in the shape of Chinese characters by organizing the letters of each English word into a character-shaped structure. For this font, Xu Bing employs the same strategy, but instead of the English language, he uses Pinyin. To be able to write the font, the user enters a Chinese word in Pinyin, which generates a list of possible characters. After selecting the desired character, the character would then

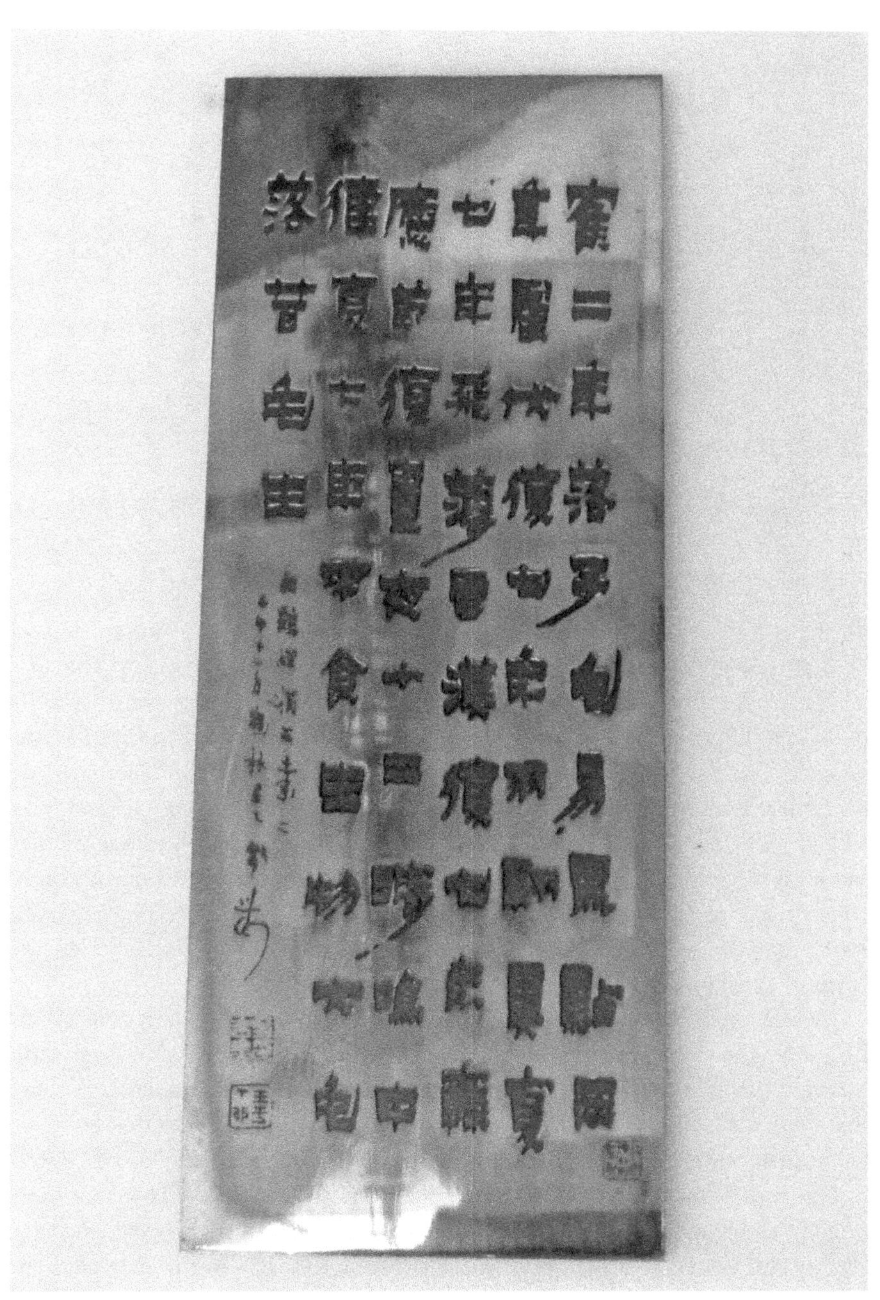

Figure 5.8: Paper-weight decorated with the calligraphy of Jin Nong.

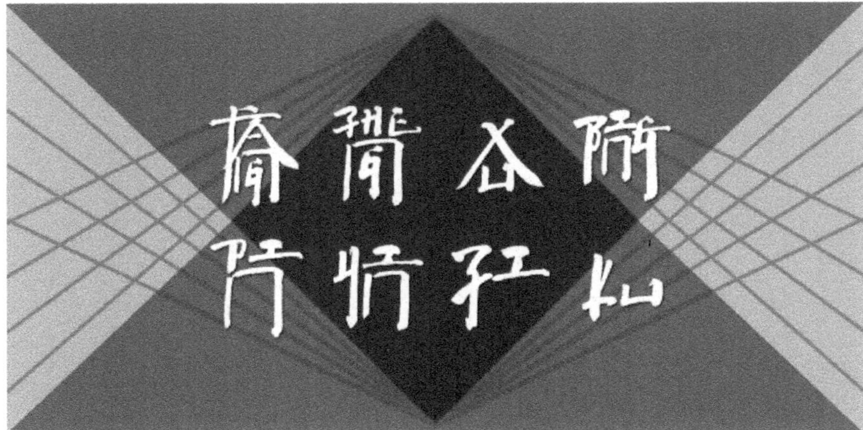

Figure 5.9: Font designed by Xu Bing, developed by FounderType. © FounderType.

normally appear on the screen in the font of choice. Xu Bing's font appears to be a structure of strokes instead, resembling Chinese woodblock characters. These strokes make up Latin letters, which spell out the Chinese word according to the Pinyin transcription method, as seen in Figure 5.9. Xu Bing, as has become a trait of his, plays with different layers of linguistic confusion and expectations with this font, creating a cognitive dissonance: visually it resembles a Chinese woodblock character, but the digital font is neither a Chinese character nor is it really English—it is Pinyin. The website of developer FounderType, where the font is listed with other creative fonts (创意书写 *chuangyi shuxie*), states that the font is useful "for art institutions and propaganda design for cultural exchange."[41] The font is also found on T-shirts.

Contemporary artist Feng Mengbo is also in the process of designing a font. Feng Mengbo creates his font not completely by hand, but is aided by a software program that is able to generate a font bank after the modeling of a few characters that Feng made on the computer—Feng disclosed in our interview that he is not a font designer, but is just interested in the project as an artist. The font displayed in Figure 5.10 looks playful and dynamic. None of the strokes have kept their original calligraphic features, and the lines are blotched as if the characters are leaking ink from out of their original shapes. Empty spaces in the characters are filled up with black ink, which makes the characters difficult to read. Again, the font does not immediately link visually to anything particularly traditional. Yet, Feng Mengbo also explains that he became creatively inspired by old-style Chinese

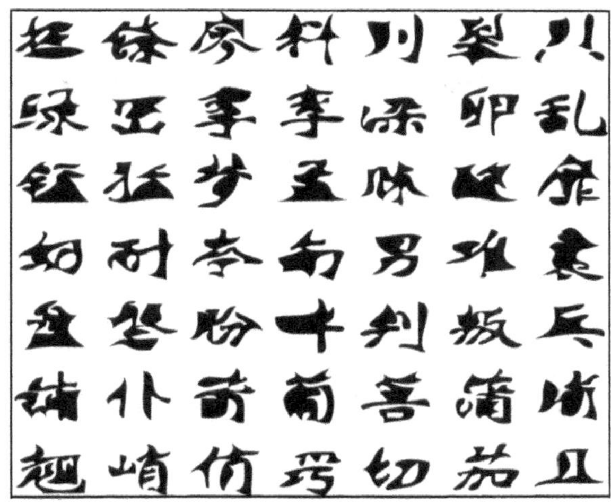

Figure 5.10: Font designed by Feng Mengbo. Courtesy of Feng Mengbo © Feng Mengbo.

writing methods: the lower quality rubbings of ancient steles inspired the blotched shapes of his digital characters. Rubbings made from eroded or damaged steles show white marks where the stone or inscription had been before, often rendering the characters illegible. In calligraphic jargon, these are called stone flowers (石花 *shihua*). Instead of choosing a perfect model from the past, Feng Mengbo chose to revive these stone flowers, normally seen as a damaged—or, according to Wu Hung, as a rubbing of ruins[42]—to preserve in an artistic digital remediation.

While the font designer is limited by demands for uniformity, legibility and salability of the font bank, their margin to be creative is fully utilized in a search for creative models from the past. In the next section, I introduce a few typographic designs that are published on ZCOOL, a popular interactive platform for Chinese designers. The website provides a platform for a creative community of designers, to display and sell their designs—ranging from font design to photography as well as offering opportunities to learn design at home.

Typographic Design

> When you look at it from traditional people's point of view, characters are not really meant for playing, like I am doing, right? It is just that according to us, younger people, we are just a small community playing around, it's fine, we are relaxed!
>
> —Interview with Lin Du

Lin Du, a young creative worker from Beijing, previously held a stable job as a web designer, but felt constrained in realizing his creative potential. He started making creative character designs after work, and published them on designer platforms such as ZCOOL.[43] Receiving positive feedback and managing to sell one of his designs through the platform encouraged him to quit his job and work freelance as a commercial font designer. His success not only motivated him to work harder and believe in himself, but it inspired him to start learning hand-written calligraphy, because, according to Lin Du, calligraphic designs are highly in demand right now. Moreover, he feels that working with calligraphy in his design is a way to put his emotions into his work. On his personal ZCOOL page, Lin published a tutorial on how to write calligraphy, stressing the importance of studying and copying the works of Liu Gongquan, Yan Zhenqing, Wang Xizhi and other traditional model calligraphers. Yet, in our interview, he is hesitant to use the word "calligraphy" to describe what he does:

> Actually, I don't dare to say it is calligraphy. Because calligraphy has such an important place in Chinese traditional culture, and has evolved over so many years. If I would say to you that I make calligraphy, it would be like I am just switching to a job I am not trained for. And I have only been writing for two years, I have no foundation. Moreover, when I am writing, I don't want to be constrained by these traditional shapes. For me, I would like to make a bit more innovative stuff.
>
> —Interview with Lin Du

Lin's account relies heavily on the narrative of self-realization and self-determination—those opportunities that the creative industries are assumed to offer.[44] Online platforms such as ZCOOL enable such a discourse, by simultaneously guiding and fostering creative workers' aspirations. Founded in 2006, ZCOOL has over 6.5 million users, and 20,000 original works are published daily in the fields of design, photography and illustration. It is both a visual content provider, as the designs are saleable, as well as an educational platform—ZCOOL offers training courses and job matching services. As such, it serves as a potent research site. First, the designs uploaded on this platform are often aspiring toward recognition from the market and can therefore give an indication of what is being made, for what intended audience. Second, the platform also operates as a place to practice, experiment and learn from each other and to exchange ideas. We find a vast range of designs, and specifically for this chapter, typographic designs for food packaging, music, movies and the like.

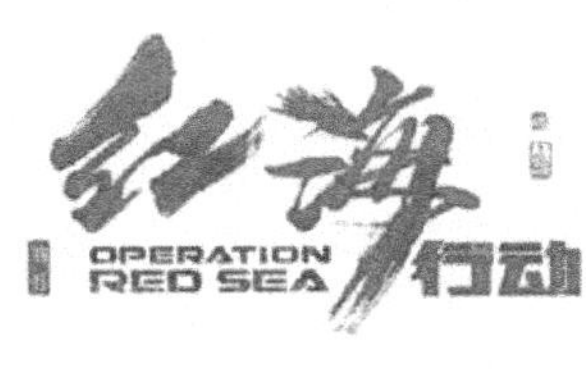

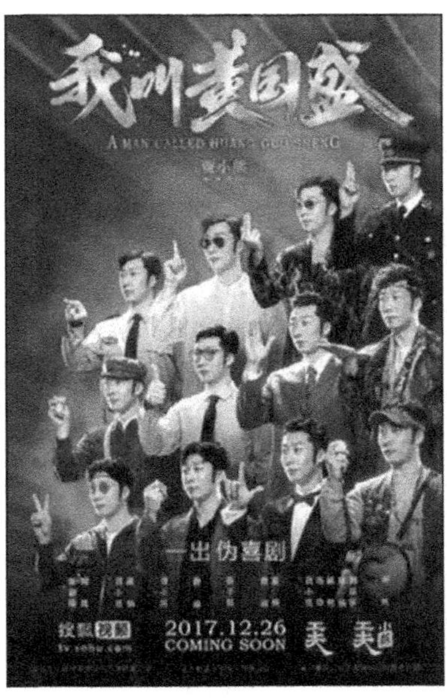

Figure 5.11: Two designs made by Di Sheng. Courtesy of Di Sheng © Di Sheng. Retrieved from ZCOOL.cn

A final example here are two creative font designs made by young designer Di Sheng specifically for movie posters (电影海报 *dianying haibao*), published on ZCOOL in 2018 (Figure 5.11). The blockbuster war movie *Operation Red Sea* (红海行动 *Honghai Xingdong*) by Dante Lam premiered in 2018, and is already the second highest grossing film ever made in China. The film was presented to the audience as a gift for the 90th anniversary of the founding of the Chinese People's Liberation Army—the army provided real weapons and other equipment. Jia Xiaoxiong's satirical comedy series *A Man Called Huang Guosheng* (我叫黄国盛 *Wo jiao Huang Guosheng*) was launched by Sohu Video in 2017. What both productions have in common is that Di Sheng, a young designer from Beijing who publishes his work on ZCOOL, created the design for their advertisements.

The calligraphic inspiration is immediately apparent in both works, as is the contrast with font bank design: the characters are not uniform, stylized or easily legible. In bold red and gold, the characters depart from black ink calligraphy, but remain traditional in color—gold and red are two colors readily associated with traditional Chineseness. The strokes deviate further from calligraphic standards: the shapes are very cursive and unorthodox, and the designer plays with the width of the strokes, rendering the characters out of balance. In both posters, there are many white stripes discernible within the body of the strokes—the previously mentioned flying white (飞白 *feibai*) that hints at a passionate and speedy wielding of a dryish brush. Flying white is also used to bring a variety of texture and multidimensionality into the calligraphy. *Operation Red Sea* is a patriotic army film: the red and gold calligraphy conveys an easily readable nationalistic message. The calligraphic design for *A Man Called Huang Guosheng* is less obviously linked to its content, but as a satirical series that critically takes up issues of societal abuse, the bold calligraphic design could well serve here as a tactic of irony.

The aesthetics of the two designs illustrate a growing trend. An overriding number of movie posters currently feature calligraphic main titles that share these commonalities (for example, *Anaconda Mountain* (蟒山 *mang shan*, 2022), *Action for Heaven* (天堂行动 *Tiantang Xindong*, 2022) or Zhang Yimou's *Sniper* (狙击手 *jujishou*, 2022).) The characters look convincingly calligraphic and hand-drawn: thick, bold, deliberately unbalanced and uneven characters, with flying white appearing in at least one stroke per character. But these characters are, from a calligraphic point of view, not necessarily very skillfully made. They rather aim to match the visual effect that the poster hopes to ignite in the viewer: exciting, surprising, bold and a movie worth watching.

These designs, my interviewees disclose, are first written by hand with ink and brush, then scanned and further modified with editing software. Many tutorials on how to create similar designs circulate on ZCOOL, as can be seen in Figure 5.12 made by car advertising designer Liang Dingli. His tagline on the platform is "Let calligraphy meet life" (让书法遇见生活 *rang shufa yujian shenghuo*). With his designs he aims to "innovate traditional calligraphy and carry forward national culture," and his simple motto is: handwriting–scanning–retouching (手写–扫描–修图 *shouxie–saomiao–xiutu*).[45] His tutorials show a piece of rice paper with his brushed calligraphy, and next to it, the remediated version embedded in a photographic design.

Although these types of designs are obviously inspired by calligraphy, they are not recognizable copies of earlier, well-known models. It is important for my argument here that they do not claim any descendancy from a calligraphic model. Therefore, these designs do not align with a specific historical period but instead establish their own style and brushwork. Consequently, I contend that these designs are expansive yet specific enough to evoke a vague yet recognizable sense of "Chineseness," appealing to a broad audience today. Wide-ranging, because this idea of Chineseness is not rooted in any specific historical timeframe but, as Boym noted, "explores ways of inhabiting many places at

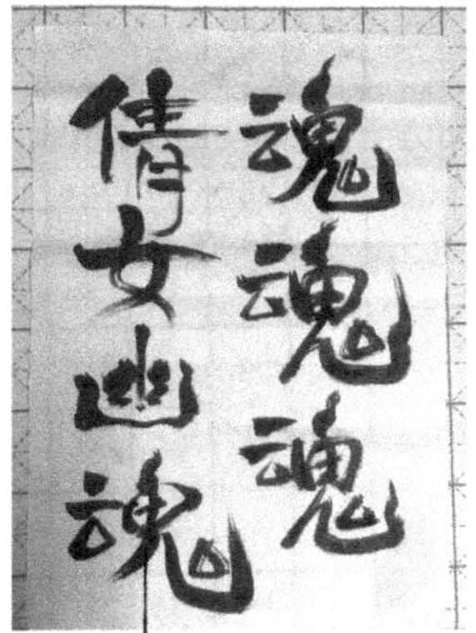

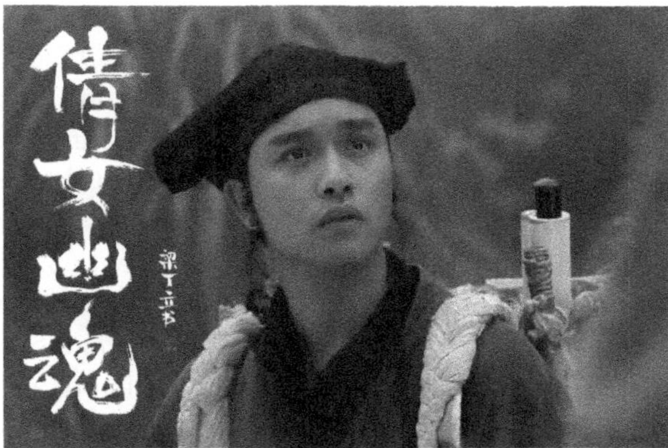

Figure 5.12: Two excerpts of a tutorial for calligraphic movie poster design by Liang Dingli. Courtesy of Liang Dingli © Liang Dingli. Retrieved from ZCOOL.cn

once and imagining different time zones."[46] They can therefore easily be employed for commercial purposes, since, as Wu Jing argues, "Commercial media are much less orthodox and more open-minded than political-oriented media, in that in an effort to churn out low-cost, stable, familiar and marketable cultural goods, the past is fully explored and exploited."[47] A notable feature of these works is that commercial font designers do not need to be skilled in calligraphy to create and sell these in-demand calligraphic designs. The designers I spoke to in this field, like Lin Du, are even hesitant to call their works calligraphy. They rather refer to it as simply "handwritten" (手写 *shouxie*), a term that can refer to any type of writing done by hand, circumventing the intricate value assessments of calligraphy. However, from the many calligraphy tutorials, templates and designs circulating on ZCOOL, we can conclude that ink and brush calligraphy remains the foundational framework for commercial font designers as well, always lurking in the background, as a promise: improve your calligraphic skill, and your design will benefit—and you will have more commercial success.[48]

Calligraphy in this discourse has become a timeless marker of Chineseness. The careful choosing of upright models, precision in following their aesthetics or worries about the calligraphic or painterly line are not that much of a concern here. We have seen how and why calligraphic qualities are mobilized, revisited and appropriated in Chinese type font design, and what is taken from the calligraphic sign to be remediated in the digital font: what (dis)continuities allow for innovation. Walter Benjamin has contended that "'Construction' presupposes 'destruction'."[49] Through a critique of the idea that the past can be reconstructed, Benjamin stresses the importance of the present as, simultaneously, a condition for legibility and a transformation of that same past. Things have to be moved, ripped apart and disintegrated first to allow for new creation. In the case of "character making" in the broad sense, techno-linguistic innovations have moved handwritten calligraphy to the carved woodblock, the typewriter, and finally the digital screen, but none of this has led to a complete erasure of its predecessor. Brokaw and Chow noted, for example, that for reasons of nostalgia, "woodblock publishers outnumbered publishers of lithographic and lead-type texts through the Revolution of 1911, despite the fact that the machinery of the new technology had been introduced to the city in the 1890s,"[50] showing that the idea of chronological innovation is untenable.

The most significant disruption throughout this timeline of innovations lies in the way in which the digital has managed to separate input from output, and the visual representation of the Chinese character is now based on a shared technological agreement, contingent upon the skill and creativity of the designer as well as market and governmental demands. Instead of leading to an erasure of these earlier methods, as we have seen, the opposite has happened: we see that the hallmarks of older writing methods increasingly reappear in the output now that the field of font design is maturing. These reappearances are creative negotiations, in which the designer can choose from a wide range of historical materials: the rubbings of eroded stone steles, square shapes of woodblocks, eccentric Qing dynasty calligraphers and the handwriting of Chinese historical figures. Visual hallmarks associated with previous writing methods have thus not only become more visible, but creative interpretations of these signs have allowed the more obscure and unknown a place in the present.

These tactics are reminiscent of the idea put forward by Arjun Appadurai, who has argued that today there is a role for the imagination in social life. Imagination steps in to construct how the past is experienced, and how that past is employed in the present: "The past is now not a land to return to in a simple politics of memory. It has become a synchronic warehouse of cultural scenarios, a kind of temporal central casting, to which recourse can be taken as appropriate, depending on the movie to be made, the scene to be enacted, the hostages to be rescued."[51] The calligraphic past becomes, as Appadurai frames it aptly, a warehouse of possibilities to choose from. In this case, innovation or inspiration means returning to an imagined creative Chinese past, now easily accessible due to technological affordances. I approached this imagining as a specific articulation of Chineseness that ties in with the Party's directive to grow national cultural self-confidence. The organizer of the "Everyone is an expert in creativity" workshop mentioned that "The project will carry forward the tradition of China's excellent culture. We will strengthen our national cultural self-confidence, and at the same time, we can share the newest contemporary innovation stories with society."[52] This almost verbatim reiteration of Xi Jinping's speech, in which he encourages a cultural rejuvenation through innovation based on the Chinese past, shows how the government succeeds in arranging things in such a way that it guides and directs creative workers to act toward the objectives of the state. Not only those working at national museums or SOCEs such as FounderType, but also young designers who internalize the same values and governmental objectives: they observe a growing trend for calligraphic design, and adjust their creative output accordingly, because it sells.

The designers that I have followed throughout this chapter construct and employ a creative Chinese past which serves them as a warehouse of inspiration and feel a sense of responsibility to carry elements of it forward. It is significant that this inspiration is not always obviously translated, as the "Rubber Stamp Square Characters" designs of Lan Zezhen illustrate. It seems that the mere mentioning of inspiration of previous methods suffices. This lack of precision is evident in the calligraphic designs of movie posters, which convey a non-specific, perhaps even "neutral," but unmistakably recognizable calligraphic feel. Creative design does not clash with the strict calligraphic mold, but does quite the opposite. What is creative, as I have shown, is to use calligraphy; it is not to be daring, illegible or avant-garde. The designers refer to calligraphy as their main source of inspiration, and font designers working at SOCEs, contemporary artists and freelance designers alike now create calligraphic designs. The dream of a creative past envisioned in the calligraphic heritage is a productive fantasy, as it is supported and actively promoted by the state, sought after by the market and thus produced by (freelance) designers, and promoting the idea of a common creative, Chinese heritage that should be unearthed by the creatives of today.

Coda

On one of my last visits to the calligraphy school of my friend Ranran, she tells me that she is invited to the Republic of Kazakhstan next summer, to give private calligraphy lessons to an aristocrat there. "It is so exciting," she says enthusiastically, "it is part of the Belt and Road Initiative, now we will be able to show Chinese calligraphy to the world. This is just the beginning!" Just the beginning. Her optimistic tenor has become familiar to me, talking to calligraphers over the years, and captures much of the sentiments expressed through the different case studies analyzed in this book. She imagines a future for calligraphy that may shine just as bright as the calligraphic past, not knowing yet that the trip would be canceled due to COVID-19 travel restrictions, halting so much of the calligraphic activity, all activity, in China and abroad. Yet, all the efforts of rejuvenation, mobilization and creative remediation have rendered calligraphy to be imagined now as an exciting art form. So exciting that Ranran, with her brush and inkstone, hopes to cross national borders as a torchbearer of a perhaps not-so-slow art—the calling card of a confident nation.

In this book, I have analyzed five different modes of calligraphy in contemporary China. In the years spanning this research, a few central questions kept returning that, as it turned out, are not exclusively relevant for practices of calligraphy. Rather, on numerous occasions, calligraphy turned into a prism through which to understand contingent notions of creativity, the role of everyday practices in cultural politics, the processes of building cultural identity and subsequent governing strategies and tactics. The project that started out with the desire to understand what a historically deeply imbedded art form practiced in contemporary Chinese society can do to its practitioners today, became, much more than I anticipated, a route toward a broader understanding of contemporary Chinese society as a whole. In this book I have attempted to analyze calligraphy as an everyday social practice; one that might change in accordance with the values ascribed to it by individuals and society as a whole.

These values, as this book has shown, remain by and large similar within the various practices of calligraphy. Yet, the increase of interpretations of the calligraphic sign demonstrates that its ascribed meaning is increasingly fluid and non-fixed, carrying several implications for calligraphy practice. In Chapter 2, I ascribed the inventive interpretation of calligraphy as an ephemeral water play in the park to a mode of making called "vernacular creativity." In Chapter 3, I developed how Zeng Xiang and Wang Dongling create from the desire to "serve modernity," and in the final two chapters, I argued that new practices of calligraphy are necessarily built on older practices: remediations. All these interventions might be understood as stemming from the same core—this core is a mode of working, thinking and creating that is deeply informed by earlier practices, and then consciously ventures beyond into something new.

This book has included a wide range of calligraphic practices in contemporary China, but has left many more out. I have not dwelled on hard-pen calligraphy (硬笔书法 *yingbi shufa*); on socially engaged art projects concerning calligraphy; on calligraphy TV shows and contests; on the way Confucius Institutes promote calligraphy outside of China; or on the calligraphies of the Uyghur, Tibetan or other ethnic minorities in China; or a comparative analysis between Chinese and Arabic or Japanese calligraphy, to name just a few directions. All these would open up a whole new range of questions. There is always more, and I am convinced there will be even more yet in the future, since calligraphy has revealed itself as a remarkably dynamic art form—constantly negotiated and negotiating, contingent and mobilized by a wide variety of actors for an even wider array of reasons. In this final section of the conclusion, I look back and take cues from all my case studies, suggesting two directions that scholarship on calligraphic practices in contemporary China could take in the future, summarizing them under the headings of Chineseness and creativity. These two themes have been consistently present throughout all the case studies and warrant a more in-depth examination.

Chineseness

This study has explored a range of different ways in which a nation cherishes and cultivates an art form that is so deeply understood as quintessentially theirs. Theirs now increasingly applies to all Chinese people, as it has become a quotidian practice for everyone—both voluntarily and involuntarily—to participate in. I have suggested in the Introduction, and in Chapters 1, 4 and 5, that a search, or a reclaiming of a national identity and Chineseness, underpins the practice of calligraphy in education, online community shaping and font design. This has proven such a resourceful discourse that it is mobilized by government structures, pointing at calligraphy as an expression of love for the motherland and an embodied participation in a strong and culturally confident China, relating directly to the rise of Chinese nationalism. Future research would do well to unpack this further, in particular to read the more mundane, intimate and daily practices of calligraphy as everyday routines that perpetuate nationalism. Michael Billig argues famously that "the world of nations is the everyday world, the familiar terrain of contemporary times."[1] Performing everyday national acts, Billig argues, and making them routines rather than performing grand sacral displays of national ceremony, is more effective with regards to constructing a sense of nation. Where Billig mainly mentions official national symbols, such as raising flags or singing anthems, I think that the wide variety of everyday calligraphies as I have sketched them in this book may well work similarly. This conclusion has relevance beyond the geopolitical setting of China—it might help toward a better understanding of the various and contingent ways in which nationalism is constructed or deconstructed through mundane and everyday artistic practices in diverse international contexts.

A study on these modes of nationalism could further propel research that takes on a more comparative approach between Chinese calligraphy and other types of contemporary calligraphies such as those practices within Tibetan, Uyghur or Arabic contexts. This could question the alleged essential Chineseness of this practice, and the naturalness with which Chinese writing and Chineseness are associated. One might find out that practices of beautiful writing are always associated with the culture, or nation, in which this writing is embedded.

Creativity

A considerable part of this book has dealt with the thorny question of creativity—I have attempted to let the various notions of creativity develop in each case study, showing how creativity is not a fully developed concept, but is contingent and transforms constantly through the changing practices of contemporary calligraphy. I suggested in the Introduction that the way to value creativity in traditional calligraphy discourse is by assessing how a calligrapher enters the spirit of a former model (入神 *rushen*) with the aim to achieve a likeness in essence. When this happens, a moment of inspired creativity occurs. This complex interplay between creativity and imitation now lives side by side with an increasing number of interpretations of calligraphy practice, all of which might well change again according to the needs of society in the future—I hasten to add here that transformation or change does not equate progress. In Chapter 2, I suggested that the creativity displayed in water calligraphy is temporal and located in the adaptations and rearrangements of pre-existing ideas and, as such, is not based on novelty. In doing so, practioneers disregard the imperative of the new that is believed to be necessary for "real" creativity, and might help us, I proposed, to further rethink the idea of creativity itself as more organically developed, convivial, healthy, less productive, ephemeral and, perhaps, more *fun*, as water calligraphers insistently refer to their practice. As Scott[2] has argued, "any push to achieve urban creativity in the absence of a wider concern for conviviality and camaraderie (which need to be distinguished from the mechanical conception of 'diversity') in the urban community as a whole is doomed to remain radically unfinished."

The subsequent chapters further show creativity as necessity—as an opportunity that calligraphy should embrace in order to remain significant and relatable, while the social and networked creative practices that exist in relation to the fast-changing affordances of digital media offer yet another typology of creativity. All these sites reveal that in the collision of tradition and contemporaneity, tradition reveals its dynamism, while the contemporary situation of China today discloses an overwhelming willingness to rehabilitate it. In the Introduction, I posed how calligraphy is often juxtaposed with claims of creativity, serving as the prime example of the well-known trope of the Chinese tradition of copying, finding its origins in calligraphy, as opposed to a creative tradition based on newness in the west. This book is one of the attempts to start breaking down these alleged dichotomies, and can be taken as exploratory research that, I suggest, should be used as a springboard for a deeper discussion and analysis of the many forms of valuing creativity, and, by extension, the notion of creativity itself. Again, this bears cross-cultural significance. Creativity is globally and increasingly framed as manageable, and used for wealth creation in the context of the creative industries. Within that context, as Dany Jacobs has argued, we are increasingly dealing with a "more disciplined form of creativity with professionalism and purpose."[3] Here, I argue, the practice of calligraphy might serve as a potent research site with regards to disciplined creativity. I close with innovative expert Jeffrey Baumgarter, who offers advice on creative thinking: "If you're stuck for an idea, open a dictionary, randomly select a word and then try to formulate ideas incorporating this word. You'd be surprised how well this works. The concept is based on a simple but little-known truth: freedom inhibits creativity. There are nothing like restrictions to get you thinking."[4] If freedom inhibits creativity, and discipline thus might generate it, then those in this dissertation who are—knowing and unknowingly—creative within the confines of predetermined brushstrokes might well serve as the answer, one of the answers, on how to value creativity.

Notes

Preface

1. Yuehping Yen, *Calligraphy and Power in Contemporary Chinese Society*. New York and London: Routledge Curzon, 2004.
2. Lily Chumley, *Creativity Class: Art School and Culture Work in Postsocialist China* (Princeton, NJ: Princeton University Press, 2016), p. xi.

Introduction

1. Amy McNair, "Engraved Calligraphy in China: Recension and Reception," *Art Bulletin* 160 (1) (1995): 106–14.
2. Yiu Fai Chow and Jeroen de Kloet, "The Spectre of Europe: Knowledge, Cultural Studies and the 'Rise of Asia'," *European Journal of Cultural Studies* 17 (1) (2014): 3–15.
3. Meaghan Morris, "Banality in Cultural Studies," in *Logics of Television: Essays in Cultural Criticism*, ed. Patricia Mellencamp (Bloomington and Indianapolis: Indiana University Press, 1990), pp. 14–43.
4. Even an extensive mentioning of important works on calligraphy in the Chinese language would not do justice to the sheer volume of Chinese encyclopedia entries, commentaries, anthologies, reference works, volumes, magazines and articles written on calligraphy throughout the centuries. The largest and most complete collection of books covering the most important texts from the Zhou to the Qing dynasty is the "Complete Library in Four Sections" (四库全书 *sikuquanshu*) that includes the subcategory "Books on Art" (艺术类 *yishulei*) containing 71 books on painting and calligraphy. In this subcategory, theoretical discussions on the art of calligraphy, biographical information and aesthetic discussions on calligraphy can be found. For a complete contemporary overview of traditional calligraphic script types throughout history two works are most comprehensive and often used: "Collection of Chinese Calligraphy" (中国书法全集 *Zhongguo shufa quanji*) (100 volumes) by Zhengcheng Liu 1991; and "Complete Works of Calligraphy" (*Shodō zenshū*) (26 volumes and 2 suppl. volumes) by Shimonaka 1973 [1954–68].

5. See for example, Chiang Yee, *Chinese Calligraphy: An Introduction to Its Aesthetic and Technique* (Cambridge, MA: Harvard University Press, 1974); Lothar Ledderose, *Mi Fu and the Classical Tradition of Chinese Calligraphy* (Princeton, NJ: Princeton University Press, 1979); Marilyn W. Fu and Shen C.Y. Fu, *Traces of the Brush: Studies in Chinese Calligraphy* (New Haven, CT: Yale University Press, 1980); John Hay, "The Human Body as a Microcosmic Source of Macrocosmic Values in Calligraphy," in *Theories of the Arts in China*, ed. Susan Bush and Christian Murck (Princeton, NJ: Princeton University Press, 1983); Yujiro Nakata, *The Art of Japanese Calligraphy* (New York: Weatherhill, 1983); Alfreda Murck and Wen C. Fong, *Words and Images: Chinese Poetry, Calligraphy, and Painting* (New York: Metropolitan Museum of Art, 1991); Wen C. Fong, *Beyond Representation: Chinese Painting and Calligraphy, 8th–14th Century* (New York and New Haven, CT: Metropolitan Museum of Art; Yale University Press, 1992); Craig Clunas, *Art in China* (Oxford: Oxford University Press, 1997); Amy McNair, *The Upright Brush: Yan Zhenqing's Calligraphy and Song Literati Politics* (Honolulu: University of Hawaii Press, 1998); Dora C.Y. Ching, "The Aesthetics of the Unusual and the Strange in Seventeenth-Century Calligraphy," in *The Embodied Image: Chinese Calligraphy from the John B. Elliott Collection*, ed. Robert E. Harrist Jr and Wen C. Fong (Princeton, NJ: The Art Museum, Princeton University Press, 1999); Harrist, Robert E., Jr and Wen C. Fong, *The Embodied Image: Chinese Calligraphy from the John B. Elliott Collection* (Princeton, NJ: The Art Museum, Princeton University, 1999); Liu, Cary Y., Dora C.Y. Ching and Judith G. Smith, *Character & Context in Chinese Calligraphy* (Princeton, NJ: Art Museum, Princeton University, 1999); Gordon Barrass, *The Art of Calligraphy in Modern China* (Berkeley: University of California Press, 2002); Zhongshi Ouyang and Wen C. Fong, *Chinese Calligraphy* (New Haven, CT: Yale University Press, 2008); Antje Richter, *Letters and Epistolary Culture in Early Medieval China* (Seattle: University of Washington Press, 2015).
6. Xu Shen. 1963. *Shuowen jiezi*. ed. Xu Xuan (Beijing: Zhonghua Shuju).
7. Ming Dong Gu, "Patterns of Tao (Dao): The Birth of Chinese Writing and Aesthetics," *The Journal of Aesthetics and Art Criticism* 74 (2) (2016): 151–63; Krzysztof Gawlikowski, "The Concept of Two Fundamental Social Principles: Wen and Wu in Chinese Classical Thought," *Annali* 47 (1989): 397–433; Angela Zito and Tani E. Barlow, *Body, Subject & Power in China* (Chicago, IL: The University of Chicago Press, 1994).
8. William Boltz, *The Origin and Early Development of the Chinese Writing System* (New Haven, CT: American Oriental Society, 1994), p. 31.
9. John DeFrancis, *The Chinese Language: Fact and Fantasy* (Honolulu: University of Hawaii Press, 1986), p. 133.
10. Clunas, *Art in China*; Shao-Lan Hertel, "The Inner Workings of Brush-and-Ink: A Study on Huang Binhong (1865–1955) as Calligrapher, with Special Respect to the Concept of Interior Beauty (Neimei)," PhD diss., Freie Universität Berlin, 2017.

11. Robert E. Harrist, Jr, "Copies, All the Way Down: Notes on the Early Transmission of Calligraphy by Wang Xizhi," *The East Asian Library Journal* 10 (1) (2001): 176–96.
12. Wang Xizhi too regarded this piece the best work of calligraphy he had ever written. Already in Wang's lifetime, scribes, officials and students began to copy his work, a practice that continues all the way from the Eastern-Jin through the Six Dynasties periods, and then reaching its peak during the reign of Emperor Taizong (r. 627–649) of the Tang dynasty. Emperor Taizong deeply admired the work of Wang Xizhi, and subsidized the production of numerous copies of his pieces. Upon seeing a copy of the *Orchid Pavilion*, Emperor Taizong decided he had to have the original, and he summoned search parties to find the authentic piece. Hunting for it all over the country, the manuscript was finally stolen from Buddhist monk Biancai, and came into the possession of the emperor. The emperor then treasured it to the extent that when he died, he had it buried with him in his tomb, leaving the original forever lost (Harrist, "Copies, All the Way Down"; Yuehping Yen, *Calligraphy and Power in Contemporary Chinese Society* (New York and London: Routledge Curzon, 2004)).
13. I start with characters on paper, but it should be noted that bamboo slips were widely used before the invention of paper as carriers of characters. Bamboo slips date back to the Shang dynasty (17th century BCE) and were in use at least until the Jin dynasty (300 CE). Tsien and Needham (1985: 146) further argue that stencils were made as early as the second century BCE, animal skin or thin silk fabric treated with varnish or some other tree sap have been used at this time.
14. Cynthia Brokaw and Kai-Wing Chow, eds, *Printing and Book Culture in Late Imperial China* (Berkeley: University of California Press, 2005).
15. Andreas Reckwitz, *The Invention of Creativity: Modern Society and the Culture of the New* (Cambridge and Malden: Polity Press, 2017), p. 1.
16. David Hesmondhalgh and Sarah Baker, *Creative Labour Media Work in Three Cultural Industries* (London: Routledge, 2011), p. 2.
17. Xin Gu and Justin O'Connor, "A New Modernity? The Arrival of 'Creative Industries' in China," *International Journal of Cultural Studies* 9 (2006): 271–83; Michael Keane, "From Made in China to Created in China," *International Journal of Cultural Studies* 9 (2006): 285–96; Michael Keane and Ying Chen, "Entrepreneurial Solutionism, Characteristic Cultural Industries and the Chinese Dream," *International Journal of Cultural Policy* (2017): 1–13.
18. Keane, "From Made in China," pp. 285–96; David Craig, Jian Lin and Stuart Cunningham, *Wanghong as Social Media Entertainment in China* (London, UK: Palgrave Macmillan, 2021).
19. Harrist, "Copies, All the Way Down," p. 178.
20. David Bolter and Richard Grusin, *Remediation: Understanding New Media* (Cambridge, MA: The MIT Press, 2000).

Chapter 1

1. Sébastien Billioud and Joël Thoraval, *The Sage and the People: The Confucian Revival in China* (Oxford: Oxford University Press, 2015).
2. Janette Ryan, *Education in China* (Cambridge: Polity Press, 2019).
3. Ministry of Education (henceforth, MOE), "MOE Calls for High Quality Education at 2022 National Education Conference," 2022. http://en.moe.gov.cn/news/press_releases/202201/t20220124_596108.html [accessed 21 January 2022].
4. Andrew Kipnis, *Governing Educational Desire: Culture, Politics, and Schooling in China* (Chicago, IL: University of Chicago Press, 2011), p. 7.
5. Suzanne Pepper, *Radicalism and Education Reform in 20th Century China: The Search for an Ideal Development Model* (Cambridge: Cambridge University Press, 1996); Ryan, *Education in China*.
6. Ibid.
7. Kipnis, *Governing Educational Desire*; Ruyu Hung, *Education Between Speech and Writing: Crossing the Boundaries of Dao and Deconstruction* (London: Routledge, 2017); Tongdong Bai, "Against Democratic Education," *Journal of Curriculum Studies* 43 (5) (2011): 615–22.
8. Pepper, *Radicalism and Education Reform in 20th Century China*, p. 57.
9. Ibid., p. 84.
10. Richard Curt Kraus, *Brushes with Power: Modern Politics and the Chinese Art of Calligraphy* (Berkeley: University of California Press, 1991).
11. Ibid., p. 63.
12. Dongping Han, *The Unknown Cultural Revolution: Educational Reforms and Their Impact on China's Rural Development, 1966–1976* (New York: Routledge, 2000).
13. Orville Schell, *Mandate of Heaven: The Legacy of Tiananmen Square and the Next Generation of China's Leaders* (New York: Simon and Schuster, 1995), p. 354.
14. Ruth Hayhoe, *China's Universities, 1895–1995: A Century of Cultural Conflict* (New York: Routledge, 1996).
15. Sohu, "*Nian Shufa Gaokao, ni suo guanzhu de dou zai zheli* 年书法高考，你所关注的都在这里 [Everything You Want to Know About This Years' Calligraphy *Gaokao* Is Here]," 2022. www.sohu.com/a/405224242_584699 [accessed July 2, 2024].
16. MOE, "*Jiaoyu bu guanyu yinfa 'zhongxiaoxue shufa jiaoyu zhidao gangyao' de tongzhi* 教育部关于印发《中小学书法教育指导纲要》的通知 [Ministry of Education on the Issuance of Primary and Secondary School Calligraphy Education Guideline]," 2013. www.moe.gov.cn/srcsite/A26/s8001/201301/t20130125_147389.html [accessed August 2, 2020]; Mary Wiseman Bittner and Yuedi Liu, eds. *Subversive Strategies in Contemporary Chinese Art* (Leiden, Boston: Brill, 2011), p. xxiv.
17. MOE, "*Jiaoyu bu dui shisan jie quanguo renmin dashi yici huiyi di 7496 hao jianyi de dapufu* 教育部对十三届全国人大一次会议第 7496 号建议的答复 [Ministry of Education's Meeting of the 13th National People's Congress Reply to Recommendation No. 7496]," 2018. www.moe.gov.cn/jyb_xxgk/xxgk_jyta/jyta_jijiaosi/201812/t20181229_365452.html [accessed April 12, 2019].

18. MOE, "*Jiaoyu bu guanyu chengli jiaoyu bu zhongguo shufa jiaoyu zhidao weiyuanhui deng san ge jiaoyu zhidao weiyuanhui de tongzhi* 教育部关于成立教育部中国书法教育指导委员会等三个教育指导委员会的通知 [Notice of the Ministry of Education on the Establishment of Three Education Steering Committees Including the Chinese Calligraphy Education Steering Committee]," 2021. www.moe.gov.cn/srcsite/A17/s7059/202105/t20210514_531576.html [accessed August 2, 2022].
19. Ibid.
20. Jiemo Dui, "*Suzhi jiaoyu fengkou zhi shang, zhengce chengyao de 'shufa jiaoyu' jiang ying lai de baofa*? 素质教育风又之上，政策撑腰的'书法教育'将迎来大爆发? [Beyond the Promises of Carrico Quality Education, Carrico Will There Be an Explosion Of The Policy Supported Carrico Calligraphy Education Carrico?]" 2018. www.iyiou.com/p/70713 [accessed July 2, 2022]; Sohu, Carrico *Nian shufa gaokao, ni suo guanzhu de dou zai zheli*. Carrico
21. Chumley, *Creativity Class: Art School and Culture Work in Postsocialist China* (Princeton, NJ: Princeton University Press, 2016), p. 60.
22. 魏碑 *Weibei* refers to the clear and angular regular calligraphy style of stone inscriptions made in the Northern Wei dynasty (386–534). The inscriptions on stone were carved by craftsmen rather than calligraphers. They were seen as the opposite of the flowing elegant style represented by Wang Xizhi. During the Qing dynasty, groups of literati led by Kang Youwei, as discussed in the Introduction, started to rediscover and appreciate the stone inscriptions of the Wei dynasty. They believed that the stone inscriptions showed what calligraphy should look like: honest, unadorned and fresh (see also Chapter 3).
23. Michel Foucault, *Discipline and Punish: The Birth of the Prison* (New York: Vintage Books, 1975), p. 170.
24. Mu Qian, *Guoxue Gailun* 国学概论 [Discussion on National Learning] (Shanghai: Guji Chubanshe, 1998); Shaobo Xie, "Guoxue Re and the Ambiguity of Chinese Modernity," *China Perspectives* 1 (2011): 39–45.
25. Ibid., pp. 39–45.
26. Ibid., p. 45.
27. Chiang Yee, *Chinese Calligraphy: An Introduction to Its Aesthetic and Technique* (Cambridge, MA: Harvard University Press, 1974), p. 107.
28. Francesca Bray, *Technology and Gender* (Berkeley: University of California Press, 1997), p. 371.
29. Yuehping Yen, *Calligraphy and Power in Contemporary Chinese Society* (New York and London: Routledge Curzon, 2004); Bray, *Technology and Gender*; Krzysztof Gawlikowski, "The Concept of Two Fundamental Social Principles: Wen and Wu in Chinese Classical Thought," *Annali* 47 (1989): 397–433; Angela Zito and Tani E. Barlow, *Body, Subject & Power in China* (Chicago, IL: The University of Chicago Press, 1994); Ming Dong Gu, "Patterns of Tao (Dao): The Birth of Chinese Writing and Aesthetics," *The Journal of Aesthetics and Art Criticism* 74 (2) (2016): 151–63.
30. Yen, *Calligraphy and Power*, p. 84.

31. Eric Hobsbawm and Terence Ranger, *The Invention of Tradition* (Cambridge: Cambridge University Press, 1983), p. 1.
32. Shufaedu.com. Hanxiang Shufa Jiaoyu 汉翔书法教育 [Hanxiang Calligraphy Education], n.d. www.shufaedu.com/ [accessed April 11, 2022].
33. Svetlana Boym, *The Future of Nostalgia* (New York: Basic Books, 2001), p. 34.
34. Ibid., p. 31.
35. Ya-hwei Hsu, *Reshaping Chinese Material Culture: The Revival of Antiquity in the Era of Print, 960–1279* (New Haven, CT: Yale, 2010); Hung Wu, *Reinventing the Past: Archaism and Antiquarianism in Chinese Art and Visual Culture* (Chicago, IL: Art Media Resources, 2010).
36. Boym, *The Future of Nostalgia*, p. 33.
37. Jeroen de Kloet and Anthony Fung, *Youth Cultures in China* (Malden, MA: Polity, 2017).
38. See, for example, Yee, *Chinese Calligraphy*; Alfreda Murck and Wen C. Fong, *Words and Images: Chinese Poetry, Calligraphy, and Painting* (New York: Metropolitan Museum of Art, 1991); Amy McNair, *The Upright Brush: Yan Zhenqing's Calligraphy and Song Literati Politics* (Honolulu: University of Hawaii Press, 1998); Michael Nylan, "Calligraphy, the Sacred Text and Test of Culture," in *Character and Context in Chinese Calligraphy* Liu, Cary Y.; Dora C.Y. Ching & Judith G. Smith (Eds.) (Princeton, NJ: The Art Museum, Princeton University Press, 1999), pp. 16–77; Wei-Ming Tu, *Humanity and Self-Cultivation: Essays in Confucian Thought* (Boston, MA: Cheng & Tsui, 1999); Yen, *Calligraphy and Power*; Antje Richter, *Letters and Epistolary Culture in Early Medieval China* (Seattle: University of Washington Press, 2015).
39. Xu Liu, 165.4310; 887–946 劉昫. *Jiu Tang Shu*. Beijing: Zhong Hua Shu Ju, 1975.
40. McNair, *The Upright Brush*, p. 6.
41. Lothar Ledderose, *Mi Fu and the Classical Tradition of Chinese Calligraphy* (Princeton, NJ: Princeton University Press, 1979), p. 29–30.
42. Amy McNair, "Looking at Chinese Calligraphy: The Anxiety of Anonymity and Calligraphy from the Periphery," in *Looking at Asian Art*, ed. Katherine R. Tsiang and Martin J. Powers (Chicago: University of Chicago, 2012), p. 54.
43. McNair, *The Upright Brush*.
44. Michel Foucault, *The Foucault Reader*, ed. Paul Rabinow (New York: Pantheon, 1984), p. 73.
45. Bray, *Technology and Gender*, p. 369.
46. Foucault, *Discipline and Punish*.
47. Susan Bush, *The Chinese Literati on Painting; Su Shih (1037–1101) to Tung Ch'i-Ch'ang (1555–1636)* (Cambridge, MA: Harvard University Press, 1971), p. 49.
48. Roland Barthes, "The Death of the Author," in *Image, Music, Text*, trans. Stephen Heath (New York: Hill and Wang, 1977), p. 146.
49. Hannah Arendt, "Introduction: Walter Benjamin 1892–1940," in *Walter Benjamin, Illuminations: Essays and Reflections* (New York: Schocken Books, 2007), p. 48.

50. Susan Bush and Hsio-Yen Shih, comps. and eds., *Early Chinese Texts on Painting* (Cambridge, MA.: Harvard University Press, 1985), p. 16.
51. Liang in Xiongbo Shi, "Zhang Yinlin: A Preface to Chinese Calligraphy Criticism (1931)," *Journal of Art Historiography* 13 (2015): 13–25.
52. Wendan Li, *Chinese Writing and Calligraphy* (Honolulu: University of Hawaii Press, 2010), p. 33. For an in-depth overview on brushstroke techniques and correct physical positions, see Yen, *Calligraphy and Power*, pp. 83–9.
53. Shaogang Liu, *Shufa lianxi zidao* 书法练习指导 [Guidance for Calligraphy Practice] (Qingdao: Qingdao Chubanshe, 2014).
54. 柳体 *Liuti* refers to the calligraphy of Liu Gongquan (778–865 CE) and 欧体 *Outi* is the writing style of Ouyang Xun (557–641 CE). Both are Tang dynasty calligraphers, whose writings are often used as model.
55. Foucault, *Discipline and Punish*, p. 152.
56. Foucault, *The Foucault Reader*, p. 61.

Chapter 2

1. Excerpt from a poem written by water calligrapher Huang Songbai, published in the *Taorandi shubao* 陶然 地书报 [Taoran Water Calligraphy Newspaper] of January 2017.
2. An interviewee mentioned that her group of water calligraphers that practice in Taoranting Park started to proudly call themselves "ground writers" (地书人 *dishu ren*) three years ago, when they realized other groups in the park have been referring to them as such, and, liking the sound of it, they adopted the name.
3. On the other hand, semantically, 地书 *dishu* is actually closer connected to the names of calligraphic styles. They are all made up of two characters, the first one stressing the kind of style (楷书 *kaishu* regular script, 草书 *caoshu* cursive script, 隶书 *lishu* clerical script, etc.), and the second character denominating the act of writing, 书 *shu*. Following this, 地书 *dishu* could be considered a calligraphic style. Yet this is problematic as well, as water calligraphy is actually written in the abovementioned styles rather than being one of them.
4. Zitui Li, "*Dishu Laonian Shenghuo You Yidao Liangli Fengjing* 地书老年生活有一道亮丽风景 [Water Calligraphy: Another Way to Beautiful Landscapes in the Lives of the Elderly]," *Zhongguo Laonian* 3 (2011): 22–24; Chen Shan, "*Jie Shifu de Xiaosa 'Dishu'* 解师傅的潇洒 '地书' [Understanding the Confident and Free 'Water Calligraphy' of Older Men]," *Xintiandi* 10 (2007): 24; Zhang Li, "*Xie dishu' shijian buyi guochang* 写地书'时间不宜过长 [Don't Practice 'Writing Water Calligraphy' For Too Long]," *Kaixin Laonian* 4 (2007): 34. Zhang Li argues that although it is a healthy practice, one should also be aware of health dangers: looking down at the characters for too long might cause a lack of blood in the head, and the long hours of standing might lead to a stiff back.
5. Judith Farquhar, "The Park Pass: Peopling and Civilizing a New Old Beijing," *Public Culture* 21 (3) (2009): 551–76; Judith Farquhar and Qicheng Zhang, *Ten*

Thousand Things: Nurturing Life in Contemporary Beijing (New York: Zone Books, 2012).
6. Piper Gaubatz, "New Public Space in Urban China: Fewer Walls, More Malls in Beijing, Shanghai and Xining," *China Perspectives* 4 (2008): 72–83.
7. Jean Burgess, "Hearing Ordinary Voices: Cultural Studies, Vernacular Creativity and Digital Storytelling," *Continuum* 20 (2) (2006): 201–14.
8. Jean Burgess, "Vernacular Creativity and New Media" (PhD diss., Queensland University of Technology, 2007), p. 32.
9. Richard Florida, *The Rise of the Creative Class* (New York: Basic Books, 2002).
10. Ibid., p. 232.
11. Jamie Peck, "Struggling with the Creative Class," *International Journal of Urban and Regional Research* 29 (4) (2005): 740–70; Pierre-Michel Menger, "Artistic Labor Markets: Contingent Work, Excess Supply and Occupational Risk Management," in *Handbook of the Economics of Art and Culture*, ed. Victor A. Ginsburg and David Throsby (Amsterdam: Elsevier, 2006), pp. 765–811; David Hesmondhalgh and Sarah Baker, *Creative Labour: Media Work in Three Cultural Industries* (London and New York: Routledge, 2011); Angela McRobbie, *Be Creative: Making a Living in the New Culture Industries* (Cambridge, UK and Malden, MA: Polity, 2016); Christoph Lindner, "Boredom and Creativity in the Era of Accelerated Living," in *Boredom, Shanzhai, and Digitisation in the Time of Creative China*, ed. Jeroen de Kloet, Yiu Fai Chow and Lena Scheen (Amsterdam: Amsterdam University Press, 2019), pp. 110–20.
12. Yiu Fai Chow, "Exploring Creative Class Mobility: Hong Kong Creative Workers in Shanghai and Beijing," *Eurasian Geography and Economics* 58 (4) (2017): 361–85.
13. Oli Mould, *Against Creativity* (New York: Verso, 2018).
14. Lindner, "Boredom and Creativity," p. 114.
15. McRobbie, *Be Creative*, p. 157.
16. Farquhar, "The Park Pass."
17. Mingzheng Shi, "From Imperial Gardens to Public Parks: The Transformation of Urban Space in Early Twentieth-Century Beijing," *Modern China* 24 (3) (1998): 219–54.
18. Ibid.
19. Ibid., p. 245.
20. Shaoguang Wang, "The Politics of Private Time: Changing Leisure Patterns in Urban China," in *Urban Spaces in Contemporary China: The Potential for Autonomy and Community in Post-Mao China*, ed. Debora Davis et al. (Cambridge: Cambridge University Press, 1995), p. 154.
21. Mary Padua, "Hybrid Modernity: Framing the Public Park in Post-Mao China," in *Council of Educators in Landscape Architecture CELA 2007: Negotiating Landscapes Proceedings*, August 14–19, University Park, Penn State University (2007), pp. 65–80.

22. Unn Målfrid Rolandsen, *Leisure and Power in Urban China* (London: Routledge, 2014).
23. Farquhar, "The Park Pass," p. 558.
24. Ibid., p. 554.
25. Caroline Chen (2010) remarks that in addition, the One Child Policy instituted in 1978 has liberated grandparents from babysitting responsibilities, allowing them more leisure time for themselves. That might not be altogether true: they simply have to babysit smaller numbers of infants (Caroline Chen, "Dancing in the Streets of Beijing: Improvised Uses within the Urban System," in *Insurgent Public Space: Guerrilla Urbanism and the Remaking of Contemporary Cities*, ed. Jeffrey Hou (London: Routledge, 2010), pp. 21–35.
26. Angela Zito, "Writing in Water, or, Evanescence, Enchantment and Ethnography in a Chinese Urban Park," *Visual Anthropology Review* 30 (1) (2014): 11–22.
27. Farquhar, "The Park Pass."
28. Often referred to as the "three jewels" (三宝 *sanbao*) in Daoist contexts, these concepts are the cornerstones of traditional Chinese medicine. 精 *jing* refers to the basis of the material body, 气 *qi* is the life force, energy, breath or spirit, and 神 *shen* refers to the mind, soul.
29. Judith Farquhar and Qicheng Zhang, *Ten Thousand Things: Nurturing Life in Contemporary Beijing* (New York: Zone Books, 2012), p. 122.
30. Ibid., p. 122.
31. Elsewhere, Farquhar and Zhang argue that this is also closely related to the withdrawal of national support for health care after the 1980s. The 1990s brought a massive growth in health insurance schemes that proved unaffordable for many. They argue that in this climate the "aging population is bombarded with state-sponsored public health information and free disease screenings. They have realized that when it comes to their own health, they are 'on their own'" (Judith Farquhar and Qicheng Zhang, "Biopolitical Beijing: Pleasure, Sovereignty, and Self-Cultivation in China's Capital," *Cultural Anthropology* 20 (3) (2005): 320).
32. Farquhar and Zhang, *Ten Thousand Things*, p. 143.
33. Michel Foucault, *The Use of Pleasure. The History of Sexuality, Vol. 2.* (Harmondsworth, Middlesex: Penguin, 1992), p. 11.
34. Farquhar and Zhang, *Ten Thousand Things*, p. 183.
35. The two concepts carry similar semantic origins, as Hay (1983) has illuminated: 书体 *shuti* translates as "script-body," and 身体 *shenti* "the self-body," further supporting the idea of their interconnectedness (John Hay, "The Human Body as a Microcosmic Source of Macrocosmic Values in Calligraphy," in *Theories of the Arts in China*, ed. Susan Bush and Christian Murck (Princeton, NJ: Princeton University Press, 1983), pp. 74–102. For more on traditional Chinese concepts of the body, see Roger T. Ames, "The Meaning of Body in Classical Chinese Thought," *International Philosophical Quarterly* 24 (1) (1984): 39–54; Jean François Billeter, *Chinese Art of Writing* (New York: Rizzoli, 1990); Angela Zito, *Of*

Body and Brush: Grand Sacrifice as Text/Performance in 18th Century China (Chicago: University of Chicago Press, 1997); Yuehping Yen, *Calligraphy and Power in Contemporary Chinese Society* (New York and London: Routledge Curzon, 2004).

36. Yutang Lin, *My Country and My People* (London: W. Heinemann, 1936).
37. Yen, *Calligraphy and Power*, p. 76.
38. Hay, "The Human Body as a Microcosmic Source of Macrocosmic Values in Calligraphy," pp. 74–102.
39. This folk-style poem describes how a gentleman can live crudely, but is enriched not by objects but by noble teachings. Zhao Mengfu famously copied this piece in regular script, and it is a popular piece for calligraphy practice.
40. The poem describes a folk story of the annual meeting of two stars in love in the sky and is associated with the Qixi festival, on the seventh day of the seventh lunar month, when these two stars are seen close together in the firmament.
41. Dating back to around the seventh century CE, the *The Heart Sutra* is one of the most famous sutras in Mahayana Buddhism, and a few water calligraphers disclosed that they come to the park every day just to write this sutra as part of a Zen-like practice. The short-lived nature and the gradual disappearing of the water-written characters relate to the content of the sutra, as it describes how ultimately all phenomena are empty in essence.
42. Anna Dezeuze, *Almost Nothing: Observations on Precarious Practices in Contemporary Art* (Manchester: Manchester University Press, 2017).
43. Ibid., p. 103.
44. Michel de Certeau, *Culture in The Plural*, ed. Luce Giard (Minneapolis: University of Minnesota Press, 1997), p. 139.
45. Michel de Certeau, *The Practice of Everyday Life* (Berkeley: University of California Press, 1984); Ben Highmore, *Everyday Life and Cultural Theory: An Introduction* (London and New York: Routledge, 2002), p. 148.
46. François Chastanet, *Dishu: Ground Calligraphy in China* (Årsta: Dokument Press, 2013).
47. Burgess, "Hearing Ordinary Voices."
48. Michael Gardiner, *Critiques of Everyday Life: An Introduction* (London and New York: Routledge, 2000), p. 13.
49. BJWMB.gov.cn, "*Xicheng: Taoran dishu wenhuajie shuhuai xin shidai* 西城：陶然地书文化节抒怀新时代 [Xicheng: Taoran Water Calligraphy Culture Festival Embracing the New Era]," 2018. www.bjwmb.gov.cn/xxgk/xcjy/t20181022_885072.htm [accessed March 27, 2018].
50. *Renminwang*, "*Beijing Taoran dishu wenhuaji: fendou xin shidai shuxie xin Taoran* 北京陶然地书文化节: 奋斗新时代 书写新陶然 [Beijing Taoran Water Calligraphy Culture Festival: Struggling in the New Era, Writing a New Taoran]," 2018. http://bj.people.com.cn/n2/2018/1019/c82846-32175537.html [accessed March 27, 2018].

51. See, for example, *China Daily*, "*Jing shou jia dishu xiehui chengli minjian yishu xieyi di tan shenghuo* 京首家地书协会成立民间艺术写意低碳生活 [Beijing's First Ground-Writing Association Was Established to Express Folk art and Low-Carbon Life]," 2010. www.chinadaily.com.cn/dfpd/2010-04/09/content_9707332.htm [accessed March 27, 2022].
52. Zito, "Writing in Water."
53. More works by Song Dong are inspired by writing in water, for example: *Stamping with Water* (1996), a performance piece taking place in Tibet in which he spent an hour stamping the water with a wooden stamp bearing the character "water," and *Writing the Time with Water* (2000), which is an artwork attempting to capture fading time.

Chapter 3

1. Britta Erickson, *The Art of Xu Bing: Words Without Meaning, Meaning Without Words* (Washington, DC and Seattle: University of Washington Press, 2001), p. 13.
2. Ibid., p. 16.
3. Minglu Gao, *Total Modernity and the Avant-Garde in Twentieth-Century Chinese Art* (Cambridge, MA: MIT Press, 2011).
4. Mary Wiseman Bittner and Yuedi Liu, eds, *Subversive Strategies in Contemporary Chinese Art* (Leiden, Boston: Brill, 2011), p. xxiv.
5. Gordon Barrass, *The Art of Calligraphy in Modern China* (Berkeley: University of California Press, 2002), p. 29.
6. Gao, *Total Modernity and the Avant-Garde*, p. 219.
7. Jiang Xu and Wang Dongling, eds, *Shu feishu—kaifang de shufa shikong* 书非书—开放的书法时空[The Act of Writing and of Non-writing: The Open Space for Chinese Calligraphy] (Beijing: Zhongguo Meishuxueyuan Chubanshe, 2005), p. 9.
8. Minglu Gao, *The '85 Movement: Avant-Garde Art in the Post-Mao Era* (Cambridge, MA: Harvard University Press, 1999).
9. Birgit Hopfener, "'Embodied Criticality' in Moving-Image Installations by Wang Gongxin and Zhang Peili," *Journal of Visual Art Practice* 11 (2012): 193–208.
10. Hsingyuan Tsao and Roger T. Ames, *Xu Bing and Contemporary Chinese Art: Cultural and Philosophical Reflections* (New York: SUNY Press, 2011), p. 8.
11. In Erickson, *The Art of Xu Bing*, p. 14.
12. Often dated from 1990–95, Meiling Cheng, however, corrects the inception of Qiu's *The Preface of the Orchid Pavilion* to 1990–97 (Meiling Cheng, "De/Visualizing Calligraphic Archaeology: Qiu Zhijie's Total Art," *TDR: The Drama Review* 53 (2) (2009): 17–34, p. 33), and I will follow her amendment, as Hopfener has argued that Qiu Zhijie himself corrected the dates in a conversation with Cheng (Hopfener, "'Embodied Criticality'," p. 3).

13. Jerome Silbergeld and Dora C.Y. Ching, eds, *Persistence/Transformation: Text as Image in the Art of Xu Bing* (Princeton, NJ: Princeton University Press, 2006).
14. In Erickson, *The Art of Xu Bing*, p. 41.
15. In Adriana Iezzi, "Contemporary Chinese Calligraphy Between Tradition and Innovation," *Journal of Literature and Art Studies* 3 (2013): 167.
16. Jeroen de Kloet and Edwin Jurriëns, eds, *Cosmopatriots: On Distant Belongings and Close Encounters* (Amsterdam: Rodopi, 2007), p. 41.
17. Jacques Rancière, *The Politics of Aesthetics: The Distribution of the Sensible*, ed. and trans. Gabriel Rockhill (London: Continuum, 2004).
18. Ibid., p. 3.
19. Ibid., p. 46.
20. In Alexandra Berlina, ed., *Viktor Shklovsky: A Reader* (London: Bloomsbury Academic, 2016).
21. Gu Gan, "*Xiandai shufa Manyi* 现代书法漫议 [Free Discussions on Modern Calligraphy]," *Meishu Yanjiu* (4) (1992): 52.
22. Statement by Lin Fengmian at The Great Beijing Art Meeting in 1927, in Michael Sullivan, *Art and Artists of Twentieth-Century China* (Berkeley: University of California Press, 1996), p. 44.
23. Ralph Croizier, "Post-Impressionists in Pre-War Shanghai: The Juelanshe (Storm Society) and the Fate of Modernism in Republican China," in *Modernity in Asian Art*, ed. John Clark (Broadway, Australia: Wild Peony, 1993), p. 135; Hui Guo, "Writing Chinese Art History in Early Twentieth-Century China," PhD diss., Leiden University, 2010, p. 35.
24. On the semantic origins of 国画 *guohua* and 中国画 *zhongguohua* and the adoption of Japanese modern concepts in the Chinese lexicon, see Guo, "Writing Chinese Art History," pp. 22–4.
25. Guo, "Writing Chinese Art History."
26. Xiongbo Shi, "Zhang Yinlin: A Preface to Chinese Calligraphy Criticism (1931)," *Journal of Art Historiography* 13 (2015): 13–25.
27. Qianshen Bai, *Fu Shan's World: The Transformation of Chinese Calligraphy in the Seventeenth Century* (Cambridge, MA: Harvard University Asia Center, 2003); Shi-yee Liu, "In Pursuit of Authenticity: The Epigraphic School of Chinese Calligraphy," *Netmuseum.org*, 2014. www.metmuseum.org/blogs/now-at-the-met/2014/epigraphic-school [accessed August 24, 2020]; Lothar Ledderose, "Aesthetic Appropriation of Ancient Calligraphy in Modern China," in *Chinese Art: Modern Expressions*, ed. Maxwell K. Hearn and Judith Smith (New York: Metropolitan Museum of Art, 2001), pp. 222–7.
28. Yuli Wang, *The Mirror of Writing: Kang Youwei's Curriculum for Chinese Calligraphy Art* (Washington, DC: New Academia Publishing/The Spring, 2017), p. 4; See also Guo, "Writing Chinese Art History"; Shi, "Zhang Yinlin."
29. In Wang, *The Mirror of Writing*, p. 7.
30. Zhang Yinlin in Shi, "Zhang Yinlin," p. 11.

31. Mao Tse-Tung, *Mao Tse-Tung Talks at the Yenan Forum on Literature and Art. World Communism: Pamphlets from McMaster University* (Beijing: Foreign Languages Press; The People's Republic of China, 1967), p. 88.
32. Richard Curt Kraus, *Brushes with Power: Modern Politics and the Chinese Art of Calligraphy* (Berkeley: University of California Press, 1991).
33. Ibid., p. 66.
34. Ibid., p. 72. In addition, as Yen notes, Mao's calligraphic works were often found in people's homes, on porcelain busts, mugs, vases and calendars, thus making the calligraphy of Mao and the other revolutionary leaders visible for everyone and thoroughly permeating the everyday lives of common people (Yuehping Yen, *Calligraphy and Power in Contemporary Chinese Society* (New York and London: Routledge Curzon, 2004), p. 3). Until today, this visibility of Mao Zedong's handwritings persists, for example in the phrase "Serve the People" (为人民服务 *wei renminfuwu)* that is seen often on public buildings and squares all over China as well as newspapers and paraphernalia.
35. Established by Mao, the Hunan–Hubei–Jiangxi Soviet (湘鄂赣苏维埃 *Xiang egan suwei ai*) was a liberated zone in the 1930s, and a self-governing region under CCP control. The resolution was adopted within the Hunan–Hubei–Jiangxi Soviet, and while the Soviet itself was a political and military entity, the resolution was a cultural policy.
36. Kraus, *Brushes with Power*, p. 63.
37. Geremie Barmé, "History Writ Large: Big-Character Posters, Red Logorrhoea and the Art of Words," *Portal Journal of Multidisciplinary International Studies* 9 (3) (2012): 9; see also Goran Leijonhufvud, *Going Against the Tide: On Dissent and Big-Character Posters in China* (London: Curzon Press, 1990).
38. In Hua Sheng, "Big Character Posters in China: A Historical Survey," *Journal of Chinese Law* 4 (1990): 238.
39. Ibid., p. 240.
40. See Leijonhufvud, *Going Against the Tide.*
41. Barrass, *The Art of Calligraphy in Modern China*, p. 163.
42. Tsao and Ames, *Xu Bing and Contemporary Chinese Art*, p. 14.
43. Kraus, *Brushes with Power*, p. 76.
44. Even before the 20th century, missionaries developed versions of romanized Chinese to facilitate the reading of religious texts for Chinese people. Other efforts included the creation of the Gwoyeu Romatzyh system in 1928, the Latinxua Sinwenz system in collaboration with Soviet sinologists, and ultimately, Hanyu Pinyin in 1958, the state-led initiative distinct from those missionary efforts.
45. Shouhui Zhao, "Chinese Character Modernisation in the Digital Era: A Historical Perspective." *Current Issues in Language Planning* 6 (2005): 315–78, 333.
46. Gu, "*Xiandai shufa Manyi*," p. 52.
47. Ibid., p. 53.

48. Gu Gan, "Cong Xiandai Shufa dao Hanzi Yishu 从现代书法到汉字艺术 [From Modern Calligraphy to Chinese Character Art]," Meishu Bao, August 15, 2016. https://news.artron.net/20160815/n856919.html [accessed May 23, 2017].
49. Xu and Wang, *Shu feishu*, p. 9.
50. Qi Gong in Alfreda Murck and Wen C. Fong, *Words and Images: Chinese Poetry, Calligraphy, and Painting* (New York: Metropolitan Museum of Art, 1991), p. 12.
51. That this situation might lead to conflicts of interest is evident, and is showcased for example in the polemic article by Nanming Wang in 2017 where he attacks fellow modern calligraphy pioneer Qiu Zhenzhong for selecting the list of calligraphers as well as participating in the 2000 Chengdu exhibition "Gate of the Century." Wang states: "Qiu Zhenzhong shamelessly said to me: 'because the formation of "modern calligraphy" is related to me, I am of course qualified to participate'" (Nanming Wang, "*Yishu, Zhidu yu Falu—Zhongguo yi Guoji Jiaowang de Jieguo* 艺术、制度与法律—中国与国际交往的结果 [Art, Institutions and Laws—the Results of China's International Relations]," 2017. https://news.artron.net/20170315/n915996.html [accessed August 15, 2018].
52. A comprehensive overview of these classifications has been made by Adriana Iezzi in "Contemporary Chinese Calligraphy"; and "What Is 'Chinese Modern Calligraphy'? An Exploration of the Critical Debate on Modern Calligraphy in Contemporary China," *Journal of Literature and Art Studies* 5 (2015): 210.
53. In Iezzi, "What Is 'Chinese Modern Calligraphy'?"
54. Wang Dongling, "*Jufu Dazi Kuangfang Dacao Xiandai Shufa* 巨幅大字 狂放大草 现代书法 [Large Characters, Crazy Grass Script, Contemporary Calligraphy]," 2013 https://news.artron.net/20131011/n518934.html [accessed May 30, 2020].
55. Barrass, *The Art of Calligraphy in Modern China*. See also Iezzi, "Contemporary Chinese Calligraphy" and Iezzi, "What is 'Chinese Modern Calligraphy'?"
56. Author's intent aside, this did not mean that their works were always apolitical. Eva Cockcroft argues, for example, that their works were appropriated by government agencies as a vehicle for Cold War propaganda (Eva Cockcroft, "Abstract Expressionism, Weapon of the Cold War," *Art Forum* 15 (10) (1974): 39–41.
57. Gu Gan, *The Three Steps of Modern Calligraphy*, English edition, trans. Hu Yunhuan (Beijing: China Books Publishing House, 1990), p. 126. In reply, Gu notes that the lines and the vigor in the strokes of, for example, the works of Kline and Miro are very similar to calligraphy, and studying a sculpture of Henry Moore, he asks: "Shall we take in this way of creation to design Chinese characters—the reformation of line and space?" (Gu, *The Three Steps of Modern Calligraphy*, p. 129).
58. Eugenia Bogdanova-Kummer, "The Line Between Calligraphy and Painting: A View from Post-War Japan," in *The Power of Line*, ed. Marzia Faietti and Gerhard Wolf (Munich: Hirmer, 2015), p. 118.
59. Interview with author.
60. Online, however, articles criticizing his work do abound. See, for example, Wenming Zhi Chuang, "中國年度`丑書' 最高榮譽獎，花落誰家？[Who Won the

Highest Honor of China's 'Ugly Book' Award of the Year?]." KK News, October 9, 2016. https://kknews.cc/news/exr4gr.html [accessed February 6, 2025].

61. Jiang Xu, *The Way of Calligraphy: Wang Dongling's Work*, English Edition (Shanghai: Shanghai Fine Arts Publishing House, 2011), p. 22.
62. Ibid., p. 32.
63. Gordon Barrass, *The Art of Calligraphy in Modern China* (Berkeley: University of California Press, 2002), pp. 140, 143.
64. Ibid., p. 140.
65. Ibid., p. 164.
66. Shao-Lan Hertel, "The Inner Workings of Brush-and-Ink: A Study on Huang Binhong (1865–1955) as Calligrapher, with Special Respect to the Concept of Interior Beauty (Neimei)" (PhD diss., Freie Universität Berlin, 2017) p. 274.
67. Dongling Wang, "*Xiandai Shufa Jingshen Lun* 现代书法精神论 [Discussing the spirit of contemporary calligraphy]," *Xin Meishu* 新美术 1 (28) (2007), 10–11.
68. Interview with author.
69. The poem is "Drinking by the Lake: Clear Sky at First, then Rain" (饮湖上初晴后雨 *Yin hushang chu qing hou yu*).
70. Kraus, *Brushes with Power*, p. 57.
71. Hertel, "The Inner Workings of Brush-and-Ink," p. 102.
72. In an interview with Yan Liang: www.sohu.com/a/223868780_676789 [accessed July 29, 2024]. Yan Liang, "Wang Dongling: `Luan Shu' shi Mao Tianxia zhi Da Bu Wei de Shi [王冬龄 | `乱书' 是冒天下之大不韪的事]," Sohu, 2018. https://www.sohu.com/a/223868780_676789 (accessed July 29, 2024).
73. Ibid.
74. I am part of several calligraphy-related WeChat groups in which participants chat about calligraphy, share articles, and share their own calligraphic works. In all these groups, Zeng Xiang's work was heavily debated at the time of the exhibition, even in a group dedicated to font design.
75. Liu Zongchao Liu, "*'Choushu' zhong de 'Zhen' he 'Shan'* 丑书'中的'真'与 '善' [The 'Real' and the 'Good' in 'Ugly Calligraphy']," *Renmin Taolun* 36 (2016): 139.
76. Wo Xinghua Wo, "*Lun Choushu* 论丑书 [Discussing Ugly Calligraphy]," *Shufa Daobao* 2 (2002).
77. Liu, "*'Choushu' zhong de 'Zhen' he 'Shan'*," p. 139.
78. Imre Galambos, "Correction Marks in the Dunhuang Manuscripts," in *Studies in Chinese Manuscripts: From the Warring States Period to the 20th Century*, ed. Imre Galambos (Budapest: ELTE Institute of East Asian Studies, 2013), pp. 191–210.
79. Bai, *Fu Shan's World*, p. 13.
80. Dora C.Y. Ching, "The Aesthetics of the Unusual and the Strange in Seventeenth-Century Calligraphy," in *The Embodied Image: Chinese Calligraphy from the John B. Elliott Collection*, ed. Robert E. Harrist Jr and Wen C. Fong (Princeton, NJ: The Art Museum, Princeton University Press, 1999), p. 355.

81. Retrieved from Wen C. Fong, "Prologue: Chinese Calligraphy as Presenting the Self," in *Chinese Calligraphy*, trans. Wang Youfen (New Haven, CT and London: Yale University Press and Beijing: Foreign Language Press, 2008), pp. 1–31.
82. In Bai, *Fu Shan's World*, p. 101.
83. In Wo, "*Lun Choushu*," translation taken from Bai, *Fu Shan's World*; *Ning wu qiao, ning chou wu mei, ning zhili wu qinghua, ning zhen shuai wu anpai* 宁毋巧宁丑毋媚宁支离毋轻滑宁真率毋安排.
84. Jacques Rancière, *Dissensus: On Politics and Aesthetics*, trans. Steven Corcoran (London: Bloomsbury, 2015), p. 36.
85. Wei, Wei, "*Qianyi Choushu* 浅议'丑书' [Talking about 'Ugly Calligraphy']," *Xiandai funu (xiaxun)* (2014): 344–45.
86. Fuming Wang, "*Liuxing shufeng yu choushu* 流行书风与丑书 [Popular Calligraphy and Ugly Calligraphy]," *Qingshaonian Shufa* (10) (2004).
87. Zhenji, "*Zeng Xiang feng le! Zaici dianwule Zhongguo shufa* 曾翔疯了！再次玷污了中国书法 [Zeng Xiang Is Crazy! Once Again Polluting Chinese Calligraphy]," 2018. www.sohu.com/a/228871152_482079 [accessed July 23, 2018].
88. Daojun Lin, "'*Shufa yi si' yu Zeng Xiang de yiyi* '书法已死'与曾翔的意义 ['Calligraphy Is Already Dead' and the Meaning of Zeng Xiang]," 2018. www.douban.com/note/665238839/ [accessed May 12, 2021].
89. Ibid.
90. Andrea Bachner, *Beyond Sinology: Chinese Writing and the Scripts of Culture* (New York: Columbia University Press, 2014), p. 171.
91. Mingjun Lu, *Hui 'wan' de Zeng Xiang* 会'玩' 的 曾翔 [Zeng Xiang Knows How to 'Play']," 2018. https://news.artron.net/20140114/n559118.html [accessed August 1, 2019]; Zeng Xiang, *Wo shi yishu zhuimengren* 我是艺术追梦人 [I Am an Art Dreamcatcher], 2018. www.jingduzhai.com/mobile/article-5352.html [accessed November 30, 2018].

Chapter 4

1. MOE. "*Jiaoyu bu guanyu yinfa 'zhongxiaoxue shufa jiaoyu zhidao gangyao' de tongzhi* 教育部關於印發《中小學書法教育指導綱要》的通知 [Ministry of Education on the Issuance of 'Primary and Secondary School Calligraphy Education' Guidelines]," 2013.
2. Jing Tsu, *Kingdom of Characters* (New York: Riverhead, 2022), p. 243.
3. Nick Couldry and Andreas Hepp, *The Mediated Construction of Reality* (London: John Wiley & Sons, 2016).
4. Jing Tsu, *Kingdom of Characters*, p. 242.
5. Victor Mair, "Character Amnesia," *Language Log*, 2010. http://languagelog.ldc.upenn.edu/nll/?p=2473 [accessed July 23, 2022].
6. Jennifer Lee, "Where the PC Is Mightier Than the Pen," *New York Times*, February 1, 2001.
7. David Berry, *Critical Theory and the Digital* (New York: Bloomsbury Academic, 2014), p. 13.

8. Benedict Anderson, *Imagined Communities: Reflections on the Origin and Spread of Nationalism* (London: Verso, 1998).
9. Yingjie Guo, *Cultural Nationalism in Contemporary China: The Search for National Identity Under Reform* (London: Routledge Curzon, 2004).
10. Florian Schneider, "Emergent Nationalism in China's Sociotechnical Networks: How Technological Affordance and Complexity Amplify Digital Nationalism," *Nations and Nationalism* 28 (1) (2022): 268.
11. Ibid., p. 268.
12. Michael Billig, *Banal Nationalism* (London, Thousand Oaks and New Delhi: Sage, 1995), p. 38.
13. Ibid., p. 43.
14. Ben Light, Jean Burgess and Stephanie Duguay, "The Walkthrough Method: An Approach to the Study of Apps," *New Media & Society* 20 (3) (2018): 881–900.
15. Ibid., p. 882.
16. Ibid., p. 892.
17. Ibid., p. 882.
18. Andrea Bachner, *Beyond Sinology: Chinese Writing and the Scripts of Culture* (New York: Columbia University Press, 2014), p. 202.
19. David Bolter and Richard Grusin, *Remediation: Understanding New Media* (Cambridge, MA: The MIT Press, 2000).
20. Ibid., p. 15.
21. Ibid., p. 272.
22. See, for example, Likun Zhang, Xiaoyan Li, Yi Tang, Fangbin Song, Tian Xia and Wei Wang, "Contemporary Advertising Text Art Design and Effect Evaluation by IoT Deep Learning under the Smart City," *Security and Communication Networks*, (2022): 1–14.
23. Sara Su, Ying-Qing Xu, Heung-Yeung Shum and Falai Chen, "Simulating Artistic Brushstrokes Using Interval Splines," in *Proceedings of the 5th IASTED International Conference on Computer Graphics and Imaging*, Kauai, Hawaii (2002), pp. 85–90; CADAL https://cadal.edu.cn/index/home [accessed May 20, 2020]. Also Xiafen Zhang and George Nagy, "The CADAL Calligraphic Database," in *Proceedings of the 2011 Workshop on Historical Document Imaging and Processing* (HIP '11), Association for Computing Machinery, (2011), pp. 37–42; Songhua Xu, Frances C. Lau and Yunhe Pan, *A Computational Approach to Digital Chinese Painting and Calligraphy* (Hangzhou/Berlin: Zhejiang UP/Springer-Verlag, 2009).
24. Ibid., p. 14.
25. Victor Mair, "How Many More Chinese Characters Are Needed?" *Language Log*, 2016. https://languagelog.ldc.upenn.edu/nll/?p=29034 [accessed October 22, 2022].
26. Matt Anderson, "Numbers of Characters," in *Encyclopedia of Chinese Language and Linguistics*, vol. 3, ed. Rint Sybesma et al. (Leiden: Brill, 2017), p. 255.
27. Ibid.
28. Victor Mair, "Modern Chinese Writing," in *The World's Writing Systems*, ed. Pete T. Daniels and William Bright (Oxford: Oxford University Press, 1996), pp. 200–8.

29. Su et al., "Simulating Artistic Brushstrokes," p. 85.
30. Ibid.
31. Siuchi Hsu, Irene Lee and Neil Wiseman, "Skeletal Strokes," in *Proceedings of the 6th Annual ACM Symposium on User Interface Software and Technology* (New York: ACM Press, 1993), pp. 197–206.
32. Helena Wong and Horace Ip, "Virtual Brush: A Model-Based Synthesis of Chinese Calligraphy," *Computers & Graphics* 24 (1) (2000): 99–113.
33. Ross Girshick, "Simulating Chinese Brush Painting: The Parametric Hairy Brush" (PhD diss., Waltham: Brandeis University, 2004, p. 1.
34. Jinhui Yu and Qunsheng Peng, "Realistic Synthesis of Cao Shu of Chinese Calligraphy," *Computers & Graphics* 29 (1) (2005): 145–53.
35. Bolter and Grusin, *Remediation: Understanding New Media*, p. 21.
36. Xu et al., *A Computational Approach to Digital Chinese Painting and Calligraphy*, p. 5.
37. Cao Shi, Jianguo Xiao, Wenhua Jia and Canhui Xu, "Automatic Generation of Chinese Character Based on Human Vision and Prior Knowledge of Calligraphy," in *Natural Language Processing and Chinese Computing: Proceedings of the First CCF Conference, NLPCC 2012*, Beijing, China, ed. Ming Zhou et al. (Heidelberg: Springer, 2012), pp. 23–33.
38. Ibid., p. 30.
39. Jean Baudrillard, *Simulacra and Simulation*, trans. Sheila Glaser (Ann Arbor, MI: University of Michigan Press, 1994 [1981]).
40. José van Dijck, *The Culture of Connectivity: A Critical History of Social Media* (Oxford: Oxford University Press, 2013).
41. Ibid., p. 6.
42. Tarleton Gillespie, "The Platform Metaphor, Revisited," *Digital Society Blog*, August 27, 2017. www.hiig.de/en/the-platform-metaphor-revisited/ [accessed April 5, 2022].
43. Guobin Yang, *Engaging Social Media in China: Platform, Publics and Production*, ed. Guobin Yang and Wei Wang (East Lansing: Michigan State University Press, 2021); Michael Keane, "Going Global or Going Nowhere? Chinese Media in a Time of Flux," *Media International Australia* 159 (1) (2016): 13–21.
44. José van Dijck, Thomas Poell and Martijn de Waal, *The Platform Society: Public Values in a Connective World* (New York: Oxford University Press, 2018), p. 4.
45. Ibid., p. 8.
46. Thomas Poell, Erin Duffy Brooke and David Nieborg, *Platforms and Cultural Production* (Cambridge: Polity Press, 2021), p. 200.
47. Cyberspace Administration China (CAC), "*Chuanbo wangluo zheng nengliang rang wangluo kongjian tian lang qi qing* 传播网络正能量 让网络空间天朗气清 [Spreading Positive Energy on the Internet to Make Cyberspace Clear and Bright]," 2017. https://www.cac.gov.cn/2017-04/20/c_1120846141.htm [accessed March 21, 2023]; Jian Lin and Jeroen de Kloet, "Platformization of the Unlikely Creative Class: Kuaishou and Chinese Digital Cultural Production," *Social Media + Society* 5 (4) (2019), 1–12, p. 3.

48. Xu Chen, David Bondy Valdovinos Kaye and Jing Zeng, "Positive Energy Douyin: Constructing 'Playful Patriotism' in a Chinese Short-Video Application," *Chinese Journal of Communication* 14 (1) (2021): 97–117.
49. On August 19, 2013, during a speech at the National Propaganda and Ideology Work Conference, Xi Jinping introduced the idea of 'telling China's story well', urging Party-state media and quasi-private actors to strengthen and enhance external propaganda through 'new concepts, categories, and expressions'. The phrase quickly became a key political slogan, driving various 'storytelling' campaigns in China. Media Project, "The CMP Dictionary: Telling China's Story Well," China Media Project, 2021. https://chinamediaproject.org/the_ccp_dictionary/telling-chinas-story-well [accessed February 7, 2025].
50. I have included the period from April 30, 2018 to May 15, 2018 in this analysis. It should be noted that this particular group was dissolved in September 2018, and different subgroups have emerged that are structured similarly, in which I have participated ever since.
51. Billig, *Banal Nationalism*, p. 43.

Chapter 5

1. "*Renren dou shi chuangyijia* 人人都是创意家 [Everyone Is an Expert in Creativity]" is the slogan of the Cultural Innovation Center of the National Museum of Art in Beijing.
2. Ghost Street is the name commonly used in English for this street, but it is actually a mistranslation of the original 簋街 *guijie*, in which 簋 *gui* means a type of vessel, and not 鬼, *gui* ghost.
3. Andrea Bachner, *Beyond Sinology: Chinese Writing and the Scripts of Culture* (New York: Columbia University Press, 2014), p. 168. As Bachner explains in a footnote, this is an argument based on a small selection of submissions for the FounderType (方正 *Fangzheng*) Prize, a well-known contest in the field of Chinese typographical design organized by FounderType, the largest font design company in China. However, these designs are not representative of all design submissions, nor of the designs of FounderType that are commercially available in general.
4. Rey Chow, "Introduction: On Chineseness as a Theoretical Problem," *Boundary 2*, 25 (3) (1998): 1–24; Anthony Reid, "Escaping the Burdens of Chineseness," *Asian Ethnicity* 10 (3) (2009): 285–96; Ien Ang, "Can One Say No to Chineseness? Pushing the Limits of the Diasporic Paradigm," *Boundary 2*, 25 (3) (1998): 223–42; Allen Chun, "Fuck Chineseness: On the Ambiguities of Ethnicity as Culture as Identity," *Boundary 2*, 23 (2) (1996): 111–38; Jeroen de Kloet, *China with a Cut: Globalisation, Urban Youth and Popular Music* (Amsterdam: Amsterdam University Press, 2010).
5. Pengzhi Feng, "*Cong 'san ge zixin' dao 'si ge zixin'* 从'三个自 信' 到'四个信' [From 'Three Confidences' to 'Four Confidences'']," *Zhongguo Gongchandang Xinwen*

中国共产党闻 [Chinese Communist Party News], 2016. http://theory.people.com.cn/n1/2016/0707/c49150-28532466.html [accessed July 21, 2022].

6. "*Yi guren zhi guiju kai zhiji zhi shengmian* 以古人之规矩，开自己之生面." For this phrase I follow the interpretation as suggested by Baidu: https://zhidao.baidu.com/question/330712591028865005.html [accessed May 12, 2022].
7. Xi Jinping, "*Jianding wenhua zixin, jianshe shehuizhuyi wenhua Qiangguo* 坚定文化自信，建设社会主义文化强国 [Strengthening Cultural Self-Confidence and Building a Strong Socialist Culture]." www.qstheory.cn/dukan/qs/2019-06/15/c_1124626824.htm [accessed July 25, 2024].
8. In the 1990s, digital font design flourished, but many of the companies failed to survive. To date, the market is dominated by two companies: FounderType (方正 *Fangzheng*) and Hanyi Fonts (汉议字库 *Hanyi Ziku*).
9. Jian Lin, "Be Creative for the State: Creative Workers in Chinese State-Owned Cultural Enterprises," *International Journal of Cultural Studies* 22 (1) (2018): 53–69.
10. They connect through an active WeChat group, called FONT&type, which had 447 members in July 2022.
11. Thomas S. Mullaney, *The Chinese Typewriter: A History* (Cambridge, MA: The MIT Press, 2017), p. 79.
12. Tsuen-Hsuin Tsien and Joseph Needham, *Science and Civilisation in China: Volume 5, Chemistry and Chemical Technology; Part 1, Paper and Printing* (Cambridge: Cambridge University Press, 1985), p. 146.
13. Earlier practices of duplicating images and prints include seals on clay, and later paper or silk, and impressions from finger tips or from the palm, according to Tsien and Needham, *Science and Civilisation in China*, p. 135.
14. Ibid., p. 132.
15. Ibid., p. 146.
16. Cynthia Brokaw and Kai-Wing Chow, eds, *Printing and Book Culture in Late Imperial China* (Berkeley: University of California Press, 2005), p. 10.
17. Tsien and Needham, *Science and Civilisation in China*, p. 159; Joseph McDermott, "The Ascendance of the Imprint in China," in *Printing and Book Culture in Late Imperial China*, ed. Cynthia Brokaw and Kai-Wing Chow (California: University of California Press, 2005), p. 56.
18. Brokaw and Chow, eds, *Printing and Book Culture in Late Imperial China*.
19. Ibid., p. 16.
20. Hang Lin, "Printed as Handwritten: The Importance of Calligraphy in Printing in Late Ming China," *The Polish Journal of the Arts and Culture. New Series* 1 (2015): 51–76, p. 56.
21. Tsien and Needham, *Science and Civilisation in China*.
22. Christopher Reed, *Gutenberg in Shanghai: Chinese Print Capitalism, 1876–1937* (Honolulu, HI: University of Hawaii Press, 2004), p. 86.
23. Ibid., p. 87.

24. Jing Tsu, *Kingdom of Characters* (New York: Riverhead, 2022); Mullaney, *The Chinese Typewriter*.
25. Reed, *Gutenberg in Shanghai*.
26. Pingxin Guo and Sun Qiangnan, "General Review of Computer Technology and Application in China," *Computers in Industry* 8 (2) (1987): 113–15; Mullaney, *The Chinese Typewriter*; Michael Pecht and Weifeng Liu, "Computers in China," 2019. www.researchgate.net/publication/265422783_COMPUTERS_IN_CHINA [accessed August 2, 2019].
27. Tsu, *Kingdom of Characters*.
28. Mullaney, *The Chinese Typewriter*.
29. Guo and Qiangnan, "General Review of Computer Technology and Application in China."
30. Tsu, *Kingdom of Characters*, p. 269.
31. *Ziti shi wenhua de biaopi* 字体是文化的表皮 is a statement by font designer Zhou Bai, and quoted at the opening of the lecture.
32. Phoenix Art 凤凰艺术, "*Mei zai shenghuo, renren dou shi chuangyijia Zhongguo meishu guanyong chuangyi dianliang shenghuo* 美在生活人人都是创意家 中国美术馆用创意点亮生活 [Beauty in Life, Everyone Is a Creative Person, and the National Art Museum of China Lights Up Life with Creativity]," 2017. http://art.ifeng.com/2017/0830/3374205.shtml [accessed August 2, 2018].
33. Fang Cao, *Wenzi Yishu Sheji* 文字艺术设计 [Typography Art Design] (Beijing: Gaodeng Jiaoyu Chubanshe, 2009).
34. A calligraphic concept that refers to the inner square of the grid paper, used as a reference for determining where the strokes should be positioned when copying a character.
35. FounderType *Fangzheng Ziti* 方正字体, "*Ziti wei Wuhan jiayou | Fangzheng ziku kaifang quanbu zhongwen ziti, kang yi xuancuan mianfei shiyong* 字体为武汉加油 | 方正字库开放全部中文字体，抗疫宣传免费使用 [Fonts Cheer for Wuhan: Founder Font Library Opens All Chinese Fonts, Free to Use for Anti-Epidemic Propaganda]," 2020. www.foundertype.com/index.php/FontInfo/index/id/205 [accessed July 28, 2022].
36. Wang Wen taped lecture at the National Museum in Beijing organized by the Cultural Innovation Center in Beijing on April 21, 2018.
37. Yi Xing, "They're Just Your Type," *China Daily Asia*, December 17, 2016. https://covid-19.chinadaily.com.cn/weekend/2016-12/17/content_27696749_2.htm [accessed December 21, 2018].
38. Kevin Carrico, "The Imaginary Institution of China: Dialectics of Fantasy and Failure in Nationalist Identification, as Seen through China's Han Clothing Movement" (PhD diss., New York: Cornell University, 2013), p. 3.
39. Zhijie Ke and Yuxiang Su, *Zixing Sanbu: Richang Shenghuo de Zhongwen Zixingxue* 字型散步日常生活的中文字型學 [A Font Walk: The Study of Fonts in Everyday Life] (Chengdu: Lianpu, 2014).

40. FounderType *Fangzheng Ziti* 方正字体, "*Di Jiu Jie Fangzheng Ziti Dasai Huojiang Zuopin Xinshang (Zhongwen Zhuanye Zu)* 第九届方正字体大赛获奖作品欣赏(中文专业组) [Winners of FounderType Design Competition 2018 Chinese Professional Group)]," 2018. https://ztds.foundertype.com/index.php/previous_works/index.html?id=9&cid=31 [accessed July 21, 2022].
41. FounderType *Fangzheng Ziti* 方正字体, "*Fangzheng Xu Bing xin Yingwen shuti* 方正徐冰英文书 [FounderType Xu Bing New English Font]," 2015. www.foundertype.com/index.php/FontInfo/index/id/333.html [accessed April 14, 2024].
42. Hung Wu, *A Story of Ruins: Presence and Absence in Chinese Art and Visual Culture* (London: Reaktion Books, 2013).
43. Lin Du's designs can be found here: https://zfa053711.zcool.com.cn. [accessed June 8, 2024].
44. David Hesmondhalgh and Sarah Baker, *Creative Labour: Media Work in Three Cultural Industries* (London and New York: Routledge, 2011).
45. Liang Dingli's designs can be found here: www.ZCOOL.com.cn/work/ZMjE0NDg5ODg=.html [accessed July 28, 2022].
46. Svetlana Boym, *The Future of Nostalgia* (New York: Basic Books, 2001), p. 31.
47. Jing Wu, "Nostalgia as Content Creativity: Cultural Industries and Popular Sentiment," *International Journal of Cultural Studies* 9 (2006): 362.
48. An example of a tutorial can be found here: https://zfa053711.ZCOOL.com.cn/moments#tab_anchor. An example of a template is here: www.ZCOOL.com.cn/work/ZMTgxNTQ3ODA=.html [accessed July 28, 2022].
49. Walter Benjamin, *The Arcades Project* (Cambridge, MA: Harvard University Press, 1999), p. 470.
50. Brokaw and Chow, eds, *Printing and Book Culture in Late Imperial China*, p. 25.
51. Arjun Appadurai, *Modernity At Large: Cultural Dimensions of Globalization* (Minneapolis: University of Minnesota Press, 1996), p. 30.
52. Phoenix Art 凤凰艺术, "*Mei zai shenghuo.*"

Coda

1. Michael Billig, *Banal Nationalism* (London, Thousand Oaks and New Delhi: Sage Publications, 1995).
2. Allen Scott, "Creative Cities: Conceptual Issues and Policy Questions," *Journal of Urban Affairs* 28 (2009): 1–17.
3. Dany Jacobs, "Creativity and the Economy." Background paper for the Innovation Lecture "Compete with Creativity" 2005, organized by the Dutch Ministry of Economic Affairs (Amsterdam: The Dutch Ministry of Economic Affairs, 2005), p. 9.
4. In Yale Hirsch and William J. O'Neil, *The Capitalist Spirit: How Each and Every One of Us Can Make a Giant Difference in Our Fast-Changing World* (Hoboken, NJ: Wiley, 2009), p. 31.

Bibliography

Ames, Roger T. "The Meaning of Body in Classical Chinese Thought." *International Philosophical Quarterly* 24, 1 (1984): 39–54.

Anderson, Benedict. *Imagined Communities: Reflections on the Origin and Spread of Nationalism*. London: Verso, 1998.

Anderson, Matt. "Numbers of Characters." In *Encyclopedia of Chinese Language and Linguistics*, vol. 3, ed. Rint Sybesma, Wolfgang Behr, Yuego Gu, Zev Handel, C.-T. James Huang and James Myers. Leiden: Brill, 2017, pp. 255–9.

Ang, Ien. "Can One Say No to Chineseness? Pushing the Limits of the Diasporic Paradigm." *Boundary 2* 25, 3 (1998): 223–42.

Appadurai, Arjun. *Modernity at Large: Cultural Dimensions of Globalization*. Minneapolis: University of Minnesota Press, 1996.

Arendt, Hannah. "Introduction: Walter Benjamin 1892–1940." In *Walter Benjamin, Illuminations: Essays and Reflections*, trans. Harry Zohn. New York: Schocken Books, 2007, pp. 1–55.

Bachner, Andrea. *Beyond Sinology: Chinese Writing and the Scripts of Culture*. New York: Columbia University Press, 2014.

Bai, Qianshen. *Fu Shan's World: The Transformation of Chinese Calligraphy in the Seventeenth Century*. Cambridge, MA: Harvard University Asia Center, 2003.

Bai, Tongdong. "Against Democratic Education." *Journal of Curriculum Studies* 43, 5 (2011): 615–22.

Barmé, Geremie. "History Writ Large: Big-Character Posters, Red Logorrhoea and the Art of Words." *Portal Journal of Multidisciplinary International Studies* 9, 3 (2012): 1–20.

Barrass, Gordon. *The Art of Calligraphy in Modern China*. Berkeley: University of California Press, 2002.

Barthes, Roland. "The Death of the Author." In *Image, Music, Text*, trans. Stephen Heath. New York: Hill and Wang, 1977, pp. 142–8.

Baudrillard, Jean. *Simulacra and Simulation*, trans. Sheila Glaser. Ann Arbor, MI: University of Michigan Press, 1994 [1981].

Benjamin, Walter. *The Arcades Project*. Cambridge, MA: Harvard University Press, 1999.

Berlina, Alexandra, ed. *Viktor Shklovsky: A Reader*. London: Bloomsbury Academic, 2016.

Berry, David. *Critical Theory and the Digital.* New York: Bloomsbury Academic, 2014.

Billeter, Jean François. *Chinese Art of Writing.* New York: Rizzoli, 1990.

Billig, Michael. *Banal Nationalism.* London, Thousand Oaks and New Delhi: Sage Publications, 1995.

Billioud, Sébastien, and Joël Thoraval. *The Sage and the People: The Confucian Revival in China.* Oxford: Oxford University Press, 2015.

Bilton, Chris. "Manageable Creativity." *International Journal of Cultural Policy* 16, 3 (2010): 255–69.

Mary Wiseman Bittner and Yuedi Liu, eds. *Subversive Strategies in Contemporary Chinese Art.* Leiden, Boston: Brill, 2011, p. xxiv.

BJWMB.gov.cn. "*Xicheng: Taoran dishu wenhuajie shuhuai xin shidai* 西城：陶然地书文化节抒怀新时代 [Xicheng: Taoran Water Calligraphy Culture Festival Embracing the New Era]." www.bjwmb.gov.cn/xxgk/xcjy/t20181022_885072.htm [accessed March 27, 2018).

Bogdanova-Kummer, Eugenia. "The Line Between Calligraphy and Painting: A View from Post-War Japan." In *The Power of Line*, ed. Marzia Faietti and Gerhard Wolf. Munich: Hirmer, 2015, pp. 118–28.

Bolter, David, and Richard Grusin. *Remediation: Understanding New Media.* Cambridge, MA: The MIT Press, 2000.

Boltz, William. *The Origin and Early Development of the Chinese Writing System.* New Haven, CT: American Oriental Society, 1994.

Boym, Svetlana. *The Future of Nostalgia.* New York: Basic Books, 2001.

Bray, Francesca. *Technology and Gender.* Berkeley: University of California Press, 1997.

Brokaw, Cynthia. "Book History in Premodern China: The State of the Discipline I." *Book History* 10, 1 (2007): 253–90.

Brokaw, Cynthia, and Kai-Wing Chow, eds. *Printing and Book Culture in Late Imperial China.* Berkeley: University of California Press, 2005.

Burgess, Jean. "Hearing Ordinary Voices: Cultural Studies, Vernacular Creativity and Digital Storytelling." *Continuum* 20, 2 (2006): 201–14.

Burgess, Jean. "Vernacular Creativity and New Media." PhD diss., Queensland University of Technology, 2007.

Bush, Susan. *The Chinese Literati on Painting: Su Shih (1037–1101) to Tung Ch'i-Ch'ang (1555–1636).* Cambridge, MA: Harvard University Press, 1971.

CADAL (China Academic Digital Associative Library). 2010. "Resources Introduction." https://cadal.edu.cn/index/home [accessed May 20, 2020].

Cao, Fang. *Wenzi Yishu Sheji* 文 字艺术设计 [Typography Art Design]. Beijing: Gaodeng Jiaoyu Chubanshe, 2019.

Carrico, Kevin. "The Imaginary Institution of China: Dialectics of Fantasy and Failure in Nationalist Identification, as Seen through China's Han Clothing Movement." PhD diss., Cornell University, 2013.

Chastanet, François. *Dishu: Ground Calligraphy in China.* Årsta: Dokument Press, 2013.

Chen, Caroline. "Dancing in the Streets of Beijing: Improvised Uses within the Urban System." In *Insurgent Public Space: Guerrilla Urbanism and the Remaking of Contemporary Cities*, ed. Jeffrey Hou. London: Routledge, 2010, pp. 21–35.

Chen, Shan. "*Jie Shifu de Xiaosa 'Dishu'* 解师傅的潇洒'地书 [Understanding the Confident and Free 'Water Calligraphy' of Older Men]". *Xintiandi* 10 (2007): 24.

Chen, Xu, David Bondy Valdovinos Kaye and Jing Zeng, "Positive Energy Douyin: Constructing 'Playful Patriotism' in a Chinese Short-Video Application." *Chinese Journal of Communication* 14, 1 (2021): 97–117.

Cheng, Meiling. "De/Visualizing Calligraphic Archaeology: Qiu Zhijie's Total Art." *TDR: The Drama Review* 53, 2 (2009): 17–34.

China Daily. "*Jing shou jia dishu xiehui chengli minjian yishu xieyi di tan shenghuo* 京首家地书协会成立民间艺术写意低碳生活 [Beijing's First Ground-Writing Association Was Established to Express Folk art and Low-Carbon Life]". December 17, 2016. www.chinadaily.com.cn/dfpd/2010-04/09/content_9707332.htm, 2010. [Accessed March 27, 2022].

Ching, Dora C.Y. "The Aesthetics of the Unusual and the Strange in Seventeenth-Century Calligraphy." In *The Embodied Image: Chinese Calligraphy from the John B. Elliott Collection*, ed. Robert E. Harrist Jr. and Wen C. Fong. Princeton, NJ: The Art Museum, Princeton University, 1999, pp. 342–59.

Chow, Rey. "Introduction: On Chineseness as a Theoretical Problem." *Boundary 2* 25, 3 (1998): 1–24.

Chow, Yiu Fai. "Exploring Creative Class Mobility: Hong Kong Creative Workers in Shanghai and Beijing." *Eurasian Geography and Economics* 58, 4 (2017): 361–85.

Chow, Yiu Fai, and Jeroen de Kloet. "The Spectre of Europe: Knowledge, Cultural Studies and the 'Rise of Asia'." *European Journal of Cultural Studies* 17, 1 (2014): 3–15.

Chumley, Lily. *Creativity Class: Art School and Culture Work in Postsocialist China*. Princeton, NJ: Princeton University Press, 2016.

Chun, Allen. "Fuck Chineseness: On the Ambiguities of Ethnicity as Culture as Identity." *Boundary 2* 23, 2 (1996): 111–38.

Clunas, Craig. *Art in China*. Oxford: Oxford University Press, 1997.

Cockcroft, Eva. "Abstract Expressionism, Weapon of the Cold War." *Art Forum* 15, 10 (1974): 39–41.

Couldry, Nick, and Andreas Hepp. *The Mediated Construction of Reality*. London: John Wiley & Sons, 2016.

Craig, David, Jian Lin and Stuart Cunningham. *Wanghong as Social Media Entertainment in China*. London: Palgrave Macmillan, 2021.

Croizier, Ralph. "Post-Impressionists in Pre-War Shanghai: The Juelanshe (Storm Society) and the Fate of Modernism in Republican China." In *Modernity in Asian Art*, ed. John Clark. Broadway, Australia: Wild Peony, 1993, pp. 135–54.

Cyberspace Administration China (CAC). "*Chuanbo wangluo zheng nengliang rang wangluo kongjian tian lang qi qing*. 传播网络正能量 让网络空间天朗气清. [Spreading Positive Energy on the Internet to Make Cyberspace Clear and

Bright].” 2017. https://www.cac.gov.cn/2017-04/20/c_1120846141.htm [accessed March 21, 2023].

de Certeau, Michel. *The Practice of Everyday Life*. Berkeley: University of California Press, 1984.

de Certeau, Michel. *Culture in The Plural*, ed. Luce Giard. Minneapolis: University of Minnesota Press, 1997.

DeFrancis, John. *The Chinese Language: Fact and Fantasy*. Honolulu: University of Hawaii Press, 1986.

de Kloet, Jeroen. *China with a Cut: Globalisation, Urban Youth and Popular Music*. Amsterdam: Amsterdam University Press, 2010.

de Kloet, Jeroen, and Anthony Fung. *Youth Cultures in China*. Malden, MA: Polity, 2017.

de Kloet, Jeroen, and Edwin Jurriëns, eds. *Cosmopatriots: On Distant Belongings and Close Encounters*. Amsterdam: Rodopi, 2007.

Dezeuze, Anna. *Almost Nothing: Observations on Precarious Practices in Contemporary Art*. Manchester: Manchester University Press, 2017.

Dui, Jiemo. “*Suzhi jiaoyu fengkou zhi shang, zhengce chengyao de 'shufa jiaoyu' jiang ying lai de baofa*? 素质教育风又之上，政策撑腰的‘书法教育’将迎来大爆发?” [Beyond the Promises of ‘Quality Education,’ Will There Be an Explosion of the Policy Supported ‘Calligraphy Education’?]” 2018. www.iyiou.com/p/70713 [accessed July 2, 2022].

Erickson, Britta. *The Art of Xu Bing: Words Without Meaning, Meaning Without Words*. Washington, DC: University of Washington Press, 2001.

Farquhar, Judith. “The Park Pass: Peopling and Civilizing a New Old Beijing.” *Public Culture* 21, 3 (2009): 551–76.

Farquhar, Judith, and Qicheng Zhang. “Biopolitical Beijing: Pleasure, Sovereignty, and Self-Cultivation in China's Capital.” *Cultural Anthropology* 20, 3 (2005): 303–27.

Farquhar, Judith, and Qicheng Zhang. *Ten Thousand Things: Nurturing Life in Contemporary Beijing*. New York: Zone Books, 2012.

Feng, Pengzhi. “*Cong 'san ge zixin' dao 'si ge zixin'* 从‘三个自 信’ 到‘四个信’ [From ‘Three Confidences’ to ‘Four Confidences’].” *Zhongguo Gongchandang Xinwen* 中国共产党闻 [Chinese Communist Party News], 2016. http://theory.people.com.cn/n1/2016/0707/c49150-28532466.html [accessed July 21, 2022].

Florida, Richard. *The Rise of the Creative Class*. New York: Basic Books, 2002.

Fong, Wen C. *Beyond Representation: Chinese Painting and Calligraphy, 8th–14th Century*. New York and New Haven, CT: Metropolitan Museum of Art; Yale University Press, 1992.

Fong, Wen C. “Prologue: Chinese Calligraphy as Presenting the Self.” In *Chinese Calligraphy*, trans. Wang Youfen. New Haven, CT and London: Yale University Press; Beijing: Foreign Language Press, 2008.

Foucault, Michel. *Discipline and Punish: The Birth of the Prison*. New York: Vintage Books, 1975.

Foucault, Michel. *The Foucault Reader*, ed. Paul Rabinow. New York: Pantheon, 1984.

Foucault, Michel. *The Use of Pleasure: The History of Sexuality, Vol. 2*. Harmondsworth, Middlesex: Penguin, 1992.

FounderType *Fangzheng Ziti* 方正字体. "*Di Jiu Jie Fangzheng Ziti Dasai Huojiang Zuopin Xinshang (Zhongwen Zhuanye Zu)* 第九届方正字体大赛获奖作品欣赏(中文专业组) [Winners of FounderType Design Competition 2018 Chinese Professional Group]." 2018. https://ztds.foundertype.com/index.php/previous_works/index.html?id=9&cid=31 [accessed July 21, 2022].

FounderType *Fangzheng Ziti* 方正字体. "*Ziti wei Wuhan jiayou | Fangzheng ziku kaifang quanbu zhongwen ziti, kang yi xuancuan mianfei shiyong* 字体为武汉加油｜方正字库开放全部中文字体，抗疫宣传免费使用 [Fonts Cheer for Wuhan: Founder Font Library Opens All Chinese Fonts, Free to Use for Anti-Epidemic Propaganda]." 2020 [accessed July 28, 2022].

FounderType *Fangzheng Ziti* 方正字体. "*Fangzheng Xu Bing xin Yingwen shuti* 方正徐冰英文书 [FounderType Xu Bing New English font]." 2015. www.foundertype.com/index.php/FontInfo/index/id/333.html [accessed April 14, 2024].

Fu, Marilyn W., and Shen C.Y. Fu. *Traces of the Brush: Studies in Chinese Calligraphy*. New Haven, CT: Yale University Press, 1980.

Galambos, Imre. "Correction Marks in the Dunhuang Manuscripts." In *Studies in Chinese Manuscripts: From the Warring States Period to the 20th Century*, ed. Imre Galambos. Budapest: ELTE Institute of East Asian Studies, 2013, pp. 191–211.

Gao, Minglu. *The '85 Movement: Avant-Garde Art in the Post-Mao Era*. Cambridge, MA: Harvard University, 1999.

Gao, Minglu. *Total Modernity and the Avant-Garde in Twentieth-Century Chinese Art*. Cambridge, MA: MIT Press, 2011.

Gardiner, Michael. *Critiques of Everyday Life: An Introduction*. London and New York: Routledge, 2000.

Gaubatz, Piper. "New Public Space in Urban China: Fewer Walls, More Malls in Beijing, Shanghai, and Xining." *China Perspectives*, 4 (2008): 72–83.

Gawlikowski, Krzysztof. "The Concept of Two Fundamental Social Principles: Wen and Wu in Chinese Classical Thought." *Annali* 47 (1989): 397–433.

Gillespie, Tarleton. "The Platform Metaphor, Revisited." *Digital Society Blog*, August 27, 2017. www.hiig.de/en/the-platform-metaphor-revisited/ [accessed April 5, 2022].

Girshick, Ross. "Simulating Chinese Brush Painting: The Parametric Hairy Brush." PhD diss., Brandeis University, 2004.

Gu, Gan. *The Three Steps of Modern Calligraphy*. English edition, trans. Hu Yunhuan. Beijing: China Books Publishing House, 1990.

Gu, Gan. "*Xiandai shufa Manyi* 现代书法漫议 [Free Discussions on Modern Calligraphy]." *Meishu Yanjiu* 4, 68 (1992): 52–53.

Gu, Ming Dong. "Patterns of Tao (Dao): The Birth of Chinese Writing and Aesthetics." *The Journal of Aesthetics and Art Criticism* 74, 2 (2016): 151–63.

Gu, Xin, and Justin O'Connor. "A New Modernity? The Arrival of 'Creative Industries' in China." *International Journal of Cultural Studies* 9 (2006): 271–83.

Guo, Hui. "Writing Chinese Art History in Early Twentieth-Century China." PhD diss., Leiden University, 2010.

Guo, Pingxin, and Qiangnan Sun. "General Review of Computer Technology and Application in China." *Computers in Industry* 8, 2 (1987): 113–17.

Guo, Yingjie. *Cultural Nationalism in Contemporary China: The Search for National Identity Under Reform*. London: Routledge Curzon, 2004.

Han, Dongping. *The Unknown Cultural Revolution: Educational Reforms and Their Impact on China's Rural Development, 1966–1976*. New York: Routledge, 2000.

Harrist, Robert E., Jr. "Copies, All the Way Down: Notes on the Early Transmission of Calligraphy by Wang Xizhi." *The East Asian Library Journal* 10, 1 (2001): 176–96.

Harrist, Robert E., Jr. and Wen C. Fong. *The Embodied Image: Chinese Calligraphy from the John B. Elliott Collection*. Princeton, NJ: The Art Museum, Princeton University, 1999.

Hay, John. "The Human Body as a Microcosmic Source of Macrocosmic Values in Calligraphy." In *Theories of the Arts in China*, ed. Susan Bush and Christian Murck. Princeton, NJ: Princeton University Press, 1983, pp. 74–102.

Hayhoe, Ruth. *China's Universities, 1895–1995: A Century of Cultural Conflict*. New York: Routledge, 1996.

Hertel, Shao-Lan. "The Inner Workings of Brush-and-Ink: A Study on Huang Binhong (1865–1955) as Calligrapher, with Special Respect to the Concept of Interior Beauty (Neimei)." PhD diss., Freie Universität Berlin, 2017.

Hesmondhalgh, David, and Sarah Baker. *Creative Labour Media Work in Three Cultural Industries*. London: Routledge, 2011.

Highmore, Ben. *Everyday Life and Cultural Theory: An Introduction*. London and New York: Routledge, 2002.

Hirsch, Yale, and William J. O'Neil. *The Capitalist Spirit: How Each and Every One of Us Can Make a Giant Difference in Our Fast-Changing World*. Hoboken, NJ: Wiley, 2009.

Hobsbawm, Eric, and Terence Ranger. *The Invention of Tradition*. Cambridge: Cambridge University Press, 1983.

Hopfener, Birgit. "'Embodied Criticality' in Moving-Image Installations by Wang Gongxin and Zhang Peili." *Journal of Visual Art Practice* 11 (2012): 193–208.

Hsu, Siuchi, Irene Lee and Neil Wiseman. "Skeletal Strokes." In *Proceedings of the 6th Annual ACM Symposium on User Interface Software and Technology*. New York: ACM Press, 1993, pp. 197–206.

Hsu, Ya-hwei. *Reshaping Chinese Material Culture: The Revival of Antiquity in the Era of Print, 960–1279*. New Haven, CT: Yale University Press, 2010.

Hung, Ruyu. *Education Between Speech and Writing: Crossing the Boundaries of Dao and Deconstruction*. London: Routledge, 2017.

Iezzi, Adriana. "Contemporary Chinese Calligraphy Between Tradition and Innovation." *Journal of Literature and Art Studies* 3 (2013): 158–79.

Iezzi, Adriana. “What Is ‘Chinese Modern Calligraphy’? An Exploration of the Critical Debate on Modern Calligraphy in Contemporary China.” *Journal of Literature and Art Studies* 5 (2015): 206–16.

Ink Pool. *Mochi* 墨池. https://mc.mochiapp.cn/website/ [accessed April 23, 2022].

Jacobs, Dany. “Creativity and the Economy.” Background paper for the Innovation Lecture “Compete with Creativity” 2005, organized by the Dutch Ministry of Economic Affairs. Amsterdam: The Dutch Ministry of Economic Affairs, 2005.

Jinping, Xi. “*Jianding wenhua zixin, jianshe shehuizhuyi wenhua Qiangguo* 坚定文化自信，建设社会主义文化强国 [Strengthening Cultural Self-Confidence and Building a Strong Socialist Culture].” www.qstheory.cn/dukan/qs/2019-06/15/c_1124626824.htm [accessed July 25, 2024].

Ke, Zhijie, and S. Yuxiang *Zixing Sanbu: Richang Shenghuo de Zhongwen Zixingxue* 字型散步日常生活的中文字型學 [A Font Walk: The Study of Fonts in Everyday Life]. Chengdu: Lianpu, 2014.

Keane, Michael. “From Made in China to Created in China.” *International Journal of Cultural Studies* 9 (2006): 285–96.

Keane, Michael. “Going Global or Going Nowhere? Chinese Media in a Time of Flux.” *Media International Australia* 159, 1 (2016): 13–21.

Keane, Michael, and Ying Chen. “Entrepreneurial Solutionism, Characteristic Cultural Industries and the Chinese Dream.” *International Journal of Cultural Policy* (2017): 1–13.

Kipnis, Andrew. *Governing Educational Desire: Culture, Politics, and Schooling in China*. Chicago, IL: University of Chicago Press, 2011.

Kraus, Richard Curt. *Brushes with Power: Modern Politics and the Chinese Art of Calligraphy*. Berkeley: University of California Press, 1991.

Ledderose, Lothar. *Mi Fu and the Classical Tradition of Chinese Calligraphy*. Princeton, NJ: Princeton University Press, 1979.

Ledderose, Lothar. “Aesthetic Appropriation of Ancient Calligraphy in Modern China.” In *Chinese Art: Modern Expressions*, ed. Maxwell K. Hearn and Judith Smith. New York: Metropolitan Museum of Art, 2001, pp. 222–7.

Lee, Jennifer. “Where the PC Is Mightier Than the Pen.” *New York Times*, February 1, 2001.

Leijonhufvud, Goran. *Going Against the Tide: On Dissent and Big-Character Posters in China*. London: Curzon Press, 1990.

Li, Wendan. *Chinese Writing and Calligraphy*. Honolulu: University of Hawaii Press, 2010.

Li, Zitui. “*Dishu Laonian Shenghuo You Yidao Liangli Fengjing* 地书老年生活有一道亮丽风景 [Water Calligraphy: Another Way to Beautiful Landscapes in the Lives of the Elderly].” *Zhongguo Laonian*, 3 (2011): 22–4.

Liang, Yan. “Wang Dongling: `Luan Shu’ shi Mao Tianxia zhi Da Bu Wei de Shi [王冬龄 | `乱书’ 是冒天下之大不韪的事],” Sohu, 2018. https://www.sohu.com/a/223868780_676789 [accessed July 29, 2024].

Light, Ben, Jean Burgess and Stephanie Duguay. "The Walkthrough Method: An Approach to the Study of Apps." *New Media & Society* 20, 3 (2018): 881–900.

Lin, Daojun. "'*Shufa yi si' yu Zeng Xiang de yiyi* 书法已死'与曾翔的意义 ['Calligraphy is Already Dead' and the Meaning of Zeng Xiang]." www.douban.com/note/665238839/ [accessed May 26, 2023].

Lin, Hang. "Printed as Handwritten: The Importance of Calligraphy in Printing in Late Ming China." *The Polish Journal of the Arts and Culture. New Series* 1 (2015): 51–76.

Lin, Jian. "Be Creative for the State: Creative Workers in Chinese State-Owned Cultural Enterprises." *International Journal of Cultural Studies* 22, 1 (2018): 53–69.

Lin, Jian and Jeroen de Kloet. "Platformization of the Unlikely Creative Class: Kuaishou and Chinese Digital Cultural Production." *Social Media + Society* 5, 4 (2019): 1–12.

Lin, Yutang. *My Country and My People*. London: W. Heinemann, 1936.

Lindner, Christoph. "Boredom and Creativity in the Era of Accelerated Living." In *Boredom, Shanzhai, and Digitisation in the Time of Creative China*, ed. Jeroen de Kloet, Yiu Fai Chow and Lena Scheen. Amsterdam: Amsterdam University Press, 2019, pp. 110–20.

Liu, Cary Y., Dora C.Y. Ching and Judith G. Smith. *Character & Context in Chinese Calligraphy*. Princeton, NJ: Art Museum, Princeton University, 1999.

Liu, Shaogang. *Shufa lianxi zidao* 书法练习指导 [Guidance for Calligraphy Practice]. Qingdao: Qingdao Chubanshe, 2014.

Liu, Shi-yee. "In Pursuit of Authenticity: The Epigraphic School of Chinese Calligraphy." *Netmuseum.org*. www.metmuseum.org/blogs/now-at-the-met/2014/epigraphic-school [accessed August 24, 2020].

Liu, Xu. *Jiu Tang Shu* 旧唐书 [Old Standard History of the Tang Dynasty]. Beijing: Zhong hua shuju. 1975.

Liu, Zhengcheng, ed. *Zhongguo shufa quanji* 中国书法全集 [Collection of Chinese Calligraphy] 100 vols. Beijing: Xinhua Publishing House, 1991.

Liu, Zongchao. "'*Choushu' zhong de 'Zhen' he 'Shan'* '丑书'中的'真'与 '善' [The 'Real' and the 'Good' in 'Ugly Calligraphy']." *Renmin Taolun* 36. 2016. http://www.rmlt.com.cn/2016/1230/454893.shtml [accessed February 7, 2025].

Lu, Mingjun. "*Hui 'wan' de Zeng Xiang* 会' 玩' 的 曾翔 [Zeng Xiang Knows How to 'Play']." 2018 https://news.artron.net/20140114/n559118.html [accessed August 1, 2019].

Mair, Victor. "Modern Chinese Writing." In *The World's Writing Systems*, ed. Pete T. Daniels and William Bright. Oxford: Oxford University Press, 1996, pp. 200–8.

Mair, Victor. "Character Amnesia." *Language Log*, 2010. http://languagelog.ldc.upenn.edu/nll/?p=2473 [accessed July 23, 2022].

Mair, Victor. "How Many More Chinese Characters Are Needed?" *Language Log*, 2016. https://languagelog.ldc.upenn.edu/nll/?p=29034 [accessed October 22, 2022].

Mao, Tse-Tung. *Mao Tse-Tung Talks at the Yenan Forum on Literature and Art*. World Communism: Pamphlets from McMaster University. Peking: Foreign Languages Press; The People's Republic of China, 1967.

McDermott, Joseph. "The Ascendance of the Imprint in China." In *Printing and Book Culture in Late Imperial China*, ed. Cynthia J. Brokaw and Kai-wing Chow. Berkeley: University of California Press, 2005, pp. 55–104.

McNair, Amy. "Engraved Calligraphy in China: Recension and Reception." *Art Bulletin* 160, 1 (1995): 106–14.

McNair, Amy. *The Upright Brush: Yan Zhenqing's Calligraphy and Song Literati Politics*. Honolulu: University of Hawaii Press, 1998.

McNair, Amy. "Looking at Chinese Calligraphy: The Anxiety of Anonymity and Calligraphy from the Periphery." In *Looking at Asian Art*, ed. Katherine R. Tsiang and Martin J. Powers. Chicago, IL: University of Chicago Press, 2012, pp. 53–74.

McRobbie, Angela. *Be Creative: Making a Living in the New Culture Industries*. Cambridge, UK and Malden, MA: Polity, 2016.

Menger, Pierre-Michel. "Artistic Labor Markets: Contingent Work, Excess Supply and Occupational Risk Management." In *Handbook of the Economics of Art and Culture*, ed. Victor A. Ginsburg and David Throsby. Amsterdam: Elsevier, 2006, pp. 765–811.

MOE (Ministry of Education). "*Jiaoyu bu guanyu yinfa 'zhongxiaoxue shufa jiaoyu zhidao gangyao' de tongzhi* 教育部關於印發《中小學書法教育指導綱要》的通知 [Ministry of Education on the Issuance of Primary and Secondary School Calligraphy Education Guidelines]." 2013.

MOE (Ministry of Education). "*Jiaoyu bu dui shisan jie quanguo renda yici huiyi di 7496 hao jianyi de dafu* 教育部对十三届全国人大一次会议第 7496 号建议的答复 [Ministry of Education's Meeting of the 13th National People's Congress Reply to Recommendation No. 7496]." 2018. www.moe.gov.cn/jyb_xxgk/xxgk_jyta/jyta_jijiaosi/201812/t20181229_365452.html [accessed April 12, 2019].

MOE (Ministry of Education). "教育部关于成立教育部中国书法教育指导委员会等三个教育指导委员会的通知 [Notice of the Ministry of Education on the Establishment of Three Education Steering Committees Including the Chinese Calligraphy Education Steering Committee]." 2021. www.moe.gov.cn/srcsite/A17/s7059/202105/t20210514_531576.html [accessed August 2, 2020].

MOE (Ministry of Education). "MOE Calls for High Quality Education at 2022 National Education Conference." 2022. http://en.moe.gov.cn/news/press_releases/202201/t20220124_596108.html [accessed January 21, 2022].

Morris, Meaghan. "Banality in Cultural Studies." In *Logics of Television: Essays in Cultural Criticism*, ed. Patricia Mellencamp. Bloomington and Indianapolis: Indiana University Press, 1990, pp. 14–43.

Mould, Oli. *Against Creativity*. London and Brooklyn, NY: Verso, 2018.

Mullaney, Thomas S. *The Chinese Typewriter: A History*. Cambridge, MA: The MIT Press, 2017.

Murck, Alfreda, and Wen C. Fong. *Words and Images: Chinese Poetry, Calligraphy, and Painting*. New York: Metropolitan Museum of Art, 1991.

Nakata, Yujiro. *The Art of Japanese Calligraphy*. New York: Weatherhill, 1983.

Nylan, Michael. "Calligraphy, the Sacred Text and Test of Culture." In *Character and Context in Chinese Calligraphy*, eds. Liu, Cary Y.; Dora C.Y. Ching and Judith G. Smith. Princeton, NJ: The Art Museum, Princeton University Press, 1999, pp. 6–77.

Ouyang, Zhongshi, and Wen C. Fong. *Chinese Calligraphy*. New Haven, CT: Yale University Press, 2008.

Padua, Mary. "Hybrid Modernity: Framing the Public Park in Post-Mao China." In *Council of Educators in Landscape Architecture CELA 2007: Negotiating Landscapes Proceedings*, August 14–19, 2007. University Park, Penn State University. Raleigh, NC: The CELA.org, 2007, pp. 65–80.

Pecht, Michael, and Weifeng Liu. "Computers in China." 2019. www.researchgate.net/publication/265422783_COMPUTERS_IN_CHINA [accessed August 2, 2019].

Peck, Jamie. "Struggling with the Creative Class." *International Journal of Urban and Regional Research* 29, 4 (2005): 740–70.

Pepper, Suzanne. *Radicalism and Education Reform in 20th Century China: The Search for an Ideal Development Model*. Cambridge: Cambridge University Press, 1996.

Phoenix Art. "*Mei zai shenghuo, renren dou shi chuangyijia Zhongguo meishu guanyong chuangyi dianliang shenghuo* 美在生活人人都是创意家 中国美术馆用创意点亮生活 [Beauty in Life, Everyone Is a Creative Person, and the National Art Museum of China Lights Up Life with Creativity]." 2017. http://art.ifeng.com/2017/0830/3374205.shtml [accessed August 2, 2018].

Poell, Thomas, Erin Duffy Brooke and David Nieborg, *Platforms and Cultural Production*. Cambridge: Polity Press, 2021.

Qian, Mu. *Guoxue Gailun* 国学概论 [Discussion on National Learning]. Shanghai: Guji Chubanshe, 1998.

Rancière, Jacques. *The Politics of Aesthetics: The Distribution of the Sensible*, ed. and trans. Gabriel Rockhill. London: Continuum, 2004.

Rancière, Jacques. *Dissensus: On Politics and Aesthetics*, trans. Steven Corcoran. London: Bloomsbury, 2015.

Reckwitz, Andreas. *The Invention of Creativity: Modern Society and the Culture of the New*. Cambridge and Malden: Polity Press, 2017.

Reed, Christopher. *Gutenberg in Shanghai: Chinese Print Capitalism, 1876–1937*. Honolulu: University of Hawaii Press, 2004.

Reid, Anthony. "Escaping the Burdens of Chineseness." *Asian Ethnicity* 10, 3 (2009): 285–96.

Renminwang. "*Beijing Taoran dishu wenhuaji: fendou xin shidai shuxie xin Taoran* 北京陶然地书文化节: 奋斗新时代 书写新陶然 [Beijing Taoran Water Calligraphy Culture Festival: Struggling in the New Era, Writing a New Taoran]." http://bj.people.com.cn/n2/2018/1019/c82846-32175537.html [accessed March 27, 2018].

Richter, Antje. *Letters and Epistolary Culture in Early Medieval China*. Seattle: University of Washington Press, 2015.

Rolandsen, Unn Målfrid. *Leisure and Power in Urban China*. London: Routledge, 2014.

Ryan, Janette. *Education in China*. Cambridge: Polity Press, 2019.

Schell, Orville. *Mandate of Heaven: The Legacy of Tiananmen Square and the Next Generation of China's Leaders*. New York: Simon and Schuster, 1995.

Schneider, Florian. "Emergent Nationalism in China's Sociotechnical Networks: How Technological Affordance and Complexity Amplify Digital Nationalism." *Nations and Nationalism* 28, 1 (2022): 267–285.

Scott, Allen. "Creative Cities: Conceptual Issues and Policy Questions." *Journal of Urban Affairs* 28 (2006): 1–17.

Sheng, Hua. "Big Character Posters in China: A Historical Survey Perspectives on Free Speech in China." *Journal of Chinese Law* 4 (1990): 234–56.

Shi, Cao, Jianguo Xiao, Wenhua Jia and Canhui Xu. "Automatic Generation of Chinese Character Based on Human Vision and Prior Knowledge of Calligraphy." In *Natural Language Processing and Chinese Computing: Proceedings of the First CCF Conference, NLPCC 2012, Beijing, China*, ed. Ming Zhou, Guodong Zhou, Dongyan Zhao, Qun Liu and Lei Zou Heidelberg: Springer, 2012, pp. 23–33.

Shi, Mingzheng. "From Imperial Gardens to Public Parks: The Transformation of Urban Space in Early Twentieth-Century Beijing." *Modern China* 24, 3 (1998): 219–54.

Shi, Xiongbo. "Zhang Yinlin: A Preface to Chinese Calligraphy Criticism (1931)." *Journal of Art Historiography* 13 (2015): 13–25.

Shimonaka, Kunihiko, ed. *Complete Works of Calligraphy* (*Shodō zenshū*). 26 vols. and 2 suppl. vols. Tokyo: Heibonsha, 1954–68 (reprinted 1973).

Shufaedu.com. n.d. *Hanxiang Shufa Jiaoyu* 汉翔书法教育 [Hanxiang Calligraphy Education]. www.shufaedu.com/ [accessed April 11, 2022].

Silbergeld, Jerome, and Dora C.Y. Ching, eds. *Persistence/Transformation: Text as Image in the Art of Xu Bing*. Princeton, NJ: Princeton University Press, 2006.

Sohu.com. "*Nian Shufa Gaokao, ni suo guanzhu de dou zai zheli* 年书法高考，你所关注的都在这里 [Everything You Want to Know About This Years' Calligraphy *Gaokao* Is Here]." 2022. www.sohu.com/a/405224242_584699 [accessed July 2, 2024].

Su, Sara, Ying-Qing Xu, Heung-Yeung Shum and Falai Chen. "Simulating Artistic Brushstrokes Using Interval Splines." In *Proceedings of the 5th IASTED International Conference on Computer Graphics and Imaging, Kauai, Hawaii*, 2002, pp. 85–90.

Sullivan, Michael. *Art and Artists of Twentieth-Century China*. Berkeley: University of California Press, 1996.

Tsao, Hsingyuan, and Roger T. Ames. *Xu Bing and Contemporary Chinese Art: Cultural and Philosophical Reflections*. New York: SUNY Press, 2011.

Tsien, Tsuen-Hsuin, and Joseph Needham. *Science and Civilisation in China: Volume 5, Chemistry and Chemical Technology; Part 1, Paper and Printing*. Cambridge: Cambridge University Press, 1985.

Tsu, Jiing. *Kingdom of Characters*. New York: Riverhead, 2022.

Tu, Wei-Ming. *Humanity and Self-Cultivation: Essays in Confucian Thought*. Boston, MA: Cheng & Tsui, 1999.

van Dijck, José. *The Culture of Connectivity: A Critical History of Social Media*. Oxford: Oxford University Press, 2013.

van Dijck, José, Thomas Poell and Martijn de Waal, *The Platform Society: Public Values in a Connective World*. New York: Oxford University Press, 2018.

van Doorn, Niels. "Platform Labour: On the Gendered and Racialized Exploitation of Low-Income Service Work in the 'On Demand' Economy." *Information, Communication & Society* 20 (2017): 898–914.

Wang, Dongling. "*Xiandai Shufa Jingshen Lun* 现代书法精神论 [Discussing the Spirit of Contemporary Calligraphy]." *Xin Meishu* 新美术 1, 28 (2007): 10–15.

Wang, Dongling. *Jufu dazi kuangfang dacao xiandai shufa* 巨幅大字 狂放大草现代书法 [Large Characters, Crazy Grass Script, Contemporary Calligraphy], 2013. https://news.artron.net/20131011/n518934.html [accessed May 30, 2020].

Wang, Fuming. "*Liuxing shufeng yu choushu* 流行书风与丑书 [Popular Calligraphy and Ugly Calligraphy]." *Qingshaonian Shufa*, 10, 2004.

Wang, Nanming. "*Yishu, Zhidu yu Falu—Zhongguo yi Guoji Jiaowang de Jieguo* 艺术、制度与法律—— 中国与国际交往的结果 [Art, Institutions and Laws—The Results of China's International Relations]." 2017. https://news.artron.net/20170315/n915996.html [accessed August 15, 2018].

Wang, Shaoguang. "The Politics of Private Time: Changing Leisure Patterns in Urban China." In *Urban Spaces in Contemporary China: The Potential for Autonomy and Community in Post-Mao China*, ed. Debora Davis, Richard Kraus, Barry Naughton and Elizabeth Perry. Cambridge: Cambridge University Press, 1995, pp. 149–72.

Wang, Yuli. *The Mirror of Writing: Kang Youwei's Curriculum for Chinese Calligraphy Art*. Washington, DC: New Academia Publishing/The Spring, 2017.

Wei, Wei, "*Qianyi Choushu* 浅议'丑书' [Talking about 'Ugly Calligraphy']." *Xiandai funu (xiaxun)* (2014): 344–45.

Wiseman Bittner, Mary and Yuedi Liu, eds. *Subversive Strategies in Contemporary Chinese Art*. Leiden and Boston, MA: Brill, 2011.

Wo, Xinghua. "论丑书 *Lun Choushu* [Discussing Ugly Calligraphy]." *Shufa Daobao* 2, 2002.

Wong, Helena, and Horace Ip. "Virtual Brush: A Model-Based Synthesis of Chinese Calligraphy." *Computers&Graphics* 24 (2000): 99–113.

Wu, Hung. *Reinventing the Past: Archaism and Antiquarianism in Chinese Art and Visual Culture*. Chicago, IL: Art Media Resources, 2010.

Wu, Hung. *A Story of Ruins: Presence and Absence in Chinese Art and Visual Culture*. London: Reaktion Books, 2013.

Wu, Jing. "Nostalgia as Content Creativity: Cultural Industries and Popular Sentiment." *International Journal of Cultural Studies* 9 (2006): 359–68.

Xie, Shaobo. "Guoxue Re and the Ambiguity of Chinese Modernity." *China Perspectives* 1 (2011): 39–45.

Xing, Yi. "They're Just Your Type." *China Daily Asia*, December 17, 2016. https://covid-19.chinadaily.com.cn/weekend/2016-12/17/content_27696749_2.htm [accessed December 21, 2018].

Xu, Jiang, ed. *The Way of Calligraphy: Wang Dongling's work*. English Edition. Shanghai: Shanghai Fine Arts Publishing House, 2011.

Xu, Jiang, and Wang Dongling, eds. *Shu feishu kaifang de shufa shikong*书非书— 开放的书法时空 [The Act of Writing and of Non-Writing: The Open Space for Chinese Calligraphy]. Beijing: Zhongguo Meishuxueyuan Chubanshe, 2005.

Xu, Songhua, Frances C. Lau and Yunhe Pan. *A Computational Approach to Digital Chinese Painting and Calligraphy*. Hangzhou/Berlin: Zhejiang UP/Springer-Verlag, 2009.

Yang, Guobin. *Engaging Social Media in China: Platform, Publics and Production*, ed. Guobin Yang and Wei Wang. East Lansing: Michigan State University Press, 2021.

Yee, Chiang. *Chinese Calligraphy: An Introduction to Its Aesthetic and Technique*. Cambridge, MA: Harvard University Press, 1974.

Yen, Yuehping. *Calligraphy and Power in Contemporary Chinese Society*. New York and London: Routledge Curzon, 2004.

Yu, Jinhui, and Qunsheng Peng. "Realistic Synthesis of Cao Shu of Chinese Calligraphy." *Computers & Graphics* 29, 1 (2005): 145–53.

Zeng, Xiang. "*Wo shi yishu zhuimengren* 我是艺术追梦人 [I Am an Art Dreamcatcher]." www.jingduzhai.com/mobile/article-5352.html [accessed November 30, 2018].

Zhang, Li, "*Xie dishu' shijian buyi guochang* 写地书'时间不宜过长 [Don't Practice 'Writing Water Calligraphy' For Too Long]." *Kaixin Laonian* 4, 34 (2007).

Zhang, Likun, Xiaoyan Li, Yi Tang, Fangbin Song, Tian Xia and Wei Wang. "Contemporary Advertising Text Art Design and Effect Evaluation by IoT Deep Learning under the Smart City." *Security and Communication Networks*, (2022).

Zhang, Xiafen, and George Nagy. "The CADAL Calligraphic Database." In *Proceedings of the 2011 Workshop on Historical Document Imaging and Processing* (HIP '11), Association for Computing Machinery, 2011, pp. 37–42.

Zhao, Shouhui. "Chinese Character Modernisation in the Digital Era: A Historical Perspective." *Current Issues in Language Planning*, 6 (2005): 315–78.

Zhenji, "*Zeng Xiang feng le! Zaici dianwule Zhongguo shufa* 曾翔疯了！再次玷污了中国书法 [Zeng Xiang Is Crazy! Once Again Polluting Chinese Calligraphy]." 2018. www.sohu.com/a/228871152_482079 [accessed July 23, 2018].

Zhi Chuang, Wenming, "中國年度`丑書' 最高榮譽獎，花落誰家？ [Who Won the Highest Honor of China's 'Ugly Book' Award of the Year?]." KK News, October 9, 2016. https://kknews.cc/news/exr4gr.html [accessed February 6, 2025].

Zito, Angela. *Of Body and Brush: Grand Sacrifice as Text Performance in 18th Century China*. Chicago, IL: University of Chicago Press, 1997.

Zito, Angela. "Writing in Water, or, Evanescence, Enchantment and Ethnography in a Chinese Urban Park." *Visual Anthropology Review* 30, 1 (2014): 11–22.

Zito, Angela, and Tani E. Barlow, eds. *Body, Subject & Power in China*. Chicago, IL: University of Chicago Press, 1994.

Index

Page numbers followed by 'n' refer to notes with the number following 'n' being the note number.

Page numbers in italics refer the reader to photographs.

Most Chinese names have been entered as they appear in the text without inversion. The names of Chinese authors follow the form used in the bibliography.

Entries that start with numbers appear in the index as if the numbers are spelt out.